A Pet of Your Own

A Doubleday Fatback

A Pet of Your Own

GEORG ZAPPLER AND
PAUL VILLIARD

Doubleday & Company, Inc.
Garden City, New York

Illustrations for Parts I, II, IV, and V by Paul Villiard
Illustrations for Part II by Richard Marshall

Library of Congress Cataloging in Publication Data

Zappler, Georg.
A pet of your own.

Includes index.
SUMMARY: Discusses keeping exotic fish, amphibians,
reptiles, birds, and wild mammals as pets.
1. Pets—Juvenile literature.   [1. Pets]
I. Villiard, Paul, joint author.   II. Title.
SF416.2.Z36   636.08′87
Library of Congress Catalog Card Number 79–7613
ISBN: 0-385-15429-1

Portions of this book first appeared in the following books:
Birds as Pets, Copyright © 1974 by Paul Villiard
Amphibians as Pets, Copyright © 1973 by Georg and Lisbeth Zappler
Wild Mammals as Pets, Copyright © 1972 by Paul Villiard
Exotic Fish as Pets, Copyright © 1971 by Paul Villiard
Reptiles as Pets, Copyright © 1969 by Paul Villiard

CONTENTS

PART I. *Exotic Fish as Pets*

Introduction   3

CHAPTER ONE   5
A Little About Water

CHAPTER TWO   13
Establishing an Aquarium

CHAPTER THREE   21
A Little About Fish

CHAPTER FOUR   24
A Little About Breeding

CHAPTER FIVE   31
Plants in the Aquarium

CHAPTER SIX   37
Foods for the Fish

CHAPTER SEVEN   44
Diseases in the Aquarium

CHAPTER EIGHT   52
Live-Bearers in the Aquarium

CHAPTER NINE   61
Egg-Scatterers in the Aquarium

CHAPTER TEN   70
Adhesive Egg Layers in the Aquarium

CHAPTER ELEVEN   76
Bubble Nest Builders in the Aquarium

CHAPTER TWELVE   83
Scavenger Fish in the Aquarium

CHAPTER THIRTEEN   88
Marine Fish in the Aquarium

PART II.   *Amphibians as Pets*

CHAPTER FOURTEEN   97
Meet the Amphibian

CHAPTER FIFTEEN   126
Some Common Amphibians

CHAPTER SIXTEEN   145
Your Own Amphibian

PART III.   *Reptiles as Pets*

Introduction   171

CHAPTER SEVENTEEN   175
A Little About Reptiles

CHAPTER EIGHTEEN   185
*How to Collect Reptiles
   and Where to Buy Them*

CHAPTER NINETEEN   197
How to Determine a Reptile's
  Health

CHAPTER TWENTY   205
Kinds of Containers for Reptiles

CHAPTER TWENTY-ONE   209
Maintenance of Reptiles in Cages

CHAPTER TWENTY-TWO   213
Reptile Food

CHAPTER TWENTY-THREE   217
The Best Kinds of Snakes
  to Keep as Pets

CHAPTER TWENTY-FOUR   231
The Best Kinds of Turtles
  to Keep as Pets

CHAPTER TWENTY-FIVE   241
The Best Kinds of Lizards
  to Keep as Pets

PART IV. Birds as Pets

Introduction   253
CHAPTER TWENTY-SIX   256
A Little About Birds

CHAPTER TWENTY-SEVEN   264
How to Care for Birds

CHAPTER TWENTY-EIGHT   278
Breeding Finches and Canaries

CHAPTER TWENTY-NINE   297
Breeding the Psittacines

CHAPTER THIRTY   308
Training Your Birds

CHAPTER THIRTY-ONE   317
Diseases of Birds

PART V.   *Wild Mammals as Pets*

Introduction   327

CHAPTER THIRTY-TWO   329
What Is a Mammal?

CHAPTER THIRTY-THREE   338
How to Handle Mammals

CHAPTER THIRTY-FOUR   351
Marsupials as Pets

CHAPTER THIRTY-FIVE   356
Insect-eaters as Pets

CHAPTER THIRTY-SIX   359
Meat-eaters as Pets

CHAPTER THIRTY-SEVEN   372
Rodents as Pets

CHAPTER THIRTY-EIGHT   394
A Wacky Mammal

Index   397

PART I

Exotic Fish as Pets

INTRODUCTION

Much has been written about exotic fish or, as many persons still call them "tropical fish." Actually, the name *tropical* is not quite accurate, because a great many of the fish kept in home aquariums are not tropical at all, but are native to temperate climates and some even from cold areas. Exotic is a much better name, because it implies that the fish is unusual in some kind of way, either because of its great beauty, strange habits, bizarre shape or in some other out-of-the-ordinary way.

It is usually the case that fish from warm climates and from the tropics, where it is actually very hot and humid, are more highly colored than those which originate in temperate zones such as the United States.

Before you even start trying to set up an aquarium, you must know certain things. One thing—the most important of all, I would say—is that an aquarium takes time and care to set up, and then takes additional time to keep in proper order. The fish, once introduced into their home, must be fed at regular intervals, and this is something that cannot be haphazard or sketchy. Fish, just like humans, must have food, proper food, and enough of it, in order to remain healthy and live their normal life span. It must be realized that fish in an aquarium in the home, or even in a large public aquarium, are living under a far different environment than they did in the wild. Even though they were hatched in captivity, their lives are lived in a few gallons of water subject to changing temperatures and unnatural lighting conditions, fed artificial foods and frightened many times each day by some great hulking person—you—approaching their tank. Under these conditions it is a marvel that fish can exist at all, let alone become content or at least tolerant of their environment, even to the point where they can be successfully mated and the young raised to maturity.

It is only because of the enormous amount of research done by amateur and professional aquarists the world over, that this is possible. Countless millions of small beautiful exotic fish have died before methods of keeping them successfully have been learned.

So, knowing all this, if you are not willing to put yourself out a bit, to take on a job that will never end as long as there is a fish left in your tank, and accept the responsibility of the lives of your little pets, then it is far better for the fish if you do something else for a hobby—something not connected with living creatures who are utterly dependent upon your care for their very lives.

On the other hand, if you do take the responsibility, then there is hardly anything more rewarding than a well-set-up aquarium, stocked with healthy, colorful exotic fish. They can give you many many hours of enjoyment and satisfaction.

The purpose here is not to catalogue all the fish that are available in the thousands of pet shops throughout the country, but to describe some of the things that exotic fish need for their comfort and welfare; to tell you how to set an aquarium up properly and how to maintain it once it has been established; to list the best kinds of plants and fish for you to start your hobby and give you some information about diseases and how to treat them; and to give you all this information in a way that you, as a beginner, can understand it.

CHAPTER ONE

A Little About Water

If you take the contents of an aquarium in the order of their importance, the most important part of it is the water. Without water, everybody knows, fish cannot live. Fish do not *breathe* water, however—they breathe the oxygen that is dissolved in the water. Since the amount of oxygen dissolved in water is quite small, you must have a tank large enough to hold enough water to supply enough oxygen to the fish you intend keeping. This is the first fundamental fact you must know about your aquarium.

The amount of oxygen dissolved in the water is controlled in several ways. One way is by an aerator or pump which continuously pumps air into the water, breaking it up into fine bubbles by forcing it through a piece of porous stone, so that the oxygen can more easily be taken up by the water.

Actually, even an aerator does not put as much oxygen into the water as many persons think it does. What an aerator is good for is to make the water circulate within the tank, bringing the water from the bottom up to the top and drawing the top water to the bottom. In this way, the gases dissolved in the water are brought to the surface where they may be dispelled into the surrounding atmosphere, allowing room for more oxygen to be dissolved into the water.

One very important item to remember is the possibility of an aerator pump pushing toxic fumes into the water. Many tanks of valuable fish have been lost by the owner forgetting his aerator and deciding to paint a room in his house. The air pump picks up the paint fumes and forces them into the water, killing everything in the tank. Make very sure, if you are using any volatile chemicals, paint thinners, turpentine, or anything that will fill the room with fumes, to shut off the air pump before you start using them. Also, an excellent precaution is to seal the entire top of the tank with a sheet of Saran Wrap, fastening it securely to the sides of the tank with masking tape. The fish can live for several days under this seal, which should be left in place until all the fumes are gone.

Another way to ensure enough oxygen for your fish is by having a large surface area in your tank. This means that the larger the tank, the more fish you can safely keep in it.

You may have heard that a "balanced" aquarium is one in which the number and kinds of plants and the number and sizes of fish balance each other, the idea being that the plants "breathe" carbon dioxide and give off oxygen, and the fish breathe oxygen and give off carbon dioxide. This is not exactly the case, although there are literally thousands of aquarists—people who keep fish in tanks—who will give you or me a very strong argument about it. For many years this was thought to be the only way to keep exotic fish—"balancing" the aquarium, and these old ideas sometimes die very hard.

It is true that fish do use oxygen and do give off carbon dioxide, the same as people do when they breathe. It is also true that in certain periods of growth and activity, the plants give off oxygen, and that they do use some carbon dioxide, but not to the point where they can, as many persons think, support the lives of the fish in a sealed tank.

Although the fish only breathe oxygen in the water, the other things dissolved in it also affect their general health and welfare.

Many different kinds of minerals are found in water. Some metals are also dissolved, and some of these can be fatal to fish, although the water looks clean and you could drink it with no ill effects. Copper, especially, is very bad for fish, and, in city water, chlorine will often kill fish if you put them into water drawn freshly from the faucet.

It is to give these gases time to be dispelled from the water that beginning aquarists are always cautioned to draw the water, then let it stand for at least a day or two before introducing the fish. There are other reasons for this, too, which will be explained later and not only beginning aquarists should let the water stand—every aquarist should do so.

In the early days of keeping exotic fish, very little was known about their requirements, and it was a lucky man, indeed, who was able to keep fish for long, or to get them to breed. Most everything was guesswork and trial and error. You bought fish, filled up a tank with water and dumped them in. As Long John Silver said in Treasure Island, "Them as died was the lucky ones!" Sometimes the poor creatures would gasp for days, before finally giving up and floating to the top. Slowly we learned, and dedicated fanciers studied the behavior of the creatures, trying out one thing after another until that condition was found under which the fish would live longest, act most contented, breed and produce young, and live their "normal" life span. Water chemistry was one of the most important studies, and as each discovery was made, it was recorded in some way—either in a book, or passed on by word of mouth.

Today you can buy a material called Start Right in almost any pet shop, which, when added to the fresh water in an aquarium, removes the chlorine and many of the dissolved minerals, as well as adding antibiotics and conditioners to the water. Theoretically, with Start Right, you can put your fish into fresh water as soon as you have added the chemical. However, it is still excellent practice even with Start Right, to let the tank stand for a day or two before introducing the fish. Actually, the very best thing to do is to fill the tank, plant it with all the plants you are going to use, put in any rocks or other things, such as filter, aerator, heater and thermometer, and then let the whole stand about a week for the plants to become established, to take root and start to grow. *Then* you put in the fish.

A good thing to remember when using any chemicals in your tank, is to follow the instructions that come with the product carefully and accurately. If the label says to add one teaspoonful to five gallons of water, do not get the idea that if one teaspoonful is good, two teaspoonfuls will be better. One spoonful may be good, and two spoonfuls can be fatal to the fish.

Water temperature is very important. You cannot transfer fish from one tank to another or from the pet shop to your tank without first equalizing the temperatures. This is done very simply, by floating the container in which you brought home the fish on the top of the tank into which they are going to be placed. Do this for about one half hour, then the fish can be liberated. If you are transferring fish from one tank to another—a very bad practice, by the way, and this is mentioned here only because sometimes in an emergency, this must be done—then net out the fish and place them into a container with water from their original tank, and float this container on the top of the new tank for one half hour before releasing the fish.

One degree or even two degrees warmer water will not be too harmful to a fish, but to place a fish from warm water into colder water, even only a degree or two colder, is asking for trouble and dead fish. The temperatures in aquariums can be accurately held with the use of aquarium heaters that are thermostatically controlled. An important item of water condition is pH. pH is the symbol given to indicate the hydrogen ion concentration in water. A pH of 7 is neutral. Acid water has a pH of less than 7 and alkaline water a pH of more than 7. To adjust the pH of water, chemically, acid and alkaline solutions of sodium phosphate may be used.

In the early days it was known that certain fish did better in old and acid water than in new alkaline water. It is now known that certain species of fish cannot live unless the pH of the water is suited to their requirements. Unless you adjust the pH of your water, you simply will not be able to keep those fish alive for any length of time. Fortunately there are kits on the market now to use for testing the pH of water, and these are so simple to use that anyone who is not color blind can test water with them. Also, chemicals are available to adjust the pH of water. I am not sure just how beneficial the use of these chemicals are to the welfare of the fish, but they are used and they seem to work in many cases. I would prefer to adjust the pH by adding rain water, or distilled water, or even filtered water from an outdoor pond, provided—and this is most important—you are absolutely certain there has been no spraying of DDT on or near the water you take.

Sodium monohydrogen phosphate (Na_2HPO_4) is dissolved in the concentration of one and one half ounces per gallon of distilled water. This solution can be used for adjusting the pH of an aquarium to the alkaline side, according to the instructions I will give you.

Sodium dihydrogen phosphate (NaH_2PO_4) is made into solution in the same concentration—that is, one and one half ounces per gallon of distilled water. This solution will be used to adjust the pH to the acid side.

To adjust a tank, you must take a measured quantity of water from the tank, and test it. A gallon would be good to start with.

If the adjustment is to be made to the acid side, add the dihydrogen solution one drop at a time, mixing it in thoroughly, and testing the pH as you go along. Keep an accurate record of the number of drops needed to bring the measured gallon to the desired pH, then it is a simple matter to calculate the total number of drops needed to bring the entire tank to the same level, taking into careful consideration the space within the tank that is taken up by the rocks and gravel. The same method is used for adjusting the water to the alkaline side.

One important thing you must remember is that a tank cannot be drastically adjusted at one time. If the adjustment is more than 0.3 or 0.5 pH step, then you must perform the change over a number of days, adjusting not more than the above steps in one day. This would mean that if a tank had to be adjusted 1.3 pH steps, you would adjust not more than 0.5 the first day, then wait two or three days to make the second adjustment of another 0.5. Another wait of two days before the final adjustment of the remaining 0.3 steps is necessary.

"New water" is a term applied to water that has been recently put into use; "old water" has been in a tank for a long time with plants and fish living in it. Usually, old water is acid as a normal condition, but this need not necessarily be so. If the water were strongly alkaline to begin with, then it is not going to become acid within the time you would keep it going in an aquarium.

When using water from outdoors (except rain water) or when aging water with leaves, you should always filter it at least twice before using. This is necessary in order to screen out as much bacterial matter as possible and also larger animal life that would be bad for the fish that will eventually live in the water. Some of the protozoan life is very small and cannot be seen with the unaided eye. This matter can be filtered out through regular filter paper. Your local drugstore should be able to supply you with this circular paper that can be folded and placed within a funnel for filtering purposes. Do not filter the water two times through the same paper. Always use a fresh sheet of paper for the second filtering.

Water containing dissolved minerals is said to be hard. Water free from these salts is soft. The hardness of water is measured in degrees of DH, and there are kits available to perform this determination. (DH is the German scale of measurement of the degree of hardness of water. It is measured in parts-per-million [ppm], and designates the amount of minerals dissolved in the water.) Rila Products of Teaneck, New Jersey, makes such a kit, and it should be used according to the directions supplied with it. No chemicals can be used to reduce hardness of water without being harmful to the fish. It is best to reduce hardness by the addition of distilled water or clean rain water. The brown water of bog areas may also be used to dilute hard water, reducing the hardness somewhat. But the addition of distilled water is the fastest and safest way.

Even if you start with soft water, it may become hard after several months of use in an aquarium, especially if you have a number of shells as ornaments, or a large number of snails which die from time to time, leaving their shells behind to dissolve and add minerals to the water. Limestone rocks also make water hard, and some gravel with limestone in it will do the same.

Green water can be the bane of the aquarist's life, and, yet, at the same time is a very valuable material if you are breeding small egg-laying fish. Green water is caused by the growth of tiny species of algae, which multiply until they are present in such numbers as to make the water actually look like pea soup. Fish do not, as a general rule, live well in green water.

This growth of algae is caused by the tank receiving too much light. If you cut the light down, the growth will slow correspondingly. Algae growth is an indication, also, that the water is hard, since most species of algae require minerals for their growth. Green water cannot be cleared by changing part of the water in the tank. This will only speed up the growth of the algae since, in changing the water, you are merely adding new supplies of the minerals that algae need to grow on.

If you have a tank that turns green, the best thing to do is to remove the fish temporarily to another tank, and let the green tank remain as it is. Within a fairly short time, you will notice that the algae stops growing, and then starts to disappear. Shortly after that, the water will clear. The reason is simple—the algae exhausted the supply of minerals in the water and then starved to death.

CHAPTER TWO

Establishing an Aquarium

Setting up an aquarium is not a hard job, but it is one that should be planned in advance. First, you should know what kind of aquarium you want to have—a tank with several species of fish mixed in it (called a community tank), one with only one kind of fish, or a tank in which to breed fish. This last kind can be either for live-bearing fish or egg layers.

The usual choice for the beginner to make is a community tank. The second choice is a tank with a school of one kind of fish or a pair of large fish. Either of these possibilities means that the tank should be set up in a place where it can be viewed conveniently, where it will get enough daylight, with perhaps a bit of sun each day, or near enough to a wall outlet so that an artificial light can be used to supply the needs of the fish and the plants. As a matter of fact, an artificial light in a reflector or hood that fits over the top of the tank is much easier to control than daylight near a window.

Aquariums used only for breeding fish need not be set up the way an ornamental tank is. That is to say, it need not be planted with exotic plants, but rather with those kinds of plants that are best for breeding the particular kind of fish you are interested in. Ornamental rocks may be left out of the breeding tank, too, using rocks that would only be of purpose in breeding.

The purpose you intend to put your aquarium to also determines the size and shape of the tank. One used for breeding need not be deep, but rather should have a larger surface area. Unless, of course, you intend trying to breed large fish like Discus, Angelfish or some of the real giants like "Oscars." Then the tank would have to be very large—not less than fifty-gallon capacity. An aquarium used for ornamental purposes should be more rectangular in shape. That is to say, it should not be long and shallow, or tall and thin, but should have more "normal" proportions. I say normal proportions, since, throughout the years of keeping fish in tanks, a kind of standard of sizes has been established.

We would strongly recommend that you set up the largest tank your budget will allow, since the larger the tank, the easier it is to maintain it for long periods of time. The temperature remains more constant in a large tank than it does in a small one. The plants do better, and certainly, so do the fish, even if they are small fish. If you bear in mind the artificial conditions under which you are keeping the animals, then you will realize that the more swimming space you have for them, the better off they will be. Having determined the type of aquarium you want to have and the location where it is going to be set up, then you can start getting all the needed items together.

First, of course, is the tank itself. When the hobby was just becoming started, aquarists usually made their own tanks, since there were no commercial ones available. They were welded up out of angle iron, glazed with cement that the person mixed himself, and painted to prevent the frames from rusting out. If the interested person was unable to make his own tank, then he had to hire some shop to make it for him to his own specifications.

Finally commercial tanks came on the market. The first of these were spot-welded out of sheet steel, then enamelled to cover the bare metal. In a few years, as the hobby of keeping exotic fish grew in leaps and bounds, tanks made with frames of stainless steel appeared. These had the advantage of not rusting, and were much better looking than those with painted frames.

Recently modern research has developed silicone adhesives which have forever changed the conditions confronting the aquarist. Manufacturers started to make tanks with no frames at all! These tanks are all glass, cemented together at the edges with one of the modern adhesives, and they are so strong that they may be lifted by an end glass, even when the tank is partly filled with water, with no failure of the joint.

The tanks are perfect for fresh-water or salt-water fish, with no need to protect the occupants, since the adhesive is non-toxic to marine life. Anyway, practically none of the adhesive comes into contact with the water. These tanks are made in all the standard sizes used in making the old-style tanks with frames of metal as well as in some new sizes. Even one-hundred-gallon tanks are produced, cemented together with no frames supporting the joints. Today, these tanks are available in most of the better pet stores, and any pet store can get them for you very easily, even if they do not regularly stock them.

Following is a table of standard sizes of tanks, as used for home aquariums:

5 gallon	8″ deep,	10″ high,	14″ long
10 gallon	10″ deep,	12″ high,	20″ long
15 gallon	12″ deep,	12″ high,	24″ long
20 gallon	12″ deep,	16″ high,	24″ long
30 gallon	12″ deep,	16″ high,	36″ long
50 gallon	18″ deep,	18″ high,	36″ long
100 gallon	18″ deep,	18″ high,	72″ long

There are more, but anything larger than one-hundred-gallon

capacity is special, and I would not recommend using anything less than a five-gallon tank. In fact, I do not recommend using anything smaller than a twenty-gallon tank for keeping fish—anything smaller is used only as a "hospital" tank, a quarantine tank, or for some special purpose other than as a home for exotic fish. The exception is for keeping the beautiful fighting fish from Siam (Thailand) which are regularly kept separated in small tanks, or kept in a specially designed long tank having several partitions inside to separate the individuals. Since these fish breathe air directly, instead of only taking oxygen from the water, they can very easily be kept in small containers. They require no aeration or a large surface to keep them in good health.

Having decided on the tank size, you can get it set up ready for the fish. Next to the water, plants are the most important part of setting up your aquarium. There are dozens of different kinds of plants that live completely submerged in water, and many of these make excellent aquarium decorations.

In order to keep plants thriving in an aquarium, you must have something to plant them in. The best thing to use for this is gravel, which can be purchased in pet stores by the pound. The entire bottom of the tank should be covered with gravel to a depth of not less than one and one half inches in front and two inches in the rear. The gravel must be washed before using it.

To do this chore, put a small amount of gravel in a clean pail and fill the pail with water, stirring up the gravel all the time. Pour off the water, letting the gravel drain well. Do this several times, until the water, when the gravel is stirred up vigorously, remains clear. When all the gravel is in the tank, spread it so that it slopes forward from the rear side of the tank to the front glass.

The gravel used should be fairly coarse, and, while all kinds of colors are available in the stores, the plain common gravel still looks best in a well-planted tank. Avoid using the very fine "bird" gravel. This is fine on the bottom of birdcages, and the snowy white color is attractive, but the grains are so fine that the gravel packs too tightly and traps gases and waste matter, turning black in a short time and fouling the water.

Black gravel looks nice under some conditions. A tank, planted heavily with low and bunchy plants, with a large school of Neons or Cardinals as the only fish, shows up the brilliant metallic colors of these fish very well if the bottom is covered with black gravel. Red, yellow, blue or green gravel is garish and out of place in the tank. First of all, these colored gravels do not occur in natural conditions; secondly, they impart a color to the water that detracts from the natural beauty of the fish; and, lastly, they look terrible against the green of the plants. Still, some people must like the effect of these colors or the stores wouldn't be selling the stuff.

Now a couple of interesting rocks may be put in place to afford planting areas, or to hide a filter in a corner. The rocks should be scrubbed with plain water and a brush before putting them into the tank. Do not wash rocks with soap or detergents. Also, in selecting rocks, make sure they are suitable for use in an aquarium. Many rocks are slightly soluble in water. That is, they contain minerals that dissolve out of them into the water. This may result in the death of the fish, the death of the plants or the death of the Scavengers used in the aquarium—fish, snails, or other kinds. Selected rocks are sold in most pet stores, and they are so cheap that it pays to use them instead of hunting for "wild" rocks.

After the washed gravel is all in place and any rocks or other additions put into position, place several thicknesses of clean newspapers on top of the gravel and s-l-o-w-l-y fill the tank about halfway with water. The water should be tempered—not icy cold right out of the faucet, nor should it be too warm. The best temperature is that which will be close to the temperature required for whatever kind of fish you are keeping. The chapter on fish tells the best temperatures for each species, so you could use that as your guide.

When the tank is about half full, gently remove the newspaper, taking care not to wring it out into the tank. Lift it out into a container so you do not drip all over the house, and dispose of it in that fashion. You are now ready to start planting your tank. You should never try to plant a tank without some water in it, since you cannot see the way the plant will naturally fall after it has been set into the gravel. Nor is it a good idea to try to plant a tank which is filled with water, since you get your sleeves wet, possibly make the tank run over as you immerse your entire arm in it, and you have to work at such an awkward angle that it is difficult to see what you are doing.

In planting your tank, try to use some system of arrangement. The taller plants should be toward the rear of the tank, short ones down in front. Short plants placed around a rock show up very nicely, and the rock affords a good hold for the roots of the plants after they have started to grow and also provides a good hiding place for the fish.

Do not be stingy with the number of plants you use. It is difficult to put in too many. After the planting has been completed, you may fill the tank to the top. That is to say, to within perhaps one half inch from the top edges. If you are going to use an aerator, or filter, or both, they are put into position during the planting, because some of the plants will be used to conceal the accessory as much as possible. If you are using an outside filter, then, of course, this is put into position after the tank is filled.

When you fill the tank after planting, you may either lay sheets of newspaper right in on top of the plants to break the fall of the water, or you can fill the tank by pouring the additional water in on one of your hands, cupped to catch and dissipate it. This will avoid digging holes in the gravel with the flow of water, uprooting plants and even shifting rocks around. The pouring should be done slowly and easily. The cover, or hood, is now put on top and the tank allowed to stand until it is ready for the fish.

A 30-gallon aquarium with a set of Decro-Corners supplied by the National Aquarium Supplies and Accessories Company. The corners and borders are self-sticking and frame a tank very nicely.

Tanks can be covered in several ways, the simplest being a sheet of glass cut to fit the top of the tank. A corner may have to be cut off to allow the introduction of a heater, thermometer, or tubes from an outside filter. Sometimes, if two or more of these accessories are used, two or more corners must be clipped off the cover glass.

Stainless steel reflectors are sold to fit all sizes of tanks. They are fitted both for incandescent bulbs and for fluorescent tubes. The latter is the best kind to get, because incandescent bulbs give off a great amount of heat and the illumination they provide is not distributed over the length of the tank, but is concentrated in one spot. Sylvania Electric Products, Inc. manufactures a fluorescent tube called Gro-Lux. This is specially designed to produce that particular quality of light best suited for the growth of plants, either in the air or in aquariums. Under Gro-Lux tube lighting, the plants thrive in the aquarium. Not only that, but the colors on the fish are greatly enhanced. They literally glow under this light and their colors become vivid and strong. Once you view your exotics under a Gro-Lux, you will never again be satisfied with ordinary lighting.

Besides the reflectors, hoods covering the entire top of the tank are also manufactured. These, too, can be bought for fluorescent tube lights, and they usually have punched-out spaces to accommodate the filters, heaters and other accessories. There is a flap which can be lifted up in order to feed the fish or work in the tank.

Wrought-iron stands are available at pet stores upon which your tank may be placed. The stands are sold in sizes to match the sizes of the tanks.

CHAPTER THREE

A Little About Fish

First of all, fish are cold-blooded. This merely means that, instead of body heat being generated by metabolism, the body of the fish is the same temperature as the water in which it is swimming. This will explain to you, perhaps, why it is of such importance to maintain constant temperature in a tank, and why it is often fatal to the fish to chill a tank suddenly. The fish cannot adapt so rapidly to these sudden changes of temperature. There are other cold-blooded creatures on earth too. The enormous group of reptiles is cold-blooded. Amphibians are also cold-blooded, as are insects. Mammals and birds are warm-blooded animals.

Most fish have seven fins. The two fins most persons will instantly recognize are the back fin, or *dorsal fin,* and the tail fin, or *caudal fin.* Just in front of the caudal fin, on the bottom of the fish, is the *anal fin.* In front of the anal fin, on both sides of the bottom of the fish is the pair of *ventral fins.* The other two fins are on the sides of the fish, just behind the gill opening, and these are called the *pectoral fins.* If you look down at the top of the fish, you will probably see that generally, even while standing still in the water, the pectoral fins are constantly moving in a paddling motion, much like the oars of a rowboat. The fish uses its pectoral fins to hold its position or to change its position in the water. It also uses them as a brake to come to a stop while swimming from one place to another.

You will note that the fins of a fish usually have rays in them. These are stiffening bones which can be used to hold the fin erect or to fold it down against the body. If a fish habitually remains with its fins folded, it is usually a sign that the fish is in poor health or poor condition.

On certain fish you will find an eighth fin. This is a very small fin on the back, behind the dorsal fin and in front of the caudal fin. It has no rays. This is called the *adipose fin,* and it is an easy way to identify one group of fish—the *Characins.* When you find any fish with an adipose fin, you are pretty certain that it is a member of this large family of small fish, very popular with aquarists the world over.

Do not confuse the adipose fin with a double dorsal fin, which some fish have. The adipose does not have rays, and the dorsal fin has. Dorsal fins are divided into two parts—spiny and soft. Usually the front part of the dorsal is spiny or stiff, and the back part is soft or very thinly rayed. Some fish have the dorsal divided so that the front part and the back part look like two different fins. Besides the Characins, some of the Catfish have an adipose fin, and this fin is supported by one spine, or ray.

Down the sides of a fish is a line, running from the gill to the caudal fin, a *lateral line,* and it is a very special sense organ to the fish. With it the fish can detect sounds, vibrations in the water and also pressure changes in the water. It is believed by many scientists that there are even more uses of this line than we know about, such as gauging distance from other fish when schooling.

Some kinds of fish have the ability to breathe air directly as well as to take their oxygen from the water. These fish are called labyrinth fish, so named because they possess a labyrinth in the head above the gills, with which chambers they breathe the air directly. To this group belong the fighting fish, the Gouramis and other species. Most of the air-breathing fish build nests out of the bubbles which they make from a mouthful of air coated with mucus, and which floats on top of the water. Into this mass of bubbles they place their eggs, watching under the nest until the young fish hatch, keeping the baby fish in among the bubbles until they are old enough to swim freely.

In the chapters that follow, no scientific order is adhered to in listing the fish. They are listed in the order of their popularity to aquarists, and their availability in pet stores.

CHAPTER FOUR

A Little About Breeding

Sooner or later most people keeping exotic fish are going to want to breed them.

If you have live-bearers there is very little you have to do with their breeding—the fish manage this all by themselves. About the only thing live-bearers need in order to reproduce is enough food, and food of the right kind for the species; clean tanks and comfortable conditions wthin the tank. There must be plants in sufficient quantity and of the proper kind to afford hiding places for the young as they are born.

Artificial spawning refuges are now sold in pet stores, made of nylon wool. They are called spawning mops, and a couple of these, either anchored in the gravel or floating on the top of the water, provide plenty of cover for the babies. I prefer natural plants, though. A few bunches of Anacharis, Cabomba, Parrot's-Feather, a very dense thicket of Corkscrew Val, or even a good-sized patch of floating plants that have trailing root structures are all one needs to protect the young and safely bring them through the trying time of early life. Floating plants are very good, because the dust-sized food that you feed the new-born live-bearers does not sink readily to the bottom of the tank, and the baby fish, hiding in floating plants, are right at the source of food when you put it in. The fine particles of food spread in around the plants.

Many, if not most of the live-bearing fish sold today are artificial strains. The original stock was something quite different from what you now find in the pet store tanks. Most of them do not even resemble their parent stock. Colors differ, size of fins and shape of fins and tails, all have been altered by selective breeding until the result is an entirely different kind of fish. While this makes for more colorful or more ornamental fish, it must be remembered that in buying stock for your own breeding, there is an excellent chance that they will not breed true.

This is to say, successive matings and breeding of your stock may result in a gradual return to the original parent stock, and you will have fish you will not even recognize. Most of the time, the parent stock from which very gaily colored fish are bred is drab and colorless in comparison. Guppies are a perfect example of this. Wild Guppies are olive-colored little fish, with a few spots of color on the males, especially when they are mating. But today, the number of different kinds of Guppies would almost fill a book by themselves. These busy little fish come in nearly any color combination you want. They come with every imaginable size and shape of fin and tail.

It is nearly impossible to get a female live-bearer which is not pregnant at the time of purchase. First of all, they can be, and usually are, fertilized when they are just a few days old. This does not mean that they bear their first young at that time, however. The females carry the sperm inside their bodies, and one injection of sperm will fertilize a female for several broods of babies. About the only way to make sure that a female remains virgin until she is bred to a particular male is to take all the baby fish within a day or so of birth, and place each one in a separate container, raising them apart until you can determine the sexes, at which time all the males can be put together and all the females in another tank.

Even this precaution may come to no good end, because it is a matter of record, and indeed, not an uncommon thing, for live-bearing fish to change sex from male to female. Also, sometimes male fish take a long time to develop their sexual characteristics, and what you thought were young females might very well have been retarded development in young males. If this happened in your female tank, you would have every female in the tank fertilized before you even knew anything was wrong. Sex changes have been recorded also in a few species of egg-laying fish, but not nearly so many as in the case of live-bearers.

Live-bearers breed more frequently in warm water. Too much cold or too little light seems to slow down their sexual activities. A temperature of 75 to 80 degrees is fine for breeding. They also require a great amount of light for good breeding. A reflector over the tank should take care of this need quite adequately. Since the newly born babies swim toward the brightest part of the tank, it would be a good idea to put a small bulb against an end of the tank where you have planted the bunch plants for cover for the young. Swimming toward the light will also bring them to safety among the plants. Newly born fry of live-bearers can be fed Miracle Fry Treet. This is a prepared balanced food manufactured by Miracle Pet Products, Inc. It is rich in protein, and contains fish and shrimp meal. It is finely powdered so the tiny fish can easily take it in their mouths.

One thing to remember when a live-bearer female is giving birth is to keep her well fed. This lessens the chance of her eating her own babies. Live food is best, and a netful of Daphnia, mosquito larvae or brine shrimp dropped into the tank as soon as the delivery of young starts is a good precaution. The female will be busy eating these preferred foods, and most of the babies will escape to the safety of the plant thicket or nylon mop.

Lustar Products Company of Springfield, New Jersey, makes

several different kinds of breeding traps for the delivery of live-bearer young, as well as for the dropping of non-adhesive eggs by such fish as Danios. Two kinds of very practical traps are the Picture Window Fish Breeder and the Five-way Breeding Trap. Both of these hang suspended in a large tank, and the gravid females are placed within them when the time draws near for them to drop their babies. The sides and bottom of the Picture Window Breeder are made of plastic mesh. The baby fish swim out of the breeder which confines the female. When she has completed her delivery she can be replaced in her own tank. The bottom of the five-way trap is made of plastic rods, and there are slots in the sides. The baby fish can swim out of this trap also, and gain safety in the large tank in which the trap is suspended.

Breeding egg layers is a quite different thing from breeding live-bearers. With very few exceptions you must condition the fish for breeding, and then, if the conditions are not just right for that particular species, you will have no success. The four important conditions for breeding any species of egg-laying fish are: correct temperature, correct lighting, correct water conditions (pH and DH) and correct feeding. Perhaps we should list five conditions rather than four, and include correct tank environment, since many egg layers require some support for the eggs, or some method of trapping the eggs so they will not be eaten.

The first thing you must do when trying to breed egg layers is to make sure you have fish of different sexes. This is not as silly as it may sound, because there is often a great difficulty in telling the males apart from the females. In some species, perhaps the only way to tell is by a slightly different fin shape. In others, the male might have a spot of color present that is missing in the female. Still others may vary in body shape, or in body size.

Some species are impossible to distinguish, and these may only be tried again and again until the breeder finally has success, and then he may be able to find differences that will enable others to sex the fish.

In the chapters on fish, the breeding requirements for each species are given, if they are known. Here we will tell you of common requirements that must be used with all egg-laying fish.

First is conditioning. This merely means that the fish are brought to the peak of health, ready for breeding. To achieve this peak, large quantities of live food must be fed to the fish. Start giving them two feedings each day—as much as they will eat. Watch them closely to see if they come into breeding color. This will vary, naturally, with each species, so look for the colors on the species you are breeding to become brighter or to change, if this is the nature of that particular fish.

At the time of conditioning on live foods, test the water, and, if it is not at the optimum pH or DH for the fish, slowly start adjusting both until it is. Do not make these changes rapidly. Take several days to raise or lower the pH a degree or two.

When the water has been adjusted, and while you are continuing the twice-daily feedings of live food, start bringing the temperature up to the breeding range of those fish you are working with, if the tank has been maintained at a slightly lower temperature—which it should have been. Again, take a few days to raise the temperature more than a degree or two, and watch the thermometer very closely to make certain the temperature does not shoot up suddenly or go too high.

Check the planting arrangement within the tank. If the species requires bunch plants in which to deposit eggs, make sure there are several bunches in different locations throughout the area of the tank. If the species is one that fastens its eggs onto a

This pair of Golden Cichlids have cleaned out the flowerpot in order to spawn within it.

support, either bladelike leaves of plants, cleaned rocks or other support, then provide such arrangements for them. Some of the stiff-leaved *Sagittaria* will do nicely for the blades. A small bar of clean slate, placed in a slanting position upright in a corner of the tank, will provide a welcome support for the eggs of Angelfish, Discus and other species. A small ceramic saucer laid on the bottom of the tank in a clearing will make an ideal "nest" for certain of the Cichlids, and for other species of Cichlids, a broken flowerpot, laid on its side to make a cave will serve very well.

All other fish except the breeders should be removed from the tank. It is far better to remove the other fish rather than to transfer the breeders. With many species, it is best to use trios for breeding. This is to say two females and one male. Some species get pretty rough when breeding, and very often, the male will kill a female, or sometimes it is the other way around. Some fish require two males to one female, and, generally, these kinds are very rough; the males getting the female between them, then ramming her sides to literally knock the eggs out of her, at the same time fertilizing them as they leave the female. After such matings the female is battered and bruised, and often dies.

CHAPTER FIVE

Plants in the Aquarium

Plants are used in aquariums for several reasons: as a refuge for those fish that are low down on the "pecking order," as a refuge for the young of live-bearing fish or as a decorative medium.

Plants in the aquarium also give off some oxygen and take up some carbon dioxide. Plants form an important base for the growth of algae, which in the case of certain species of fish is necessary or they will not live. Algae will also grow on the glass sides of the tank, and on any rocks placed for decoration or as an aid in the planting.

Plants used in aquariums fall into several groups or categories. For our purposes, however, we will consider only three groups of water plants. These are: plants that float on the surface of the water, plants that grow partly out of the water, and plants that grow completely under the surface of the water. Actually, not so many kinds grow this way as you may think. Many of the plants used in aquariums are really not underwater plants at all, they are just able to live for a time under water.

Most of the plants are kinds that live with "their feet wet." This means that the plant's normal condition is to live in wet mud or sand, with the roots under water, but with all or part of the leaves out of the water. Some of them live with the leaves submerged, but the flower or flower spike shoots up out into the air.

Cryptocorynes are important plants. They are decorative, rather than bunching or hiding plants. Usually they grow into a beautiful shrubby center plant, especially in large tanks, and they can be the focal point around which the entire tank is decorated. The family of *Cryptocorynes* is a large one, and several different species are available at one time or another in pet stores. These are not truly underwater plants but rather plants of bogs and marshes where the roots can grow under shallow water and the leaves out or partly out in the air. The plants will grow, however, completely submerged, and the group, as a whole, are about the most decorative plants we have for our aquariums. The sizes of "Crypts" range from tiny dwarf species to large, bushy, shrublike plants. The leaves are narrow or broad, some of them being almost round. They may be smooth or wavy, green or dull reddish or purplish. Some are green on top and red underneath.

Crypts like soft, acid water, and they do not need a lot of light. They do like a good amount of fertilizer, so when you plant them, try to dish out the gravel around the plants to make shallow pockets into which the fish droppings will gravitate. Then you can grade the rest of the gravel on the bottom to these pockets, and much of the droppings will be utilized by the plants.

One of the most elegant of the Crypts is *C. chordata*. A plant which is so similar that it is often sold as chordata is *C. griffithii*. Both of these plants are tall and, when in good health and growth, are large, magnificent, shrubby specimens. In fact, it is most likely that all the Crypts you buy as *chordata* are really *griffithii*. Plant them in the center of the tank or toward the back glass. Close to a rock is good.

A low Crypt with dark green leaves, red on the underneath side is *C. affinis*. These make excellent plantings in a row right in front of a low rock. You should plant three or four of them in a group. Under the right conditions they will grow and multiply, and it will not be many months before you have two or three times as many as you planted. They can be thinned out a little and the new plants used for a different aquarium.

Cryptocoryne willisii has long, narrow leaves which are beautifully wavy on their edges. The leaves usually stand upright, making the plant a good one for the back of the tank. It can grow into quite a large bush, however, so do not put it too close to the glass, but leave room for development. For some reason or other, *willisii* does not seem to thrive when a tank is heavily planted with other species of *Cryptocorynes*. It does well, though, with other plants. For this reason, it is good to use a large *willisii* as the main attraction in your planting, and then use other kinds of plants for the rest of the tank.

The next group of plants we will consider is *Echinodorus*. To this genus belongs the famous Amazon Sword plant, which has been the main centerpiece plant in aquariums almost from the very first setup. They are beautifully full and bushy, and grow very large if kept in a large tank. As a centerpiece in a fifty-gallon tank, it is ideal. There are three kinds of Sword plants. *Echinodorus brevipedicellatus* is the small-leaved Amazon Sword plant and *E. paniculatus* is the regular leaved one. The third species is *E. magdalenensis,* the Dwarf Amazon Sword plant. Both of the large kinds are excellent for the center of a tank. They should not be planted in anything smaller than a twenty-gallon size, though, or there will not be enough room for the plant to develop.

For smaller tanks than twenty gallons, you can use the Dwarf Swords. Sometimes the plant you buy will develop into a "mother" plant. This simply means that the plant will put out runners, at the ends of which new plants will develop. A mother plant is highly prized, since you will continue to get many new plants without disturbing the original one, and at no further cost to you. The ends of the runners will droop until they touch the gravel, then roots will sprout and grow into the gravel, and the tiny plant start right above. When the new plant has a good growth it can be taken off the mother plant by clipping the shoot right in front of the new growth. Plant the new one in a large tank with plenty of room around it, and soon you will have a nice showy growth. Swords are not particular as to the water they live in, but they do need lots of light.

"Bunch" plants grow in stemlike formations and are sold in bunches of short sections, usually tied together with a strip of lead. If they are planted as they come from the store, still tied, roots will form at the lower ends of each stem and the plant will grow well. You should always keep nipping off the buds at the tops of the stems. If this is done, the plants will bush out and remain dense and full. If the top or apical buds are not kept cut off, the stems will shoot up to the top of the tank and grow right out of the water, looking like a wire with a leaf stuck on here and there. These "leggy" plants are not pretty to look at, they do not afford a hiding place for the fish and they add nothing to the decoration of a tank.

Some of these plants are: *Hygrophila polysperma,* with smooth, oval leaves, a pleasant shade of bright green. This is a good plant for hiding filters in a corner of the tank or for making dense thickets for small fish to hide in. It is sold under the name of Hygrophila.

Bacopa caroliniana is sold as Bacopa. This plant has thick fleshy stems with thick rounded leaves growing opposite each other. The plant has a fragrance that is quite strong. Bacopa tends to become stringy after a short time in the tank.

Ludwigia resembles Hygrophila somewhat, but is a more

Myriophyllum proserpinacoides. Parrot's-Feather is one of the more beautiful of the bunch plants, but the tops of each stem must be pinched off or the plant will grow right out of the aquarium.

manageable plant. Its full name is *Ludwigia mullerti*. It, too, gets leggy and lank in growth, but not as fast as some of the other cutting plants. It is an old favorite.

Water Sprite is the name given to *Ceratopteris thalictroides*. This plant will run wild in your tank if you do not keep it cut back severely. In a matter of a week or two, your tank will be full of Water Sprite. Bits of leaves will break off, each one starting a new plant. Parts of the stem will float to the top, there to multiply until you have hardly any water surface left.

Myriophyllum, Cabomba and Anacharis are brushy-looking plants sold in bunches. They all tend to stretch out toward the surface of the water after a time, but they do make excellent hiding places for small fish when thickly planted. If you keep live-bearing fish, these plants are perfect refuges for the tiny babies after they are born.

For a background screen, the most effective plants are the "eel grasses." Of these, *Vallisneria spiralis* is the favorite. This is a very graceful plant, having long, thin, narrow, erect leaves, each one twisted into a spiral. You buy them by the dozen or hundred and plant them thickly in a row close to the glass. The plants will send out runners, new plants developing on them at intervals of an inch or more. Pet store owners usually call this plant Val.

Sagittaria sinensis is another favorite. This looks very much like Val, but the leaves are heavier, thicker, and not twisted. There are several species of *Sagittaria* available from time to time, and one Giant Sag that is useful as a background screen in large tanks.

CHAPTER SIX

Foods for the Fish

Fish have to be fed, and the food given them must be the proper kind in order for them to remain healthy and contented, and for them to grow and reproduce. There are literally dozens of kinds of fish foods sold in pet stores. Most of them are all right, some are no good at all, and some are excellent.

Ideally, nothing but living food should be supplied exotic fish in the home aquarium, but this is quite impractical from several points of view. The first is the cost. Live food is not cheap. True, a portion of brine shrimp or Tubifex worms only costs a quarter, but multiply this low figure by day in and day out feedings, and you will see that it comes to a respectable sum.

Live food, therefore, could be used to supplement the regular dry foods given to the fish. However, there are several species of fish which will eat nothing but live foods, and this is a factor to take into consideration before you buy them. There are several kinds of live foods available in most pet stores.

Brine shrimp are usually sold throughout the entire year. This is an excellent food for nearly every species of fish, from Guppies to Sea Horses. You can hatch your own brine shrimp very easily, and use it to feed your charges. Raising the shrimp to adult size is another thing entirely. If you want to feed adult brine shrimp to your fish, I strongly suggest you buy them from the pet store instead of trying to rear them yourself.

Brine shrimp eggs are sold in vials and packages. They look like fine brown dust. The remarkable thing about the eggs is that they can be dried out for years and still hatch when put into salt water. If you live near the seashore, it is a simple matter to dip up enough clean sea water to use for hatching the eggs. You need add nothing to sea water, but just keep it slightly warm, about 70 to 75 degrees. It can even go as high as 80 degrees, and the only result will be that the eggs will hatch a little sooner.

Brine shrimp eggs hatch best if they are placed in wide, shallow pans. The more air surface, the better. The containers must be made of glass, unchipped porcelain enamel, or other noncorroding material, since even stainless steel will disintegrate in sea water. The proportion of eggs to water should be not more than one half level teaspoon per gallon of water. These eggs should be floated on the top of the water and left undisturbed until they hatch, which, at 75 degrees, should take not more than one day, or two at the most. The newly hatched brine shrimp do not look at all like the adults. They are called *nauplii* and they are very tiny. A small amount, say one fourth teaspoonful, of baker's yeast can be added to the water after the eggs hatch. This will provide food for the little creatures. The yeast will make a cloud in the water, and you should not feed any more until this cloud has been cleared up.

If you do not have access to sea water, there is no problem. Salt can be added to fresh water and the eggs will hatch just the same. Use five or six heaping tablespoons of rock salt or regular salt to the gallon of fresh water, or otherwise, follow the directions on the label of the bottle in which your eggs are sold.

Earthworms are another excellent fish food. They should be chopped before feeding them to your fish, however, and this is a messy job. The value of earthworms is so great, though, that it is

worth the messiness and bother to prepare them. If the earthworms are very small, and your fish are very large, they may be
fed whole.

Earthworms, too, can be raised at home. Many people sell
starting cultures of earthworms by mail. Directions for feeding
accompany the cultures. These are grown for use as bait for
fishermen, as reptile food, and by aquarists. A culture kept in a
cool, dark place, will supply you with good food for a long time.
Look in the classified ads in sporting, fishing and outdoors magazines for places to buy cultures of worms.

Mealworms are the larvae of a small beetle. They can be
purchased in pet stores quite cheaply, and can be raised in the
home very easily. The only requirements for rearing mealworms
successfully is a proper container, proper food, keeping the culture as dry as you possibly can, and providing some place within
the culture for the beetles to lay their eggs, which, in turn will
hatch out into more mealworms.

Department stores and discount stores sell large plastic boxes,
fitted with lids, for use as storage boxes for sweaters or other gar-
ments. One size is about 4 inches deep, and eleven inches by
sixteen inches in the other dimensions. One of these boxes
makes a perfect mealworm culture container. To set it up, cut
about five or six pieces of clean burlap that will fit inside the
box. If you have no clean burlap sacks to get the material from,
most nursery stores and many hardware stores sell burlap for a
few cents per yard. Also, fabric stores sell it.

Lay one sheet of burlap in the bottom of the box, then sprinkle a handful of dry cereal—oatmeal, cornmeal, almost any kind
—and lay a couple of thin slices of raw potato or apple on the
burlap also. This is to provide moisture for the worms, and also
a place for eggs. Drop some mealworms on the meal and cover
with a second sheet of burlap. Continue building up the pile

this way until you have made five or six layers, with some worms in each layer. Then put the cover on top and place the box in a warm dry place to start growing. If you like, and are handy with tools, you can cut several large holes in the top, then cement some window screen over the holes on the inside of the lid, with epoxy cement. This will permit good air circulation and prevent the box from sweating. If it does sweat, you will surely have to drill a number of small holes, at least, to allow the free passage of air.

Within a short time after starting, you will see small grublike things in the culture. These are the pupal stages of the beetle. Later, the beetles will emerge from them. The beetles do not fly, nor do they live very long. About all they do is mate and lay eggs, which is all you want them to do. The eggs hatch in a few days, and, if you examine your culture at frequent intervals, you will see tiny, threadlike worms, newly hatched. When your culture has started to produce new worms, you can start to use the older ones from it for feeding to your fish. These are good only for big-mouthed fish. The butterfly fish love mealworms as do any fish large enough to swallow them.

Do not feed so heavily from your culture that you use up all your breeder worms. Leave some of the big fellows to pupate and carry on the cycle. If you have many fish and need a lot of food, two or three boxes started as cultures can be rotated and will provide you with a continuous supply of good food.

Still another worm and an excellent food that is relished by all fish is Tubifex. These worms grow in sewage, and they are a really dirty job to collect and clean, so it is wiser to buy them in small portions from the pet stores than to try to go out and gather them in. When you bring them home, the lump of worms should be put into a jar or bowl and placed under a cold water faucet, adjusting the water flow to a fast drip or very tiny trickle, right onto the worms. The worms should be left under the water drip until they have been consumed by the fish. Small bits of the lump broken off with your fingers and dropped into the tank will give the fish an important addition to their diet. If you feed Tubifex worms too heavily, they will establish a colony in the gravel. Scavenger fish and snails will root them out, but it is a lot safer to feed just what the fish will eat at a time.

Daphnia is an old mainstay in the live food list. They are called water fleas, and a common variety is named *Daphnia pulex.* These little crustaceans are sold in the pet stores. Daphnia can be raised, but it requires a large pond and a lot of time and trouble to do so and it really is not worth the trouble. When feeding Daphnia, examine the animals closely, since there are often other animals mixed in with the culture, some of them harmful to the fish, especially if you have small fish in the tank.

Many other crustaceans are good for fish food, but usually it is difficult to obtain them in large enough quantities to be of any use. Insect larvae are very good foods, too, and one that is easy to come by is mosquito larvae. If you cut the top out of an old barrel or drum and fill it with water, standing it in some out-of-the-way place in the yard, you will be sure to have a good crop of mosquito larvae in a very short time. If, before you fill the drum, you paint the inside white with a good quality enamel that will withstand the water you will be able to see the larvae very clearly, and it will be much easier to pick out the insects as you need them.

Animal organs make good fish food, too, and one of the better ones is beef heart. You can buy an entire beef heart at the butcher for a small sum, and this can be cut into small chunks and put through a food chopper set at the finest grind. The job is messy, and one which you very probably will dislike, but once you have ground up a heart, you will have a long supply of food, since the ground heart may be put into plastic bags and stored in the freezer, like any other meat, and will keep for a very long time. Be sure that the heart is thawed out completely before feeding it to your fish.

Feed organ meat sparingly, since it will quickly foul a tank, due to its fat content. Also, make sure that any uneaten food is removed from the tank, and not allowed to stand on the bottom.

Frozen heart, liver and other foods are often sold in pet stores, and can be purchased in small quantities if you do not want to go to the trouble of grinding up your own. Freeze-dried animal food is also available, and this includes freeze-dried Tubifex and brine shrimp.

The greatest bulk of fish foods are dried. In dried fish foods many ingredients are used. In many prepared foods, a lot of bulk fillers are added to make larger quantities. The fillers are not necessarily harmful to the fish. The best dried or prepared foods are those which have a high percentage of animal matter in them, although some fish, notably live-bearers like Mollies and Platies, require a high vegetable content in their diet. Algae is high on the list of vegetable foods, with spinach a close second.

Raw canned seafoods are also very good for feeding the fish. Use only those things which are packed in water—not oil-packed substances. Canned shrimp, minced clams, canned crab, canned tuna fish all are very good foods. Break up the pieces until they are the proper size for the fish's mouths, and feed sparingly, so you do not leave a large surplus of uneaten food in the tank.

A whole shrimp, slit many times with a sharp knife until it is shredded, then tied securely to a thread and suspended in the tank, is a good food item. The fish will pick at the meat, pulling off small bites. When they have finished as much as they want, the remaining piece can easily be withdrawn from the water, leaving the tank uncontaminated by the food.

When breeding fish, you must have a supply of very tiny foods for the very tiny fry. Green water is one such food, and the method of obtaining it is very simple. You merely put a number of Guppies in a well-planted tank in a sunny location and wait. Within a short time you will have a tankful of nice green water that gets thicker and thicker. This is dished out to the small fry as needed.

Infusoria cultures are also a necessary food for starting small fry of egg-laying fish. Several crushed lettuce leaves placed in a quart of water will produce a culture of infusoria in a few days. Hay in water will do the same thing. The trouble with these cultures is they start to smell very soon after being started, and the smell does not improve with age. Hard aeration helps clear the solutions and reduce the odor.

Biological supply houses sell starting cultures of many living protozoa. Among these are *Paramecia, Stentors,* various *Rotifers* and many others. If you prefer to purchase one of these cultures to use as a starting medium in your trays, you will be assured of a good supply of infusoria in this manner.

Powdered skim milk may be added to distilled water as a food medium for infusoria cultures. Do not use whole milk, either dry or liquid, since the fat in it will form a scum on the top of the water, effectively cutting off the air supply to the growing organisms.

CHAPTER SEVEN

Diseases in the Aquarium

It is out of the question to expect to keep exotic fish in an aquarium without some of them getting sick with one ailment or another. Naturally, everything you do in setting up and maintaining the tank should be directed to eliminating sickness and disease as much as possible. However, you will often buy fish that are already sick or ailing, and you will not know it until you have put them into your tank and then have them keel over in a day or two. If that is all that happens, you may consider yourself fortunate. The trouble is, that most of the time, if it is a disease which has killed the fish, it will spread through the tank and kill some or all of the fish you already had.

There isn't really a lot you can do to combat diseases in exotic fish. Remedies are sold for a number of ailments; and they are sketchy at best. Usually the "cure" is so drastic that it kills everything else in the tank, or kills even the fish you are trying to help.

The commonest ailment your fish will get is called Ich. The name of this disease, which is really a parasitic infection, is *Ichthyophthiriasis*. It is also called the white spot disease, and this is just what it looks like, white spots on the sides and fins of a fish. Sometimes the fish may be literally covered with the spots, and, if the parasite gets to this point, the fish usually dies. While all fish can be attacked by the parasite, some species are bothered more than others. Guppies, for instance, will die very quickly when infested with Ich.

Usually, robust healthy fish do not contract the disease, but if they are in poor health, the Ich can kill them very quickly. Chills are the usual cause for the onslaught of this damaging parasite. Ich organisms are present in water from the faucet, or in pond or well water, in a dormant form. If the tank is maintained at a constant warm temperature, they remain dormant, but if the tank is chilled, the organisms break their dormancy and attack the fish. Since chilling weakens fish, too, they are readily susceptible to the parasites. Ich is very contagious, and can spread through an entire tank like wildfire.

In the early days of keeping fish, about the only thing that was done for Ich was to add salt to the tank and raise the temperature, keeping it at about 80 degrees for a week to ten days. Methylene blue dye has been used as a treatment for Ich with some measure of success, but it is dangerous for the plants, stains the water until you can see nothing in the tank and then requires replacement of the water to clear it up.

Quinine hydrochloride in the quantity of two grains per gallon of water in the tank is also sometimes effective in curing Ich. This chemical should be dissolved in a quantity of water taken from the tank, then poured into the tank in four equal parts, each addition one day apart. In other words, if you had a twenty-gallon tank, allowing for the plants, rocks and gravel, you would have perhaps eighteen gallons of water. Then thirty-six grains of quinine hydrochloride should be dissolved in about one pint of water from the tank, and one quarter pint added to the tank every day for four days. Some plants may be affected by this cure.

Several of the broad spectrum antibiotics may be used in aquarium treatment. One of the best of these is Chloromycetin.

It should be used in the strength of 75 mg. per gallon. This means 75 mg. of the antibiotic to each gallon of water in the tank. If the infection is a bad one, the dose can be increased to 100 mg. per gallon. The drug should be dissolved in a pint or more of water from the tank, then added to the tank in one dose, stirring it in well. Do not ever pour drugs into the tank directly over any of the fish. If you are using an outside filter, an ideal way to add medicines is to slowly pour the water into the filter, from which point it will be pumped back into the tank.

With all treatments for Ich, it is a good idea to raise the temperature to 78 or 80 degrees and hold it there for ten days or so. Be very careful, when reducing the temperature to the normal point, to do so over a period of several days, or you will chill the tank and start trouble all over again.

There are several remedies on the market for the treatment of other diseases of aquarium fish. Some of them work well. Others do not.

Velvet, or Rust as it is also called, is another fairly common disease. Copper salts are excellent for killing Velvet. Methylene blue dye is also used, as is Acriflavine, one of the antibiotics. Combinations of these are often used too.

Velvet is a tenacious infection, and one that is very difficult to cure. The fish treated should be removed from their tank into a "hospital" tank, which can be a small two- or three-gallon aquarium, half filled with the water from the infected tank. Do not put any gravel or plants into the hospital tank, but leave it bare. Put in the fish, and if you like, an aerator may be used to ensure enough oxygen for the sick patients. The temperature of the hospital tank should be raised to 80 degrees and kept there for the duration of the treatment, which may take several days.

When using copper in the treatment of Velvet, the fish must be watched very closely, or you will kill them too. Plain copper treatment may be given in the tank in which the fish live, without removing them to a hospital tank. The simplest and safest way to get the copper into the tank is to drop pennies in the water. Use about two cents to each gallon of water in the tank. Make allowances for the gravel and rocks. An aerator should be used to circulate the water. The pennies can be grouped around the air stone, and adjust the flow of air so medium bubbles flow from it. This size will circulate the water most effectively. Watch the fish very closely, looking in on them at least every hour. If at any time you see them gasping for air at the surface of the water, remove the copper cents immediately, siphon out about 25 per cent of the water and replace it with fresh water that has been aged a day and that is the same temperature as the water within the tank. When you start the treatment, it is a good idea to put aside a vessel of water so it will be ready if needed.

When it appears that the fish are free from their infection, leave them at least a full week in the tank, and then start gradually changing the water. Change about two gallons per day until the total amount of water in the tank has been replaced. If you put new fish into the tank during the treatment, the chances are the dissolved copper in the water will quickly kill them. You should under no circumstances add or remove fish, under treatment for any ailment, from tanks.

Chloromycetin is a good cure for Velvet and could be used in the same proportions as specified for the treatment of Ich—that is to say, 75 to 100 mg. to each gallon of water.

Treatment of Velvet with dyes and copper salts, in combination, *must* be done in the hospital tank. Copper-Blue Cure, a preparation manufactured by the Miracle Pet Products, Inc. is effective in curing Velvet if careful attention is paid to the directions on the label and a watch is kept on the fish.

Fungus is the next most common disease that attacks fish in the aquarium. This trouble is not so contagious as Velvet or Ich. Healthy fish usually do not contract fungus infections. If they are poorly fed, in bad condition, or if they have been injured, either in a fight with another fish or by cutting themselves on a sharp rock or projection in the aquarium, fungus is liable to attack at the site of the wound. The commonest form of fungus attacking uninjured fish is mouth fungus. And this probably was contracted after the fish had a sore mouth from fighting or bumping into the glass. Mouth fungus *is* contagious, and will spread rapidly through a group of fish.

Salt was the earliest treatment used to combat fungus. Here the fish is placed in the bare hospital tank in a measured quantity of water, one gallon, two gallon, etc. Dissolve a teaspoonful

This Cichlid is the victim of a fungus disease that will, if not arrested, eat away the tail and fins, finally killing the specimen.

of salt for every gallon of water, in a small quantity of the water in the hospital tank, then add it gradually to the tank, not pouring it in directly on top of the fish. Repeat this treatment twice a day until you have added six doses of salt. Allow the fish to remain in the salt water until the fungus disappears, and for a day or two afterward. When the fish seems cured, gradually start replacing the salt water with fresh water of the same temperature, changing not more than 25 per cent at one time, over a period of several days. When the water has been brought back to fresh water, the fish can be returned to its tank.

Another treatment for fungus is with the dye malachite green. Put a gallon of tank water into the hospital tank, and add three to five grains of the dye. Catch the infected fish in a small net and immerse it in the dye solution, keeping it in the net, for not over thirty seconds, then drop it back into its tank, *not* dipping the dye-saturated net into the tank water. The fungus should die within a day or two after treatment. If not, repeat the treatment once more. Chloromycetin in the doses given for treatment of white spot is also effective in some cases of fungus.

Fin and tail rot is a nasty disease. It is caused by bacteria and the fins and tails rot off of the fish's body. The best thing to do when a fish is affected with this disease is to flush it down the drain. If you want to try to treat it, add about 25,000 units of water-soluble penicillin to each gallon of water in the tank and leave it there. Fin and tail rot is usually caused by poor, crowded conditions in the tank, by keeping fish not compatible with each other in a community tank, so that one or more is constantly being picked at and heckled by the others, by poor food, not enough of it, or food not graded to the proper size for that particular fish to eat. Chloromycetin can be used in place of penicillin if desired. Use it in the same doses as given for the treatment of Ich.

Swim bladder trouble. Sometimes a fish is seen as being unable to swim upright. It moves erratically through the water, sinking as soon as it stops swimming, or even rising to float on its side or back at the surface of the water. The trouble is that the swim bladder, that organ which adjusts the buoyancy of the fish, is not functioning properly. Flush the fish down the john. There really isn't any cure for this trouble.

Consumption is another trouble that is useless to try to treat. The fish becomes thin and emaciated. Usually its belly becomes hollow, and the entire body of the victim may curve. The best thing to do is dispose of the sufferer.

Dropsy causes swelling of the fish's body until the scales stand out like a burr. You may try to treat the disease with Chloromycetin in the dose of 100 mg. per gallon of water, but, here again, the best thing to do is flush the fish down the drain.

Shimmies often attack fish in the aquarium, and Barbs seem especially susceptible to this ailment. Often the fish will recover with no treatment. More often they will die. When afflicted with the shimmies, the fish stands still in the water, with its body shaking from side to side. A chill is the usual cause of shimmies, but there are other causes too. Sometimes changing up to half the water in the tank will cure shimmies. Some fish, once they get shimmies, require many weeks, or even months, to recover. Live-bearers seem especially prone to this trouble, and Swordtails in particular, most often never recover.

Sometimes a fish will become infested with anchor worms. Usually these parasites attack pool fish rather than those in aquariums. However, sometimes they will get into an indoor tank and fasten themselves to the fish. The best way to get rid of these worms is to hold the fish in a wet net and pull or scrape the worms off with your fingers.

There are a number of other diseases that attack aquarium

fish. None of them, or at best, very few of them respond to treatment. Neon tetra disease is an ailment attacking many of the "tetras" and has no known cure. In the case of neons, the vivid metallic blue color fades away, leaving the fish practically colorless. Dispose of the victims as soon as you notice the progression of the disease.

CHAPTER EIGHT

Live-Bearers
in the Aquarium

Fish which have their young alive have no definite gestation period. This means that from the time of fertilization of the female to the time of delivery of the young, the period is determined by outside circumstances rather than by a physical or physiological time cycle. The length of time it takes for a viviparous (live-bearing) fish to have her young is determined by the temperature of the water she is kept in. At 75 or 78 degrees, the time from fertilization to delivery may be four or five weeks, but if the water is maintained at 68 or 70 degrees, the time to delivery may be as long as ten weeks or even longer.

In many live-bearers, one fertilization by a male will result in the female being able to store the sperm and have as many as seven broods of young from the single mating.

While you take a male and female egg layer, put them together and obtain a mating from them with a resultant batch of eggs, live-bearers go about their sexual business in a more casual way. The males are completely promiscuous. This means that they do not single out a female and mate her to produce young, but mate with each and every available female, whether she has been mated before by other males or not. The females seem to submit, rather than to participate. The males chase them all over the tank, mating them as soon as they are cornered in a favorable position.

The anal fin of male live-bearing fish is modified into a tube called the *gonopodium*. This is the organ with which he introduces his sperm into the female. When mating, the males "dance" around the female, waiting for a timely moment in which to dash up to her and thrust with his gonopodium. Meanwhile, he keeps all his fins erect, flashing his brightest colors.

After mating, the female slowly develops a "gravid spot" on her belly just at the vent. This spot is a sign that she is full of young, and the development of this spot is an indication of the time of delivery of the baby fish. As you gain experience in raising fish, you will be able to tell quite accurately, by the appearance of the gravid spot, just how far along the female is, and just about when she should drop the young.

The young fish are expelled folded in two, and they remain this way for a short time before straightening out and swimming for cover. This, no doubt, is a carryover from their instinct in nature to escape being eaten by the parent fish by swimming into very shallow water where the larger fish could not maneuver.

Females almost ready to deliver their young should not be handled. They should be left alone in their tank, and not be transferred around, since this may cause premature delivery. You can tell if the young are born prematurely if they have the yolk sac still attached to their bellies. If this is the case, you should dispose of them, because their chance for survival is practically zero.

Newly hatched brine shrimp are ideal food for newly born live-bearers. They will also take small grained dry foods. Feed the young fish from four to six times each day, and feed them only an amount that they will consume within five or ten minutes. If uneaten food remains in the tank, especially if it is dry food, there is danger of fouling the water and killing everything

Mollienisia latipinna. The magnificent "sail" on the back of this fish will rarely be reproduced in its young. Sailfin Mollies are beautiful fish but need a large tank.

in the tank. Some Catfish should be kept in the breeding tank as scavengers, to clean up any food that settles to the bottom. The Catfish will not harm the baby live-bearers in any way.

Often a batch of young fish will survive, and seem healthy enough, but they will not grow to any appreciable size after many weeks. There are several reasons for stunting. Poor stock to begin with is one. The most usual reason is too little food, and the wrong kind of food; too small an aquarium to raise the brood in, and too large a brood, which amounts to the same thing as too small an aquarium.

NAME: *Lebistes reticulatus,* Peters.

POPULAR NAME: Guppy—Rainbow Fish.

NATIVE TO: Trinidad, northern South America and Venezuela.

SIZE: The males reach a size of 1½ inches. Females, 2¼ inches.

FOOD ACCEPTED: Guppies will take almost any kind of dry food or live food.

TEMPERATURE RANGE: Guppies do best in water maintained at 75 to 80 degrees.

ATTITUDE: Guppies are generally peaceful and good community tank subjects. They sometimes tend to pick at everything else living in the tank, even at larger fish.

Lebistes reticulatus. Guppies are known to almost everyone, and they have been bred into so many varieties that you seldom see original stock any more.

This little fish has been the subject of more experimentation, probably, than any other species. Due to its short and rapid life cycle, Guppies lend themselves well to hybridizing, fixing of exotic color strains, fin variation, and a number of other characteristics now available but not found in the wild state.

Guppies like soft water, slightly alkaline. They also must be kept in a very clean tank, although they can tolerate almost foul water. They can also tolerate crowded conditions, but do not necessarily do best under this management. One of the best things about Guppies is their resistance to diseases. Unless you have poor stock, you should not be troubled with the common ailments so easily contracted by many other species of fish. Its small size is another factor that makes the Guppy so popular—a goodly sized school of them can be kept in a tank, although school may not be exactly the best description, since Guppies do not school in the sense that other fish do. Guppies are always on the go, but as individuals, not in schooling formation. The males are always busy chasing the females, and it is every fish for itself.

NAME: *Xiphophorus hellerii,* Heckel.

POPULAR NAME: Swordtail.

NATIVE TO: Mexico.

SIZE: Nearly 3 inches without the tail "sword" of the male.

FOOD ACCEPTED: Accepts almost everything. Algae is a needed part of their diet.

TEMPERATURE RANGE: Do best from 70 to 80 degrees.

ATTITUDE: Males fight, but a male and two females make good community fish.

The Swordtail is another fish that man has tampered with until there are so many artificial variations on the market that one seldom sees a "natural" fish any longer. Its popularity is due

Xiphophorus variatus. This Platy is much more colorful than the Wagtails. No two fish are colored alike.

to the fact that it is easy to care for, has a great number of young at a time—up to two hundred—and breeds about every thirty days. A most prolific fish.

Also the males are striking, with the long extension at the bottom of the caudal fin. In some artificial strains, this extension is very highly colored, and the length has been increased considerably from that of the original parent stock. A pure red variety has been developed, and has been on the market for several years. This is indeed a fish that makes an excellent showing in any tank.

Swordtails should be kept in water about 80 degrees if you are trying to breed them regularly. They must have a considerable amount of algae in their diet, and this should be supplied to them if at all possible. A fair substitute is finely chopped boiled spinach. Some aquarists feed chopped lettuce, too, but I think this is dangerous, due to the ready decomposition of lettuce, and the danger of fouling the tank with its use. Boiled spinach is eagerly taken by the Swordtails, and seems to provide the necessary ingredients that the fish obtain from algae.

Swordtails are not susceptible to ailments in general, being a fairly hardy fish. The one thing they cannot tolerate is chilling, and a fish, once chilled, is almost certainly doomed. The result of chilling is most often shimmies. Once a Swordtail contracts shimmies, it is not likely to recover from it.

In order to obtain large-sized Swordtails, the young fish must be given large amounts of good nourishing food daily. They should be fed four to six times each day, and the diet should be varied as much as possible, including such foods as live Daphnia, brine shrimp, algae, chopped spinach, and as many other items as you can provide. The young fish must be raised in a tank not less than fifteen or twenty gallons in capacity.

NAME: *Xiphophorus maculatus,* Gunther.

POPULAR NAME: Moonfish, Platy.

NATIVE TO: Mexico.

SIZE: 1½ to 2 inches.

FOOD ACCEPTED: All foods, dry or live. Needs algae.

TEMPERATURE RANGE: Same as for Swordtails—70 to 80 degrees.

ATTITUDE: Peaceful and a good community fish.

Platies got their name from the old classification. When they were first introduced to aquarists, the scientific name was *Platy-*

poecilus, which was soon shortened to Platy. As with Guppies and Swordtails, Platies have been so line-bred, and so many hybrid varieties have been developed, that it is difficult to say what the original wild stock looks like. Two species of Platy were used in aquariums; the one listed at the heading of this section, and the *Xiphophorus variatus.* From these two stocks have come the literally dozens of varieties of Platy found on the market today. One of the most attractive strains thus produced is called Wagtail Platy. This fish has a bright golden body and jet black fins and tail, making a contrast that stands out beautifully in a tank.

Platies like their water harder than do Swordtails, Mollies and Guppies. They also like a lot of light, and heavy planting, especially if you want to raise any young. About 75 degrees is the best temperature for breeding Platies. The parent fish should be liberally fed with live food during the mating and ges-tation period, and this is particularly important when the female is dropping her young to eliminate the possibility of her eating the young. Platies are not as prone to cannibalism of their babies as are Guppies. Algae or finely chopped boiled spinach should also be provided.

NAME: *Mollienisia velifera,* Regan.

POPULAR NAME: Sailfin, Mollie.

NATIVE TO: Mexico and the Gulf Coast.

SIZE: Up to 5 inches.

FOOD ACCEPTED: Almost anything, but must have a high veg-etable diet, especially algae.

TEMPERATURE RANGE: 78 to 80 degrees.

ATTITUDE: Peaceful, but needs more care than most live-bearers, so is not a good community tank fish.

Actually, *Mollienisia velifera* is not seen in pet stores as often as the smaller *M. latipinna,* or the *M. sphenops.* Latipinna and Velifera so closely resemble each other that the beginner would have difficulty telling them apart. Sphenops is a beautiful fish, mottled black, red and blue, with silvery spots showing through.

Mollies are very popular, especially with beginners, because they are a showy fish, but they require lots of care and special conditions, which make them not really a beginner's fish. First of all, they are a pretty big fish, and they must have a pretty big tank to live in. A fifty-gallon tank is not a bit too big.

Next, Mollies need hard, alkaline water, maintained at 78 degrees for their best comfort. They do well with the addition of a small quantity of salt, say in the proportion of one fourth teaspoonful to a gallon of water. Strong light should be provided in order to induce the growth of algae, which is most important to their diet. Live food is also important to their welfare, but vegetable food forms the main part.

Frequent feeding is very important. In fact, if the fish are not fed six or eight times each day, in a quantity they will consume in ten to fifteen minutes, you will have very little success in raising them.

These fish are too big to put into breeding traps, and besides, they do not normally eat their young. If you have a tankful of Mollies and one or more females become gravid and ready to deliver, it is best to remove all the other fish and let the females remain in the established tank to drop their babies. With any species of Molly it is dangerous to move gravid females, since she will in all probability drop still-born young, or, if they are alive, premature or deformed fry.

A magnificent strain is the Black, or Midnight Molly. These fish are velvety black, with golden eyes and a very large dorsal fin, edged in red or orange. The effect is striking, and they are well worth the trouble of keeping.

CHAPTER NINE

Egg-Scatterers in the Aquarium

To this group belong the great majority of egg layers kept in aquariums. The fish that scatter eggs can be divided into two categories—those who scatter adhesive eggs that stick to whatever support they fall on and those who scatter non-adhesive eggs. The egg-laying fish as a whole may be divided further into the ones who place adhesive eggs upon a support of some kind and those who push their adhesive eggs into "nests" of bubbles floating at the surface of the water. These groups will be discussed in subsequent chapters.

Of the fish which scatter non-adhesive eggs, the most common and one of the easiest to breed is the Danio. Of the fish which scatter adhesive eggs, perhaps the easiest to breed is the Barb.

For any fish that drops its eggs in this fashion, the breeding requirements are pretty much the same. The aquarium should be large enough to permit the fish a good swimming area. There should be lots of open room in the water, and several good thickets of bushy plants. The one with finely divided leaves, like Anacharis, Myriophyllum, Parrot's-Feather or Cabomba are best for fish like Barbs and Tetras. For the non-adhesive scatterers, plants are not needed except a thicket or two for the female to use as a refuge to allow her to momentarily escape the attentions of the males.

In place of plants, the bottom should be covered at least one layer deep with smooth, rounded pebbles or marbles. Or a layer of glass or plastic rods or tubes can be laid across the tank, resting upon some support to raise them from the tank bottom an inch or two. This arrangement will permit the eggs to fall through the rods or down in between the pebbles or marbles, but hinder the fish from following them and eating them. The egg layers, are, with exceptions, of course, voracious egg eaters, and, unless you take precautions to protect their eggs, not very many are apt to survive a mating.

Egg layers are ready to breed when the female is seen to fill up with eggs. Her belly will bulge with the number of eggs inside her, and, seen from the top, there will be a decided bulge on both sides of her body. When a female is seen to be full of eggs, she should be placed in the breeding tank, and conditioning foods provided in liberal quantities. Live food, of course, is far the best, and, with certain species, the only food that will bring them into spawning condition.

While conditioning the female in the breeding tank, you should also be doing the same service for the male left behind. After the two sexes have been separated for a day or two, the male can be introduced to the female all over again. Spawning should take place fairly soon after putting the two fish back together.

When the fry of egg-laying fish are hatched, they usually still have the yolk sac attached to their bellies. Sometimes this sac is almost as large as the egg was, and the fish such a tiny thing that it is just like a thread attached to the ball of the yolk. The fry feed off the nourishment in the yolk sac at first, but this is very soon absorbed. It is then that you must have the proper kind of food ready in the proper size for the very small fish. And you must have it in sufficient quantity to start the fry on their way to growth and health. Infusoria, is, of course, the best first food for fry. It should be fed many times each day in small quantities. Not less than six to eight feedings, and preferably more, should be given the little fish.

As soon as growth has started and you see that the fry have outgrown the very small infusorian animal food, you can give them newly hatched brine shrimp. Offer some of these, watching the fry through a magnifying glass to make sure they are large enough to get the shrimp into their mouths. If they experience no difficulty in taking the shrimp, you are safe to continue feeding this to them. If they seem unable to get the shrimp into their mouths, but just grab one and swim around the tank with the body of the shrimp hanging out, it is best to continue feeding the infusoria for another couple of days, returning to the brine shrimp when a little more growth has been attained.

After the newly hatched brine shrimp, the next food the young fry can take is small Daphnia. Since you cannot keep large fish in with the fry, you cannot dump a load of Daphnia into the tank with the fry unless there is some way that the large crustaceans can be disposed of. The fry can take only the very smallest of Daphnia at this stage, and perhaps the easiest way to feed them is to sift the Daphnia through a cloth mesh, straining out all but the very smallest.

In a week or two, the young fish should look like young fish, and not like little wiggling threads. They should grow rapidly and will if enough food is available and they are in a large enough tank. It is strange, but apparently the size of the tank has a bearing on the size the fish will attain, since, if fed identical kinds and quantities of food, fish in a small tank will not grow so large as the same kind of fish started and raised in a large tank.

If Daphnia is not available to the breeder at the time the

young fry have hatched, then substitutes must be used. A raw shrimp, grated into mush, is one food that is very good. The yolk of a hard-boiled egg, mashed and mixed with a little water, is useful as a starting food, but should be fed carefully, so as not to foul the water in the tank. *After* the eggs have hatched, snails can be put into the nursery tank to act as Scavengers, since the snails, although voracious eaters of fish eggs, will not bother the fry. If egg yolk is fed, you should be sure the snails are present.

Very finely chopped earthworms are another good substitute for Daphnia, and as a matter of fact, should be given the fry even though Daphnia is obtainable and used. Raw *lean* beef heart, scraped into mush, is also good, but should be fed only once or twice a week.

If you can bring a batch of fry through the critical stage of first feedings, there is every chance that you can rear them to maturity. You will notice some thinning of the ranks as the fish grow. This is only natural. Some of the weaker ones will die, and their tiny bodies disappear. The snails or Catfish will eat them, or they will be picked apart by the remaining fish. Also, as the fry grow, some will be first to feed, getting more food than the others, and, as a consequence, grow larger and faster until they will be able to eat the stunted ones that lagged behind when feeding time came around. This is only natural, and it should neither alarm you nor should you try to prevent it. It is a method, first of all, of weeding out the unfit specimens, and you will have larger and healthier fish as a result of this natural selection.

Of the egg-laying fish, the Characins are the most abundant in terms of different species. Most of the Characins have teeth, whether or not you can see them. In small fish, teeth are necessarily so small that they would be difficult to see. However, they are there. Also, most Characins have that small fin on the back called the adipose fin. This is easily seen and is a method of identifying the fish as a Characin.

Most Characins lay eggs which are slightly adhesive, and stick to the bunch plant thickets in which they are scattered. Naturally, there are exceptions to every one of the statements I have just made, which is why I have consistently used the qualifying word, *most*. Characins come from Africa and South America, with a few species being found through Central America and Mexico, up into the southern part of the United States. So far, Characins have not been discovered in any other part of the world living in a natural, wild state.

Many Characins are called "Tetras" by both pet store owners and aquarists. This is due to the early name for them, being *Tetragonopterus*, which was quickly contracted to Tetra. That name is no longer used for these fish, but the nickname has stuck, and, in all likelihood, will continue to be used. Names like these die hard.

Although Characins come from some of the hottest points on the globe, they do not require very warm water. This is probably because the streams in which they originate run through the shaded jungles and are cool, even though the country is hot and humid. The average temperature range for Characins is from 70 to 75 degrees, and for breeding, can be raised to 78 or 80 degrees.

In the matter of food, Characins cover just about the complete range of fish foods obtainable. They will eat most dry foods, but like live foods better. Some of them will eat nothing *but* live food; others will eagerly take dry foods. Some of them live on the surface of the water, seldom going more than a few inches down, or, at least, they *feed* only at the surface, not going to the bottom for food. Among this group are the dainty "hatchet fish," which are tiny fresh-water flying fish with stiffly extended pectoral fins used to glide for long distances over the surface of the water.

Some of the Characins have most interesting breeding habits, a few of which will be described under the individual fish discussion.

NAME: *Cheirdon axelrodi*, Schultz.
POPULAR NAME: Cardinal Tetra, Cardinal Fish.
NATIVE TO: Brazil.
SIZE: Up to 1½ inches.
FOOD ACCEPTED: All dry and live foods. Not choosy.
TEMPERATURE RANGE: About 75 degrees.
ATTITUDE: Peaceful, schooling, like the Neon Tetra.

Actually, this fish looks almost identical to the Neon, at first glance. The main difference is that the Cardinal has the red extending the entire length of the body except for a small white area on the belly. The blue line is slightly gold in color, but is as bright and luminous as the stripe on the Neon.

This fish must have very soft acid water. Breeding is as difficult as breeding Neons, and the same information as given for Neons holds good for this fish. One idea that may help in reducing the loss of eggs is to have an overhang of some kind in the tank so the fish can get underneath in subdued light. This overhang may consist of a flat piece of stone—slate is best—propped up on other stones, with a couple of bunch plants planted beneath. A piece of slate or even cardboard may be placed over one end of the tank, and this may serve as well, although, being up on top of the tank, it will not afford as much shade as an overhang under the water.

Some professional breeders, in working with light-sensitive fish like Neons or Cardinals, breed them in large vats and cover these with lattices of wooden strips, making a mottled shade where the fish can seek a location to their liking.

NAME: *Hemigrammus ocellifer,* Steindachner.

POPULAR NAME: Head and Tail Light.

NATIVE TO: Brazil.

SIZE: From 1½ to about 2 inches.

FOOD ACCEPTED: Will take dry foods, but prefers live animal food.

TEMPERATURE RANGE: 75 to 85 degrees.

ATTITUDE: Peaceful. Schools with its own kind. Good community fish.

This is one of the old favorites. It was imported very early when this hobby was just starting, and is easily bred, so it is cheaply priced, always available, and is hardy and lively in the tank.

The top of the eye is bright red, and there is a spot of the same color at the top of the base of the caudal fin, making two brilliant spots on the fish, from whence came its nickname. A gold stripe runs down the center of the sides, and the rest of the body is "fish silver," with a pretty iridescence visible as the fish swims.

The breeding requirements are the same as for the Danios. The breeders must be brought into prime condition with plenty of live food, water temperature maintained at about 76 to 78 degrees with the water soft and acid. The bottom of the tank should be covered with pebbles or marbles, as described in the preliminary breeding instructions for Danios. The fish scatter non-adhesive eggs which fall to the bottom, sifting down between the marbles where the adults cannot reach them. As soon as spawning has been completed, the adults can be removed from the tank. The breeding tank should be not less than ten gallons in capacity.

NAME: *Brachydanio rerio,* Hamilton-Buchanan.
POPULAR NAME: Zebrafish; Zebra Danio; Danio; Striped Danio.
NATIVE TO: India.
SIZE: Up to 2 inches.
FOOD ACCEPTED: Any kind of food. Live foods should be included occasionally.
TEMPERATURE RANGE: From 62 to nearly 110 degrees!
ATTITUDE: Peaceful and active. Schools. Good community fish.

Many things contribute to the popularity of this fish. First, it is a small fish, so several can be kept in a tank without overcrowding. Next, it is constantly on the go, schooling with its own kind and flashing from one end of the tank to the other without stopping for a moment. The colors are bright and pleasant. A deep metallic blue is striped lengthways over the silver body. Sometimes the silver has a yellowish cast. The ventral and caudal fins are also striped with blue.

Also, Danios are fairly easy to breed. They scatter non-adhesive eggs and spawn in shallow water in a long tank having a layer of pebbles or marbles covering the bottom. Two or three males should be used for each female. The water should not be more than a couple of inches deep over the tops of the marbles, since Danios eat their eggs as fast as they are expelled if the eggs cannot drop to safety in the crevices between the pebbles or marbles. In deep water, the adult fish would merely follow the eggs down, gobbling them up as fast as they could.

The water condition for Danios is not critical, but it must be clean. They breed best at temperatures between 75 and 78 degrees. The fry hatch in about a day and a half, and infusoria is fine for the first food, followed in a week by newly hatched brine shrimp. Dust-size dry foods can also be offered, if you have Scavengers in the tank with the fry and the pebbles or marbles have been removed.

CHAPTER TEN

Adhesive Egg Layers in the Aquarium

The difference between egg-scatterers and adhesive egg layers is that the scatterers throw their eggs around indiscriminately, letting them fall where they may, and the adhesive egg layers deposit them on some particular support. Usually, scatterers eat their own eggs as fast as they can find them, and adhesive egg layers stick them to a support and leave them alone to hatch. There are, of course, exceptions to both rules. To the group of adhesive egg layers belong the Carps and Minnows, the Cichlids, the Labyrinth fish and others. The Carps and Minnows include some of the most beautiful fish that can be kept in aquariums. On the Carp side there are the large number of Barbs, some of them very colorful, all of them interesting inhabitants of the aquarium. Over with the Minnows are the jewels of the fresh-water fish—the great family of Panchax species. These are called Top Minnows or egg-laying Tooth-carps, and most of them come from Africa.

There are two kinds of adhesive egg layers—those who scatter their eggs in among plants, and who will eat their eggs for the most part, and those who carefully and patiently clean off a spot on some kind of support, then deposit their eggs, one by one in a single layer, until all have been laid. These last usually are the ones who do not eat their eggs, but who care for them, guarding them against marauders, and then guarding their fry after hatching, until the young ones are able to fend for themselves. Strangely enough, after the young fish are self-sufficient, they are in danger of being eaten by their parents!

NAME: *Danio malabaricus,* Jerdon.

POPULAR NAME: Giant Danio.

NATIVE TO: India.

SIZE: Up to 4 inches and over.

FOOD ACCEPTED: Will eat any kind of food, but require a lot of it.

TEMPERATURE RANGE: From 68 to 80 degrees.

ATTITUDE: Peaceful, but large enough to eat small fish, and does!

While the fish is called the Giant Danio, and is related to the last fish described in the previous chapter, it has been put here rather than with its relative because of its breeding habits. It lays adhesive eggs, and they breed like the Carps, rather than like the egg-scatterers.

This is a large fish. They are said to reach a length of six inches in the wild, but rarely get to be over four inches in the aquarium. This is still a lot of fish, and the Giant Danio should be kept in a tank of not less than twenty- or thirty-gallon capacity for best results. They school and are always on the move. Their colors are soft, not brilliant like their smaller cousins. The fins are washed with deep rose and the body is yellow with blue stripes.

Breeding them requires a heavily planted tank with many bunches of plants like Myriophyllum, Cabomba and Parrot's-Feather, among the fine leaves of which the eggs are laid. Two males should be used for the female breeder. Nylon spawning mops may be used in place of living plants and, if this is the case, some of the mops could be allowed to float at the top of the

water while several others can be "planted" in the gravel. Giant
Danios can be bred in outdoor pools if you live in a climate
where the summers are long and warm. The difficulty is in getting the fish out of the pool for the winter. You are bound to
lose a lot of them.

NAME: *Rasbora heteromorpha,* Duncker.
POPULAR NAME: Harlequin Fish; Rasbora.
NATIVE TO: Malay Peninsula.
SIZE: Up to about 2 inches.
FOOD ACCEPTED: Will take dry foods, but needs live food at
intervals.
TEMPERATURE RANGE: From 68 to 85 degrees.
ATTITUDE: Completely peaceful. A good community fish.

This is one of the most elegant of small aquarium fish.

While Rasboras are fairly hardy, they seem somewhat susceptible to the disease called Ich. When they get it, they really are
covered!

They are strikingly colored with a copper body bearing a velvety black triangle on the rear half. The copper color is metallic.
Unless they have soft acid water, they will not thrive.

In order to breed this very desirable fish, the adults must be
well conditioned on live foods such as Tubifex worms, chopped
earthworms, brine shrimp, white worms and Daphnia. Some
mosquito larvae will be relished as well. Conditioning should be
carried on for at least three weeks before attempting to spawn
them. Breeding is best in water that has not been aged too long
and is maintained at a temperature of about 80 degrees.

The tank should not be smaller than twenty gallons and
should be heavily planted with stiff-leaved *Sagittaria,* wide-
leaved *Cryptocorynes* such as *Chordata,* some *Bacopa,* perhaps,
and any other strong leaved plants available. *Cryptocorynes,*

being native to the habitat of these fish, are probably the best choice. The plants should be clean and free from algae. Particularly, they should be examined to make certain they are not carrying patches of snail eggs.

The female lays her eggs on the undersides of the leaves, depositing them while resting on the leaf in an upside down position. The usual clutch of eggs numbers seventy-five to one hundred, and they hatch in a little over a day. The fry are very tiny, and must be started on green water or infusoria cultures. When they have some growth, they may be graduated to new brine shrimp. It is a fairly long-lived fish.

NAME: *Rasbora trilineata*, Steindachner.

POPULAR NAME: Scissor-tail.

NATIVE TO: Malay Peninsula.

SIZE: Up to 4 inches in a tank—8 inches in the wild.

FOOD ACCEPTED: Will take dry foods, but prefers live food.

TEMPERATURE RANGE: From 75 to 78 degrees.

ATTITUDE: Peaceful and not aggressive.

This fish is popular, and usually available in pet stores. It is not very brilliantly colored, being silvery above with a purple sheen on the underside. The caudal fin has two wide black bars, bordered with white. The remainder of the tail is transparent, and, when the fish swims, the two parts of the tail are snapped together; the motion being very apparent because of the black bars. This gives basis for the nickname Scissor-tail.

The fish requires soft, acid water. It can be bred in a twenty-gallon tank, but a larger one is better. The female drops non-adhesive eggs in among bunch plants, and should be removed from the tank, together with the male, as soon as spawning has been completed.

The fry hatch in a little over a day, and are large enough to

Rasbora trilineata. This Rasbora is called Scissor-tail, because of its habit of snapping the tail fin shut each time it moves in the water.

take dust dry foods as a starter. They will soon graduate to newly hatched brine shrimp. The best breeding temperature seems to be around 70 degrees. Brown water may make the breeding of this fish a littler easier.

NAME: *Capoeta tetrazona*, Bleeker.
POPULAR NAME: Tiger Barb; Sumatra Barb.
NATIVE TO: Sumatra.
SIZE: From 2 to 2½ inches.
FOOD ACCEPTED: Will take all foods. Needs some algae.

TEMPERATURE RANGE: From 70 to 85 degrees.

ATTITUDE: Generally peaceful, but will nip fins of other fish.

This fish was known in the trade for many years as *Barbus sumatranus,* then as *Barbus tetrazona.* The scientific name has finally been fixed as that listed above.

The Tiger Barb is probably the favorite of all the Barbs, because of its color, markings and the fact that it is lively, schools with its own kind, and is always on the move. While a school of these looks very nice in a large community aquarium, they should have a tank all to themselves to properly show off.

Tiger Barbs are eager eaters and will take anything you feed them. They do require algae or chopped spinach in their diet. When in full breeding color these fish are real beauties—the noses of the males turning dark red, and the red or orange tips of the fins increasing in intensity. The black bands are velvety and the remainder of the body tinged with reddish orange.

Tiger Barbs are fairly easy to spawn if conditioned properly on lots of live food and kept in soft, acid water at a temperature of 80 degrees. Some breeders say that the spawning is hastened by the addition of some fresh water, softer than their normal tank. This may work, but I have never tried it. The eggs are laid in among bunch plants or nylon spawning mops. The fry will start on infusoria, then graduate to small brine shrimp. They must be bred in a tank not smaller than twenty gallons in capacity—a larger tank is even better.

CHAPTER ELEVEN

Bubble Nest Builders in the Aquarium

Most of the group of fish called *Anabantids* build nests that float on top of the water. These nests are made of bubbles of air coated with mucus, and they are made by the males, usually under a floating leaf or sometimes in the corner of the tank.

Anabantids are also called Labyrinth fish, because of a labyrinthine organ in the head which enables them to breathe air directly, as well as take oxygen out of the water. This is similar to the organ present in the lung fish, which can live out of water for amazing lengths of time.

When the male is ready to breed, he begins to come to the surface of the water, take a bubble of air into his mouth, coat it with saliva and eject it to float on the surface of the water. He continues to make the bubbles until he builds a small mound of foam. At this time, the female should be introduced into the tank.

Sometimes a male will not accept a female, and he may drive her all around the tank, butting and nipping at her. Very often, a male will kill a female. When you see that the female is not acceptable to the male, she should be removed and a different female introduced. Of course, it is necessary that the female be full of eggs at the time she is put in with the male. If she is not, then he is almost certain to kill her in the impatience of his spawning attacks.

The spawning tank should have many thick bunches of plants to make refuges for the female while courting. The water condition is not critical as to acidity or softness, but the temperature should be held around 80 degrees. A tank of about twenty-gallon capacity should be used for spawning, although the individual fish may be kept in as little as a quart of water each!

The spawning of Labyrinth fish is very interesting, and they are perhaps the easiest of all egg-laying fish to induce to spawn. The female swims under the bubble nest when she is ready, and the male encircles her with his body, bent into an arc. He gives the female's body a squeeze and she expels several eggs, which are fertilized by the male. The female sinks toward the bottom of the tank, as though in a faint, and the male picks up the eggs in his mouth, carrying them up to the bubble nest, spitting them in among the bubbles. The female again swims under the nest and the spawning embrace is repeated. This act is repeated until the entire lot of eggs is dropped, at which time the female must be removed from the tank, or the male will kill her.

The male cares for the eggs, catching them in his mouth as they drop out of the bubble nest, blowing new bubbles to keep the nest in good repair, until the fry hatch, which takes about two days. The tiny fry hang in among the bubbles, occasionally falling out of the nest, whereupon the male picks them up in his mouth and gently blows them back.

For three or four days after they have absorbed their egg yolk sacs the male looks after the fry. As soon as the fry become free swimming, the male must be removed, because he will now eat them if left to his own devices.

Since the fry are very small, the food they must have to start their growth must be correspondingly small. Infusoria is excellent.

The water in the spawning tank should be old, and the plants established well before the spawning takes place. Leave the old dead leaves of the plants in the tank, and do not use any snails, since they would eat these leaves, which will be decaying, providing food for the infusoria.

Green water can be added also, and this is very beneficial when the fry are just beginning to feed. This, with the infusoria, should bring them up to the point where they can accept newly hatched brine shrimp. From then on, it should be an easy matter to rear them.

The spawning tank should be covered with a sheet of glass during the building of the nest, the actual spawning, and the subsequent hatching of the fry. The cover should be kept in place for at least three or four weeks.

The group of Labyrinth fish includes the very popular "Siamese Fighting Fish," all of the different species of Gouramis, some of which are among the most highly colored of exotics, the "Kissing Gourami," and a few others. These fish are mostly belligerent among their own kind, but single specimens can be included in a community tank with no problem, since they rarely attack fish of other species.

They require a lot of live food in their diet for them really to flourish. In the warmer parts of the country, they do well as outdoor pool fish, breeding freely with no attention necessary other than to make certain there is enough food available for them.

NAME: *Macropodus opercularis*, Linnaeus.

POPULAR NAME: Paradise Fish.

NATIVE TO: China.

SIZE: Up to about 3 inches.

FOOD ACCEPTED: Live food preferred. Will take anything offered.

TEMPERATURE RANGE: From below 50 degrees to 80 degrees.

ATTITUDE: Belligerent. Not a community fish.

While Paradise Fish have been known to aquarists since the late 1800s, it has really never become a favorite. This is because it has so many bad points. This is unfortunate, because when a Paradise Fish is in glowing health and full breeding color, it is one of the most beautifully colored fish obtainable. It is really jewel-like. However, it is so quarrelsome that it cannot even be kept with its own kind, but must be segregated in individual tanks. It is even impossible to put a single specimen in a community tank, since it will attack and rip the fins off or even kill all smaller fish regardless of species.

Breeding Paradise Fish is an easy matter. They are bred as described in the beginning of this chapter. Nothing special is required except to see that they have been conditioned on live foods for a week or two before spawning, and to make sure that the female is full of eggs before she is introduced to the spawning tank. You should have several females available, all full of eggs, because the male may kill one after another until he finally finds one that is acceptable to him.

The fry are easy to rear. They can be started on finely powdered dry foods and infusoria cultures, and their growth is rapid. Within a week they will be able to eagerly take newly hatched brine shrimp. When they are about three-fourths of an inch long, they will have to be separated into individual containers or the fighting will start and you will have a tankful of torn and damaged fish.

NAME: *Betta splendens,* Regan.

POPULAR NAME: Betta; Siamese Fighting Fish.

Betta splendens. The male Siamese Fighting Fish builds the bubble nest into which he will place the eggs when the female spawns.

NATIVE TO: Thailand (Siam).

SIZE: From 2½ to 3 inches.

FOOD ACCEPTED: Prefers live food. Will take dry foods.

TEMPERATURE RANGE: From 65 to 90 degrees.

ATTITUDE: Peaceful toward other species. Belligerent to its own kind.

This is the famous Siamese Fighting Fish, about which has been written reams of misinformation. It is true that they fight —that is the males fight—when two or more are placed in the same tank. However, these fights are not the bloody combats so often described. Only rarely is blood drawn during a fight. What does happen is that the victor usually rips the fins and tail of its opponent to shreds, and the vanquished fish retreats and refuses to continue the fight.

Bettas are usually sold as mature males, and immature females. For some reason or other it is very difficult to find large mature females in pet stores, with the result that you have to buy your females and raise them to maturity before you buy the male, if you are interested in trying to spawn them. The colors of Bettas are truly gorgeous. There is a red variety, in which the entire fish is a deep blood red; a blue one flashes bright metallic electric blue; a green one also metallic in color; a peach-colored one with deep red fins, usually called Cambodias; and some few with mixed colors. There is also an albino variety.

All Bettas sold today are the result of selective breeding, both for color and for fin size. The wild Bettas have short fins and are drably colored. Betta breeding is a big commercial enterprise and tens of thousands are bred for sale each year. The best breeding temperature is about 80 degrees, and the fish must be conditioned before spawning. The females must be ready and full of eggs before being offered to the male or he will probably kill her. He may even kill her if she is full of eggs, so you should have spare females ready.

As soon as the male starts to build his bubble nest you can introduce the female. Keep both fish well fed while the nest is under construction and continue feeding during the spawning period. Live foods like Daphnia and brine shrimp are the best to use. Several thickets of plants should be in the spawning tank for refuge places for the female. The tank should not be smaller than fifteen gallons. A sheet of glass should be kept on the top to prevent evaporation of the water, bubbles, and to keep the air moist above the nest. Once or twice a day the sheet can be lifted to permit fresh air to enter the tank above the water, replacing it after a few minutes.

The fry can be started on infusoria cultures, followed by newly hatched brine shrimp. They will grow rapidly, and when they have reached one half inch in length, they must be segregated into small jars containing a pint or a quart of water. While they will survive in pint containers, quart ones are better. Unless the fry are separated, they will fight and tear each other's fins. When they have grown large enough to determine the sexes, all the females can be placed together in a large tank, and the males kept in individual containers.

The young fish should be fed live foods until their bellies bulge, and kept this way for fast growth and best fin development. Daphnia, Tubifex and brine shrimp are all good foods, and frozen brine shrimp are also eagerly taken. Beef heart ground in a meat grinder can be fed sparingly, especially in the small containers, for it will foul the water rapidly.

CHAPTER TWELVE

Scavenger Fish in the Aquarium

We come now to those poor relations of exotic fish, most of which are badly mistreated by the aquarist, even though unknowingly. The trouble is that throughout the years people have been told time and time over that the Scavengers in their tanks will eat the refuse and droppings of all the other fish, and have therefore been used as garbage collectors. As a result, very few of these very interesting fish are ever fed enough to keep them really contented, and their life span is cut considerably because of their lack of nourishment.

It would be difficult to find a more gentle group of fish than the Catfish sold as Scavengers. Never will they molest a tiny new-hatched fish. They will eat fish eggs if they are laid on the bottom of the tank simply because most of the Catfish are bottom feeders, and anything placed there is natural food for them. They will not, however, seek out eggs and eat them if they are deposited on plants or other supports.

I have never seen a fight between two Catfish, nor do I think anyone else has. They get along peacefully with every other kind of fish, going about their janitorial duties industriously and thoroughly. Because they are primarily bottom feeders, they continually turn over each grain of gravel, nose around each rock and stone, looking for food. Unfortunately, many aquarists do not take their needs into consideration when feeding their fish, and as a consequence, very little food reaches the bottom of the tank. As a result, the Catfish are usually hungry all the time.

One excellent way to ensure they receive enough to eat is to feed the fish in the tank their regular portion of food, and, while they are eating it, drop into the water food that will sink to the bottom for the Catfish. This food can be a lump of Tubifex worms, of which most Catfish are extremely fond; it can be chopped clam or crabmeat, chopped raw fish, beef heart—almost any food will be eagerly taken. Live foods are eaten if the Catfish can catch them, but they really are not equipped to chase live food through the water, unless it sinks to the bottom.

There are nearly fifty kinds of Corydoras Catfish known, as well as many other species. Some of the Catfish are really weird. Their shapes are grotesque, and one wonders what the purpose of this shape may be. Usually shape and color are determined by the environmental circumstances of an animal, so that they are either camouflaged or hidden to escape their predators. I suppose, living on the bottom, some of these very oddly shaped fish resemble old rotting roots, moss-covered rocks or other material.

Very little is known about spawning many of the Catfish, other than the Corydoras species. These have been bred many times. Many of them are nocturnal and hardly ever seen during the daytime. They hide behind rocks and plants or even bury themselves in the gravel, coming out to search for food after all is quiet and dark. I once had a pair of Banjo Catfish, which disappeared shortly after putting them in a fifty-gallon tank, I assumed they had died and been eaten by the occupants of the tank, and almost a year passed with no sign of them. Only when we were tearing down the tank to empty and restock it, did the Banjos turn up, frisky as ever. They lived under the gravel all the time, coming out only when it was dark! Evidently they had been gleaning enough food from the bottom to survive, although I am sure they must have been hungry many a time, since I made no provision for feeding them.

Another group of fish that are used for Scavengers are the Loaches. There are several species of them, most of them not too cheap, since they are almost entirely imported. One Loach has been bred, but none of them in sufficient quantities to meet the demands of the market.

NAME: *Corydoras aeneus*, Gill.

POPULAR NAME: Aeneus; Bronze Catfish.

NATIVE TO: South America.

SIZE: Up to 3 inches.

FOOD ACCEPTED: Almost anything.

TEMPERATURE RANGE: From 72 to 80 degrees.

ATTITUDE: Perfectly peaceful.

To describe one *Corydoras* is to describe every species, since they are all practically identical except for markings. For this reason, I will discuss this one, then, after its history, will list the names of many species usually available in pet stores. Their breeding habits are the same, their food requirements and temperatures are similar, and one description will serve for the entire group.

First, all these little armored Catfish are gentle and harmless. They will never eat baby fish of any species, including their own. They will not disturb the eggs of other fish or their own, unless the eggs happen to be on the bottom of the tank. They are bottom feeders, but, if dry floating foods are fed the other occupants of the tank, will often swim up to the top and vacuum-clean the underside of the surface film, eating as much of the food as possible before the other fish get to it.

They relish beef heart; Tubifex is one of their favorite foods; and chopped fish, shellfish or worms are eagerly taken. They have a comical appearance with the short barbels around their protruding mouth, with which they brush over every spot in the tank in their constant search for food.

Corydoras have the habit of dashing up to the top of the tank, gulping a mouthful of air and descending to the bottom again, to repeat the performance at intervals. These fish live for a very long time if properly cared for. Unfortunately, as I stated in the introduction to this chapter, most aquarists feed the free-swimming fish in the tank and let the Catfish get anything in the way of leftover scraps. With this kind of treatment, *Corydoras* will still live a long time, but they will rarely get into spawning condition. To do this, you should give them a twenty-gallon tank to themselves, feed them large quantities of Tubifex and chopped earthworms, and condition them to the peak of health.

When you notice one or more fish swelling with eggs—it becomes very obvious when a female is ripe—you can remove the other fish except for a male, and the chance is they will spawn. The female and the male swim together to a spot on the glass, or on a clean rock, and the male cleans the place, then deposits his sperm on it. The female then sticks a few eggs on the spot, and they go to find another location for the next batch.

The water should be old and clean. The eggs hatch in about four or five days. The temperature should be kept at about 75 degrees, and the fry, when free-swimming, can be started on dust-size prepared food. The adults may be left in with the fry as they will not molest them.

Following is a list of species of *Corydoras*, some of which are always to be found in pet stores. All species accept the same conditions as *aeneus:*

Corydoras acutus, Cope. Blacktop Catfish.
Corydoras elegans, Steindachner. Elegant Corydoras.

Corydoras multimaculatus, Steindachner. Soldier Catfish.

Corydoras agassizi, Steindachner. Agassizi's Catfish.

Corydoras metae, Eigenmann. Masked Corydoras. Bandit Catfish.

Corydoras arcuatus, Elwin. Arched Corydoras. Skunk Catfish.

Corydoras julii, Steindachner. Leopard Catfish.

Corydoras melanistius, Regan. Black-spotted Catfish.

Corydoras myersi, H. Ribeiro. Myers' Corydoras.

Corydoras punctatus, Bloch. Spotted Catfish.

Corydoras paleatus, Jenyns. Peppered Corydoras.

Corydoras reticulatus, Fraser-Brunner. Network Cat.

Corydoras rabauti, LaMonte. Dwarf Cat. Rabaut's Catfish.

There are many more species of armored Catfish of the *Corydoras* group, from time to time appearing in pet store tanks. The list above is certainly enough to give you a start with them, however, and you may add to it as you find new species.

CHAPTER THIRTEEN

Marine Fish in the Aquarium

While marine fish are certainly not for the beginner, there may be some among the readers of this book who already have enough experience with exotic fish to want to try their hand at keeping some salt-water species.

I am not going to list the life histories of marine fish the way I have done for the exotics. First of all, marine fish are not bred in tanks as are exotics. Secondly, they are very expensive, the materials and equipment needed to keep them alive are complicated and costly, and the chances are that the specimens you buy will die in a very short time after they have been established in your tank.

First is the matter of water to keep them in. This can be filtered ocean water, provided it is perfectly clean, and if you live near enough to the ocean to get it in the quantities needed.

Failing natural sea water, there are several brands of salts manufactured which, when mixed in the proper proportions, simulate sea water accurately enough to keep marine fish alive for years with no difficulty, all other conditions being met, of course. Two of these artificial sea-water salts are *Rila Marine Mix,* made by Rila Products of Teaneck, New Jersey, and *Neptune Salts,* made by the Westchester Aquarium Supply Company, Inc. in White Plains, New York. Both of these salts are excellent. Both of them will maintain marine fish without any other chemicals needed. Both of them become crystal clear when mixed according to the directions and kept in the proper light. Too much sunlight will quickly turn a marine tank green.

The tanks used for marine fish should be the all-glass type, since marine water, even that made with the artificial salts, will quickly corrode even stainless steel tanks. Also, the cement used in ordinary aquaria to hold the glasses in place is often toxic to the marine fish and will kill them in a few days. The Crystal Manufacturing Company of Buffalo, New York, manufactures all-glass tanks which are ideal for marine fish. The Eugene G. Danner Mfg. Company, Inc. of Brooklyn, New York, manufactures a model of its excellent filter and pump in which all fittings and hardware which come into contact with the marine water are made of nylon, so the pump is perfect for use in a marine tank.

One thing in keeping marine fish is the necessity for hard and fast filtration, circulation of the water within the tank, and good aeration. The gravel used should not be fine, since the waste matter will lodge in fine gravel, turn it black, and soon dissipate through the water, fouling it and killing the fish unless you can remove them. This is easier said than done, however, since to remove them, you must have another marine tank available, filled with the same kind of water used in the original tank and held at the same temperature. This can be a very costly thing.

The Eureka Products Company of Newark, New Jersey, manufactures an under-gravel filter that is excellent for keeping the water from fouling, both in fresh-water and in marine tanks. The device is a series of tubes, placed on the bottom of the tank and covered with the gravel. These tubes are perforated, and an upright tube reaches out of the water in one corner of the tank. A second upright tube is connected to the air supply of an aquarium pump.

The purpose of this filter is to pump the water from the bottom of the tank after it has passed through the gravel, aerating it simultaneously to liberate the gases held within it, then bubble the water, freed of the carbon dioxide and other harmful gases back into the tank.

The next deterrent to keeping marine fish is the matter of food. While some species can be trained to take small strips of raw fish, shrimp, clams or crabmeat, by far the greatest majority of them will eat only live food in the form of small live fish. Some of the smaller marine species will take live brine shrimp as well.

No plants will live in the marine tank, since the salt water quickly kills them. Marine plants will not live either, because they need conditions impossible to imitate in an artificial ecology. They will only die and foul the tank. Dead corals are useful as decoration, but make certain that they have been thoroughly cleaned and rinsed. A shell or two, with a hole knocked into it to eliminate the possibility of water being trapped inside it, thus becoming stale and foul, which will kill the occupants of the tank, are useful as decoration.

Invertebrates can be kept in marine tanks, but they are very difficult to keep alive, and very dangerous from the standpoint of fouling the water. Sea Anemones are probably the easiest of the invertebrates to get and to keep, but they should be fed in a separate tank and permitted to remain in the feeding tank until they have eliminated their wastes, then returned to the regular aquarium. The easiest way to move Anemones around is to let them adhere to a rock of some kind, removing the rock with the Anemone on it. It will kill the animal to try to pull it free each time it is fed.

Crabs, shrimp, especially the beautiful coral shrimp, some of the mollusks, all will do well for a while at least. The crabs and mollusks will act as excellent Scavengers too.

Crabs should never be put into a marine tank where there are small marine fish present, since they will eat the fish at night. Even if the fish are fast moving, and cannot be caught during the daytime, at night, when they are resting, one fast pounce by the wily crab, and the fish becomes its dinner! Anemones cannot be kept with fish either, since the natural food of Anemones is fish, and you will soon find all your beautiful and costly specimens going down the gullet of the insatiable Anemone. It relishes Sea Horses, too, and will suck them down one by one.

Every year thousands of Sea Horses, *Hippocampus hudsonius,* DeKay, are caught and sold in pet stores. They now are even sold through the mail, with a bag of salts to make enough water to keep them in for a short time. I say a short time, since there is not enough water supplied to fill a good-sized tank, and the Sea Horses do not live very long because of lack of the proper food and the necessary conditions for their continued welfare. With Sea Horses, the great attraction is the fact that the males are the ones which give birth to the young. The female lays her eggs in the belly pouch of the male, who carries them around until they hatch and absorb their yolk sacs. When the baby sea "ponies" are ready to swim alone, the male ejects them from his pouch with energetic spasms of his body, bending backward and shooting fifty to a hundred babies out of the opening of the pouch with each spasm! It is not uncommon for a male to give "birth" to six or seven hundred young at a time! Practically never have young Sea Horses been successfully reared in captivity. Even though they feed and plenty of live food is given to them, still they die within a few days. Baby Guppies are good Sea Horse food.

Hippocampus hudsonius. This father Sea Horse is giving birth to hundreds of "colts." The female lays her eggs in the male's pouch.

There are a great number of fancy marine fish now being imported. Their cost is high because of the trouble it takes to catch them and ship them to the market. Most of them are colored like living jewels, all of them, with very few exceptions, cannot live with other fish, even of their own species, but must be kept in an individual tank. There really is no such thing as a successful community marine tank. Sooner or later there will be fights and fin-ripping between two or more of the species kept together.

Much has yet to be learned about marine life before this part of the great hobby of keeping captive fish becomes as easy as the fresh-water species. It is a part of the hobby that takes much time, a great amount of money and a lot of special equipment.

PART II

Amphibians as Pets

CHAPTER FOURTEEN

Meet the Amphibian

It is a strange thought that at one time in the earth's long history, the only sound ever heard was the voice of an amphibian. This was because, other than a few scorpions and spiders, amphibians were the only animals alive on the land. In the surrounding waters, many forms of life flourished, but the early amphibians were the only animals with backbones on land.

Modern amphibians do not give the appearance of courageous travelers. But, of course, as with all life, appearances are deceptive and times change. Early amphibians bore little resemblance to those we know today.

The word "amphibious" means having a double life. It is quite descriptive of the class of animals bearing it. Frogs, toads, newts, salamanders, and the wormlike, tropical caecilians are modern members of the group. They are animals who are able to live on land as well as in water. Some remain in the water most of the time, while others are almost completely terrestrial. Caecilians actually live under the ground. Most amphibians employ both environments and are able to cope well with either. By and large, amphibians live a large part of their lives on land and return to the water mainly to reproduce. The young, therefore, are born in the water. For that reason, they are usually quite different in appearance from their parents. They are born equipped for aquatic life and must be transformed, as they mature, to be able to enjoy a terrestrial existence.

Amphibians are remarkably versatile animals. Although dependent upon water, they can be found in very dry areas. Even some deserts are inhabited by toads and frogs, who always manage to locate a small puddle to accommodate their needs. High mountain ridges are scaled and colonized by tiny salamanders. Deep jungles provide homes, not only on the ground, but, for some enterprising frogs, even in the trees. The only continent in which some species of amphibian cannot be found is Antarctica. No amphibian lives in salt water, so do not look for them in the oceans. Anywhere else, you may look forward to an encounter with a small double-living friend.

If you will stop to consider, for just a moment, the complexities of a life in which part of the time is spent on land and part in water, you will begin to appreciate the amphibian body: A fish is a lovely creature with its sleek torpedo shape and brilliant scales. But, removed from its watery environment, a fish could not survive for more than a few hours. The stumpy, popeyed frog, however, manages well anywhere. The reasons for this versatility can be found in the marvelous amphibian body.

No feathers, fur, or scales cover the body of an amphibian. Like people, amphibians have naked skins. Their bodies are pleasant to touch, for they feel smooth and cool. The amphibian's skin serves many purposes. It keeps the animal from drying out while on land and helps the lungs in their job of respiration. Also, nakedness increases sensitivity, as the nerve endings are close to the surface, and changes in the environment are thus quickly detected. The skin, therefore, is the most vital organ of touch possessed by amphibians.

Just beneath the skin are a number of glands. The mucous

This amphibian has an enormous voice for so small a creature. The barking tree frog (*Hyla gratiosa*) is so-named for the quality of its call, when it is up in the trees. During the breeding season, this call changes and sounds more like rapidly repeated gunshots.

glands secrete the fluid that is responsible for keeping the animal moist while on land and also lubricates while the amphibian is immersed in water. Mucous glands are scattered over the entire body and, while very tiny in size, are capable of secreting an enormous quantity of sticky fluid when stimulated.

Tree frogs have glands in the toes that release a substance like glue. This enables the climber to cling to a vertical tree trunk or an overhanging branch.

Lungless salamanders rely on secretions of glands located in the groove between nose and lips to free the nostrils of water and mud.

Some male frogs have other kinds of glands that have developed from the mucous set. These are located in the chest and in the thumbs and are there for breeding purposes. Their sticky secretions make it possible for the male to hold onto his slippery mate while in the water. Male salamanders rely on secretions from glands on their chins to attract the female's attention.

There are also granular glands in the skin of amphibians which form the main means of protection for these small animals. They secrete a substance very irritating to the eyes and mouths of animals which might like to try a diet of frog legs. In some instances, this secretion is highly poisonous and can cause nausea and paralysis in small animals. Usually, when an amphibian is capable of producing such a devastating effect upon an enemy, it is brilliantly colored. So the vivid red or yellow of some frogs forms a warning to stay away. But some amphibians, like the drab brown marine toad, are highly poisonous and do not advertise the fact.

Unlike our skin, that of the amphibian allows water to pass through in both directions. The rate of passage varies with the amount of moisture in the environment, the extent of dehydration in the animal, and the exact species involved. Toads have fairly dry skin which allows for little water loss, enabling them to live in drier areas than most frogs. Amphibians that live in the desert are particularly quick to absorb water during infrequent rainfalls.

Just as the smooth skin permits water to pass in and out of the body, it also allows for an exchange of gases. Oxygen is taken in and carbon dioxide passed out through the skin. The blood vessels are very close to the surface and able to absorb the necessary oxygen directly. Thus, the skin assists the lungs in breathing and, indeed, in some cases, as with the lungless salamander, takes over the breathing function completely. This is important to the amphibian while on land, for its lungs are not as efficient as ours and cannot handle all the oxygen the animal needs. Skin breathing is even more important when the animal hibernates underwater. During the cold months, many amphibians sink down to the muddy bottoms of lakes and ponds to sleep out the bad weather. There, with the body functions slowed down, less oxygen is needed and the amphibian is able to get all it needs through the skin without having to surface for lung breathing.

The outermost layer of skin is shed at frequent intervals throughout the year. You will be unlikely to find a frog or a salamander skin lying about as you would a snakeskin, however, for the amphibian includes this old skin in his diet. As the skin begins to peel, the amphibian begins to swallow and the swallowing motions help in loosening the skin still further. After shedding, the amphibian looks shiny bright and new, but is soon covered again with the dust that serves as camouflage.

Very young amphibian larvae have only one layer of skin. Tiny hairlike structures grow from it and the motion of these hairs sets up currents in the water around the infant. These currents move the immature tadpole forward through the water to new sources of food, until the larva is old enough to move its body and tail with its muscles.

Caecilians, which are burrowing animals, have different

needs and therefore different skins than do salamanders and frogs. The skin of a caecilian feels smooth, but beneath the top layers, tiny scales can be found imbedded.

Different ways of life demand different responses from the senses. Therefore, each group of amphibians have a unique type of development of vision, hearing, smell, taste, and touch—each of them meeting the needs of the owner.

Frogs and toads have their eyes set at opposite sides of their heads, looking out in different directions. When an object is close at hand, they are not able to focus upon it with both eyes. Therefore, these animals are usually rather farsighted. If they are the sort that live on flying insects such as butterflies and mosquitoes, this farsightedness is a decided advantage. They are able to spot their dinner at long range and judge exactly the right second at which to leap in order to intercept flight.

For a toad or frog interested in crawling things, like earthworms, somewhat nearer vision is needed. These hunters do not notice the wriggler until it is quite close. If it gets too close, however, the amphibian must back off a little way to see it properly before striking out at it.

This kind of eyesight is particularly beneficial in escaping from enemies. Frogs and toads, living on the ground, would make easy prey for larger meat-eaters if not for the fact that they can see forward, backward, sideways, and upward simultaneously.

Frogs and toads are very sensitive to differences in light. If you try to sneak up on one, you will find that, although his back may be turned, the moment your shadow falls across his body, he will be off in a bound. Those frogs and toads that feed by night are able to enlarge their pupils as do cats.

A thick fold of skin over the upper part of the eyeball forms the eyelid of toads and frogs. It is immovable as it has no muscles. Sometimes the bottom lid also lacks muscles. For this reason, some amphibians have developed an additional transparent fold of skin. This fold is called the nictitating membrane. It can be drawn over the eyes by muscles which surround the eyeball. Because of its transparency, even when the animal has drawn it up in sleep, he is able to view the outer world.

Toads and frogs have really beautiful eyes. The black pupil is

Like most frogs and toads, the bullfrog (*Rana catesbeiana*) has extraordinarily beautiful eyes. Note the eardrum or "tympanum" behind the eye.

usually horizontal, but sometimes is vertical as in cats, and, occasionally, it has a scalloped outline. The iris surrounding it is always a lovely color and is patterned by lines of gold or silver or red.

Salamanders have more pupil and less iris than their cousins, with less color in the iris. This is because they are primarily night hunters and need the enlarged pupil to receive the maximum amount of available light.

Most salamanders and newts have their eyes set closer together than do frogs and toads. But the hellbender, with its very wide head, has its eyes set so far apart that it can never focus both on a single object. However, as this animal feeds strictly by night, the senses of smell and touch are much more important than that of sight.

Some salamanders that live in dark caves are completely blind. However, in some species, where the young are born outside the cave, the larvae see well and do not lose their vision until they move into the cave at maturity. If forced to remain out in the open, they will go on seeing normally after maturing.

Many of the underground caecilians are blind, for their eye muscles and nerves have completely ceased functioning. Indeed, the bones of the skull frequently grow right over the eye sockets. For an animal living below ground, the sense of sight is unnecessary, and smell and touch play a much more important role in the business of living.

Just as it is necessary for a land-living animal to keep its skin from drying out, it must also have a way of keeping the eyes moist. To accomplish this, amphibians, like all terrestrial animals, have eye glands to lubricate the eyes. These glands and the eyelids, as well, are formed just before the larvae metamorphose. Some salamanders, therefore, that retain their larval state throughout life, never develop glands and lids at all. But, since their entire lives are spent in the water, such development is as unnecessary as it is for fishes.

You can tell which amphibians have the best hearing from the volume of sound produced by the animal. Frogs and toads, who communicate vocally, have a well-developed sense of hearing. In most frogs and toads, if you will look just behind the eye above the end of the mouth, you will see a round, shiny membrane of skin. This is the frog's "ear." It is actually the same mechanism—the eardrum—that is found in humans. There is one species of frog, however, living in Siam, which has an external opening with the eardrum well below the surface. But for most frogs and toads, the drum is clearly visible on the same plane as the side of the face. It is sometimes protected by a rim of thick cartilage, but more often it is flush with the skin. The distance at which a particular species of frog can hear sound depends on its life-style. Those species which communicate with others of their kind at a long distance hear better than those which "speak" only at close proximity. For instance, the male spadefoot toad, living in desert conditions, signals loudly after a rainfall to call the female to an available puddle to lay her eggs. It is necessary for her to hurry to the spot, from any distance whatever, to take advantage of the newly created breeding ground quickly, for it may evaporate before long.

Most salamanders and newts make only small sounds. The Pacific giant salamander is an exception and can produce a loud barking noise as well as an earsplitting scream when in danger. However, most salamanders have to be content with little squeaks. As none of them has external eardrums, all "hearing" is done by the forelegs which are able to pick up ground vibrations.

Caecilians are completely voiceless. Probably they do not hear at all, but then there is little to hear if your home is a deep burrow.

Animals that live in caves or burrows are more dependent upon their sense of smell than they are upon vision. The same applies to those who live by night. Consequently, frogs and toads that are essentially diurnal (moving about in the daytime) see better and smell less than those who are nocturnal. Also, aquatic amphibians that feed in rapidly moving water are less likely to be able to find their food by sight than they are by smell.

The sense of smell in amphibians operates not only through cells in the nostrils, but also in a special area of cells in the nasal passage. This extra smelling device is called Jacobson's organ. It is found in snakes and lizards as well as in amphibians. Some aquatic salamanders lack Jacobson's organ, but the other salamanders and newts all possess it and in the frogs and caecilians it is very well developed. When the animal takes some food into its mouth, Jacobson's organ tests it for desirability. If unsatisfactory, the animal is able to spit out the food before it reaches the vulnerable stomach.

The nostrils are on the tip of the snout, sometimes on a raised surface (like a nose), but more often on a flat plane.

Even when an amphibian, such as the lungless salamander, needs no nose mechanism for breathing in air, it still has nostrils for smelling.

Caecilians have a very well-developed sense of smell and a marvelous mechanism for using it. In a little groove between the eye and the upper lip, lies a tentacle which can be brought forward and moved from side to side. The base of the tentacle is in contact with Jacobson's organ. When some item of food is encountered by the moving tentacle of the blind caecilian, tiny bits are quickly tested by the organ. To the caecilian, the tentacle is an organ of touch as well as smell and its great sensitivity makes up for the animal's lack of vision.

As in humans, the sense of taste is very closely allied to the sense of smell in amphibians. There are, however, separate mechanisms for the two senses. The taste buds are arranged in groups of cells found in the tongue, along the jaws, and in the palate of all amphibians.

When an amphibian is responding to a taste sensation, he swallows or snaps his jaws. When the sense of smell is stimulated, he will move his head or body.

Although insects and worms are quite unappetizing to us, amphibians have definite preferences in this range of diet and unappealing ones are spit out—proving that the sense of taste is well developed.

The lateral-line organs of some amphibians indicate very clearly these animals' intermediate position between fish and fully terrestrial vertebrates. These organs, possessed by fish but not by higher vertebrates, are to be found in aquatic salamanders, frog and toad larvae, and even in some adult frogs. Lateral lines are clusters of tiny cells that form in rows of pear-shaped pits on the head and body. They pick up vibrations in the water and localize the center of gravity, and so the body stays balanced.

When an amphibian, such as the newt, becomes terrestrial for a while after an aquatic existence, the lateral-line organs disappear beneath a covering of skin. When back in the water, the organs reappear.

Amphibians have the means to conquer and digest some of the most plentiful protein available to the world. They fill their bellies regularly with worms and insects. This kind of high-protein diet provides energy for living processes, restores worn-out tissues of the body, and allows for growth. Any surplus food is transformed into carbohydrates and stored until needed. It can then be turned into sugar, which supplies the energy required by all living animals. The ability to store extra food enables the hibernating species to get through the winter in good shape. Amphibians never develop any great concentrations of fat, however, as do some birds and mammals. But their relatively slow metabolism burns up food at a slower rate and allows them to operate at maximum efficiency, even when they are very lean.

The feeding equipment of amphibians varies with the mode of life. The true toads are completely toothless. Frogs usually have teeth only in the upper jaw. These teeth are capable of gripping prey tightly, but they are never used for chewing and very rarely for biting. However, one species, the South American horned frog, is very fierce and uses his powerful jaws and sharp teeth as aggressively as a tiger.

In most frogs and toads, the teeth are well assisted by an amazing tongue. A few frogs, called aglossids, are tongueless and use their hands to stuff food into their mouths. But, usually, the tongue is all important. Unlike our tongue, the frogs' and toads' is fastened at the front of the lower jaw, while the back is loose. When the mouth is closed, the tip of the tongue faces backward, toward the throat. When ready to strike at its prey, the frog opens his mouth wide and the tongue pops out in a forward position. Within the mouth are numerous glands that coat the tongue with a sticky secretion. Any unlucky insect that is struck by this quick, mobile tongue is then hopelessly stuck.

Once the prey is in the mouth, a muscular contraction takes place which forces the eyeballs down into the roof of the mouth and assists the tongue in pushing the insect down into the gullet. This contraction accounts for the blink which accompanies every swallow of the frog.

Some salamanders also have rather sticky tongues. Many have

a fascinating mushroom-shaped tongue which they are capable of shooting out over an enormous distance. Some salamanders have teeth in the jaws, while others have only a few on the palate. In place of the jaw teeth, some have developed powerful horny plates, similar to the beak of a turtle. One almost legless salamander, *Amphiuma*, has very sharp teeth and bites viciously in self-defense.

As for the caecilians, they have two rows of teeth in the upper jaw and one or two (depending on the species) in the lower jaw. They have no trouble holding onto their prey.

Now, what becomes of the food once it leaves the mouth? As with most of us, it passes into the esophagus, which in the amphibians is a straight tube lined with small hairlike structures called cilia. The food is coated with mucus in the esophagus and the cilia help the muscles in moving the slippery food through to the stomach.

Once within the stomach, special muscles move the food around and mix it with gastric juices. If, however, the food turns out to be disagreeable, frogs are able to turn their stomachs inside out and push them straight out through the mouth (like emptying a garbage pail). If the food is good, it is treated with chemicals, such as hydrochloric acid, and enzymes like pepsin, which begin the process of digestion. Some food may be held back at this point for storage. Since it is important to the amphibian to have extra food, the stomach of many can be expanded to a tremendous degree.

Within the intestine are glands which secrete a substance carried by the blood to the pancreas. This stimulates the pancreas to begin the second stage of digestion through the release of the pancreatic juices. When the food reaches the pancreas, it is broken down and is well on the way to becoming the product necessary to the amphibian's health.

The final process of digestion is accomplished by the intestinal juices produced by mucous glands that line the walls of the intestines.

The products of digestion are absorbed by the walls of the intestine. From here, they are transported by the blood to those areas of the body needing building-up and replacement of tissues. Those not needed immediately are taken to the liver. Although the liver takes up a large area in the body of an amphibian, it does not actually contribute to digestion. Its function is to store some of the fat products formed from the protein food. Just before hibernation, the liver of some amphibians may double its size with stored food.

Breathing or respiration is the way in which all of us supply our tissues with much-needed fuel. This fuel is a gas we call oxygen. Oxygen is passed into the tissues by way of the blood stream. Just as important as the taking in of oxygen is the elimination of another gas, carbon dioxide, which is unhealthy to our system. The blood stream picks up carbon dioxide from inside the body at the same time that it releases the oxygen required by all parts of the body. That way a continuous balance is maintained. Under conditions where not enough oxygen is available, carbon dioxide accumulates in the body and the cells become paralyzed and may die. This is true of all animals.

As we have already mentioned, an amphibian's way of breathing is different from ours. We use only our lungs to take in oxygen and get rid of carbon dioxide. Amphibians usually use lungs, too, but they also have skins that are moist and porous and that function as an additional site of gas exchange. Some amphibians, having no lungs at all, are extremely dependent on this kind of skin breathing.

Young amphibians, before metamorphosing, have gills for breathing. For the aquatic way of life to which they are restricted, this means of breathing is the most efficient. It enables

Most amphibians begin life with gills for breathing; then, as they mature, develop lungs. The greater siren (*Siren lacertina*), shown here, is aquatic all its life and retains its plumelike gills.

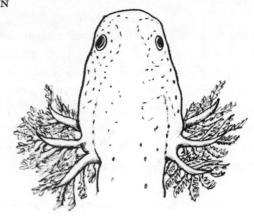

the animal to draw oxygen from the surrounding water, rather than the air. The gills of young amphibians sprout from the sides of the neck and are sometimes quite ornate. As the tadpole matures, the gills are absorbed into the body. Lungs begin to form and the mature amphibian can then leave the water, able to breathe oxygen from the air. Some amphibians never metamorphose and spend their entire lives in water. Thus, the axolotl, for instance, retains its gills throughout life.

Whether lungs, gills, or skin are used by an amphibian for breathing, the mechanism is basically the same. The large arteries carrying the blood away from the heart break down into smaller vessels which in turn split up into many tiny capillaries with thin walls. These tiny capillaries then reform into small veins which then become large veins carrying blood to the heart. Because the walls of the capillaries are so thin, gas exchange is easy there. With gills, the gas exchange is carried on between the air in the water and the blood in the capillaries. In skin breathing, the exchange can take place in water or air. Lungs are paired elastic sacs within the chest lined with blood capillaries. A very large quantity of oxygen may be brought in and a proportionately large amount of carbon dioxide released through the lungs. But the method is effective only on land.

Even those amphibians possessing lungs do not breathe exactly as we do. We breathe with the help of muscular movements within the walls of our chest. Amphibians breathe by moving the floor of the mouth, pulling air into the mouth. Then they close their nostrils and force the oxygen into their lungs. You can see a sort of quiver in the throat of a frog as it pulls in air.

The bone structure underlying the skin and flesh of an amphibian varies in the different forms. Generally speaking, even in adult amphibians, the skeleton is partly made of cartilage or gristle with the rest consisting of solid bone. The small vertebrae that make up the spine may number only nine as in the frogs and toads, but can reach as many as 250 in salamanders and caecilians. Usually there is only a single vertebra that anchors the skull to the back. Thus amphibians are a practically neckless group and do not have the ability to turn their heads without moving the whole body. The salamanders, with dozens of vertebrae between the front and hind legs, are elongated aquatic forms that swim through the water like eels. The dwarf sirens and the amphiumas, the "congo eels," are good examples. More generally, however, salamanders have only some fifteen jointed vertebrae making up the back regions—with another twenty-five or so constituting the tail. The wormlike caecilians, who appear to be all tail, have only a few tail vertebrae, but as many as two hundred vertebrae in the body proper. The tailless frogs and toads have a long bony rod rather than separate bony discs at the end of the backbone.

All vertebrates with legs have bony structures called limb girdles attached to the backbone. The pectoral or shoulder girdle carries the front legs and is attached to the column right behind the neck. The rear legs are anchored by way of the pelvic or hip girdle which is located near the vent or cloaca. The tail starts directly behind the hip girdle. Both limb girdles can be compared to V-shaped plates, closed on the underside, the open ends of each V attaching to the sides of the backbone. Each girdle is made up of separate elements fused together to form the kind of open ring just described. The shoulder girdle is attached by way of ligaments and muscles. The hip girdle is much more tightly affixed to the backbone by way of an actual bony fusion between a single vertebra, called the sacrum, and the uppermost elements of the girdle. The upper bones of all four legs are in turn socketed into round depressions on each side of the girdles. Thus, the limbs can support the weight of the body when the animal moves.

The legs themselves are made up of three main sections. There is the upper limb socketed to the girdles, followed by a lower portion which bears the hands and feet. In the hoppers, the frogs and toads, the hind legs are very powerful and the bony elements making up the spring mechanism are correspondingly large. The hind foot is tremendously lengthened and serves as a powerful lever against the ground when it pushes down, during the jump.

Salamanders have rather short limbs which they use not so much to lift themselves off the ground in the manner of a dog or horse, but more as jutting-out supports as they wriggle from side to side. Salamander limb girdles are correspondingly small. The legless amphibians, the caecilians, have no hip girdle at all, and use a strictly snakelike method for getting around, above and below the ground.

The amphibian skull doesn't look at all like the solid, long box you may have in mind, if you are thinking of a human skull. It is made up mostly of cartilage rather than bone; also it is quite flat, looking a little bit like a filled-in horseshoe. There are large holes for the eyes, and the front edge constitutes the upper jaw. The U-shaped lower jaw is slung from either side of the hind end. The brain itself is so small that it takes up only a fraction of the total skull. It is located in a small cavity at the very rear. The legless amphibians have a more solid skull than either frogs or salamanders. In line with their burrowing existence, their skulls are ramming tools for driving the body through the soil.

If any group of animals is to be truly successful, an efficient method of reproducing its own kind is an absolute essential. For many amphibians, breeding is a complex matter, for although they may be terrestrial throughout their adult lives, they must return to the water to reproduce. Some have developed the ability to produce young on land in moist surroundings, but, for most, water is necessary. True, even a mud puddle is adequate for some, but others need large bodies of fresh water in which to mate and have young.

Because of the great diversity in methods of reproduction, there is no one time of year when breeding takes place. In desert-living types, for instance, any good rainfall is the signal for mating, whatever the season. Where young need a long time to mature, early spring mating occurs. Others, that develop quickly, can be produced later in the summer.

Mating can be a very elaborate ritual or a simple matter of fertilizing the eggs as quickly as possible.

Many amphibians lay eggs, but there are also those that retain their eggs within the body until the young emerge. Some species lay thousands of eggs at a time, while others have just a few. Some young look like small replicas of their parents. Many, however, bear scarcely any resemblance to the adults. In each case, there is a good reason for the differences involved.

The business of mating in all higher forms of life, involves two individuals, one male and one female, coming together to produce young. The female manufactures the eggs and the male fertilizes them. In any group of animals, this getting-together of the sexes is a serious business attended to at more or less regular intervals. Usually, there are clear-cut differences between the sexes—which are known as secondary sexual characteristics. These characteristics may be there permanently throughout adult life, or they may only appear at mating season.

Many times, size indicates sex. In amphibians, the adult female is frequently larger than the adult male. Of course, this is not always so. The tiger salamander and the hairy frog, for instance, have males considerably larger than their females. Sometimes adults of both sexes are the same size.

Male frogs can sometimes be distinguished by dark patches on the throat. Male bullfrogs have noticeably larger eardrums than females.

All these characteristics are permanent. Of a more temporary nature is the peculiar glandular growths found on the male hairy toad. Every breeding season, long, slim, hairlike strands cover the sides and thighs of the males of this species. Later, this hair disappears.

Male European newts go through an elaborate metamorphosis during the breeding season. At other times of the year, they are terrestrial, but become completely aquatic in order to mate. The toes become webbed for swimming; the tail, too, adapts to water by becoming broad and enlarged. A lovely frilled crest appears on the back and tail. This crest is of a beautiful red color which highlights the already striking black-spotted brown body.

Usually males and females appear in equal number, but mating in amphibians is primarily a random matter. Permanent pairing-off rarely occurs.

Well, then, how do these animals meet at the appropriate times? Frogs and toads, we know, gather together at a large pool in enormous numbers every year, most frequently during the spring. It is the male who arrives at the chosen place first and from there utters his familiar croak. At breeding time, with many males croaking together, it can create quite a din. The purpose of all the noise is to lead the females to the mating grounds. Some male frogs and toads have large sacs beneath their chins which enable them to issue particularly loud calls. When relaxed, the sac appears as a loose flap of skin. But when in use, it is filled with air, forming a bubble that is sometimes so large that the male cannot see around it while in the act of calling. The first appearance of this pouch in a male frog is the indication of his new sexual maturity.

When the female frogs have answered the summons and appear on the scene, mating takes place. Each male hops from female to female without favoritism. In his enthusiasm, he might occasionally land on the back of another male, but, then, there would be a warning grunt, quite different from the mating call, to point out his mistake. A female who has already laid her eggs makes another kind of sound to ward off unwanted male attentions.

Sometimes, it is not the calling of the males that brings frogs together. The smell of certain water vegetation blooming in the spring lures the common frog to a certain pool. Frequently the sudden rush of spring water caused by increased oxygen will summon the frogs to their reproductive business.

For the voiceless newts and salamanders, mating is quite different. Males and females have to look longer and harder to find each other. When they do meet, it is up to the male to attract the female by means of his beautiful color or interesting odor.

Male and female caecilians must squiggle around underground to find each other. Males have special organs for internal fertilization of the females' eggs, so there is no danger of two members of the same sex becoming confused about each other.

Perhaps you are wondering how amphibians of different species manage to recognize the differences and remain apart at mating time. This important separation is usually provided for by the nature of courtship. Male salamanders, for instance, have involved courtship rituals to practice before the female in order to stimulate her properly. Only one routine is recognized and approved by the female, so the distinction remains clear-cut. Some North American salamanders stand in front of the female and emit glandular secretions from their cloaca, which they waft through the air to her by use of the tail. If the female is of the same species, she will follow closely behind him with her snout pressed close to his tail. No other species is likely to find his behavior pleasing.

Secondary sexual characteristics also work to indicate differences in species. No two species of frogs, for instance, sing the same song.

So we see how the right two animals get together for breeding. Now, how does the actual mating occur? Once again, it varies with the animal.

Most frogs and toads have no elaborate courtship ritual. There are a few exceptions. For instance, male and female poison frogs of Central America play an involved game of leapfrog before actual mating occurs. But mostly frogs waste no time courting. The male simply hops onto the back of the first available female as she swims by. He clasps her tightly with his forearms in an embrace called amplexus. On some of his fingers, a special rough structure assures his tight grasp on the female's body. Sometimes these warty surfaces also appear on the hind legs or the belly. The female then stretches her body and lays the eggs. At the same moment, the male releases his sperm in fluid form. The sperm enters the eggs, which are then usually dispersed by the hind legs of the male. Once all this is accomplished, the male hops off and swims away in search of the next waiting female.

Tailed frogs are so-called because of the long, tail-like organ of the male. This is actually not a tail at all, but a long extension from the cloaca. These frogs, because they live in rapidly flowing water, practice internal fertilization, with the male using his special cloaca to deposit his sperm directly into the female's cloaca.

Most salamanders have a more complex premating ritual, with great variations between species in courtship dances and display by the male. Only in a few species is the courtship casual. Hellbenders, as an example, have very nonchalant mating patterns. Here, the female simply lays her eggs and later some male she has never seen drifts by to spray them with sperm.

Usually, however, the male salamander must go to somewhat more trouble to receive a sign of approval from the female. When she does issue such a signal, he emits his sperm, wrapped up in a jellylike package called a spermatophore. The female may then press her cloaca over the package to take it into her body, or she may use her hind legs to ram it in. In some species, the male actually pushes his spermatophore into the female's cloaca. In any case, once the spermatophore is in the female's body, the gelatin dissolves and the sperms are stored in a special sac called the spermatheca located in the roof of the cloaca. Later, as each egg is laid, the sperm is freed to fertilize it. Some species store the sperm for several months, so that the time of mating and the time of fertilization are quite distinct.

Very little is known about the subterranean caecilian's mating

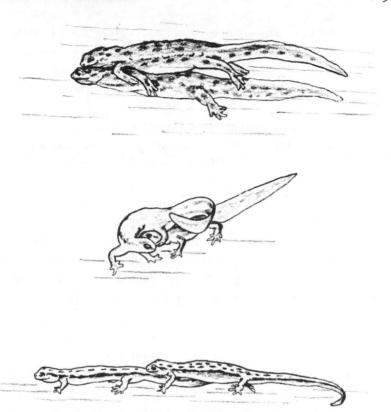

Courtship among salamanders and newts is elaborate and serves to keep the different species distinct. Illustrated here is the courtship of the waltl newt (*Pleurodeles waltl*) (top), the red-spotted newt (*Notophthalmus viridescens*) (middle), and the two-lined salamander (*Eurycea bislineata*) (bottom).

behavior. As the males have a sexual organ designed for putting in sperm, we can assume that fertilization is internal.

The kinds of eggs and the number laid by each amphibian female is once again highly variable, depending on species. One species of frog is known to lay only one egg at each breeding season, while some energetic female toads lay as many as 25,000 at one time. Some eggs are simply dropped in the water, while others are deposited in nests or watched carefully by a parent.

In general, those animals laying many eggs are less likely to make provisions for care than those with just a few offspring.

Amphibian eggs have a yolk surrounded by membranes, over which is a jellylike covering. They are usually laid in the water in clusters or strings of different lengths. But some species lay single eggs and attach them to stones or plants.

Those that lay eggs on land, and they are definitely in the minority, sometimes make small moist nests of pools in the holes of trees. There are tree frogs that build clay pools to house their eggs. A few amphibians even carry their eggs around on their bodies.

Parental care among amphibians is quite different from that shown by birds toward their eggs. Amphibians do not sit on their eggs in order for the heat of their body to help hatch the eggs. Their bodies are not warm enough to accomplish this. Instead, they must depend upon the sun to do this job for them and, therefore, in the majority of cases the eggs are simply left exposed. The incubation period varies according to the temperature of the water or air surrounding the eggs. Some eggs hatch in just a day, while others take weeks.

The tiny amphibian inside the egg may develop glands on his snout which secrete a substance that dissolves the egg membrane near his head. This helps the young creature to escape from his egg. Other amphibians develop a small egg tooth on the upper jaw which is used to split the membrane.

The young salamander or caecilian that emerges from the egg usually looks very much like its parents, except for the fact that it has gills to enable it to breathe in water. Anyone who has seen a tadpole, however, knows that this is not the case with frogs and toads.

A tadpole appears to be just a large head attached to a tail. No legs or arms are in evidence. The large gills are obvious in the newly hatched larvae. But not all tadpoles look alike. Differences in living conditions produce different kinds of tadpoles. Those that swim in still water develop high crests on the tops of their tails to aid them in their free-swimming way of life. Others are more streamlined with a flattened body and low tail. Those living in damp air rather than water have even lower and longer tails. The structure of the mouth is also different in tadpoles with varying diets.

All newly hatched tadpoles are helpless little beings, barely able to wriggle over to some nearby water plant and cling for dear life. Each one feeds itself on what is left of its yolk sac. After a time, the external gills are covered over by a flap of skin and breathing is accomplished by internal gills. Gradually, the legs begin to appear; first the front ones, and then the hind legs. Once this happens, the tail begins to be absorbed into the body. With its disappearance, the tadpole has became a charming little frog or toad, just like its parents, except for its small size.

The young salamander's metamorphosis seems merely a matter of losing the external gills. (This, by the way, is the only change in developing caecilians.) But there are a few other changes in salamanders that are not so obvious. Young salamanders have no eyelids, while the adults do.

In most amphibians, before metamorphosis is complete, the lungs appear and take over the job of the gills. A new system of blood circulation develops. The legs become strong enough to carry the animal on land.

With all these changes, it is not so surprising to find that there is also a change in diet. Salamanders, who are similar to the parents in external appearance, are also meat-eaters at an early stage, but tadpoles usually start life as vegetarians and only become carnivorous as they mature.

Some amphibians do not go through any metamorphosis at all. These are animals that are born on dry land and so hatch out of their eggs as miniature adults. Such is the case with the Alpine salamander and some lungless salamanders. Some of the narrow-mouthed toads as well as some frogs also boast fully mature offspring. In these land-born types, there is much more parental supervision of the eggs than is usual among amphibians.

There are also certain tree frogs that dam up the water in shallow areas close to the banks and make small mud-walled pools in which to lay eggs. In this protected environment, the young develop in relative safety from predators.

Some frogs make nests of foam. At the time of egg-laying, the female also extrudes a substance that looks like egg white which is beaten into a meringue by the father's hind legs until it floats at the top of the water. Here the young remain to grow and mature until the nest disintegrates. Sometimes, such foam nests are constructed on land and the foam is particularly important here, for it keeps the young from drying out.

There are foam nests made in leaves by tree frogs, but other sorts of leaf nests are also made. Here, it is the jellylike mass surrounding the egg that acts like a glue to hold the leaf rolled up.

Even the lowly caecilians practice a kind of child care. Frequently, female caecilians wrap themselves around their eggs as a way of ensuring sufficient moisture. Some salamanders also care for their eggs in this manner; many never stray from their eggs. Usually, it is the female salamander who acts as protector, but sometimes the male is the guardian. Indeed, some devoted fathers stand by constantly flicking their tails through the water, so that oxygen bubbles are formed around the eggs.

Frogs rarely stay near the eggs in this manner, but there are some who carry their eggs around with them. Some South American tree frogs actually have a pouch on the back for the carrying of eggs. In some species, the male actually places the eggs in the female's pouch with his hind legs. Others are simply rolled down into position as they are laid.

The amphibians most famous for child care are the midwife toads of Europe. In this group it is the male who assumes the role of protector. Midwife toads do their pairing off on land and as the female lays her long string of eggs, the male wraps it around his hind legs. There they remain entwined for the three or four weeks it takes to incubate them. The female goes merrily off on her way immediately after laying the eggs, leaving her patient mate to care for their twenty to sixty offspring. The male withdraws to his hole, now spending all his daylight hours there, only venturing forth in the evening to search for food and moisten the eggs attached to his legs. At the right moment, he goes for a dip in the nearest pool, leaving the eggs to hatch and develop in normal tadpole fashion.

Other male amphibians showing great parental care are the tiny, one-inch-long Darwin's frogs, who store their young in their enormously enlarged vocal sacs. To judge from the size of the pouch, one would think there would be a huge voice issuing forth from this small amphibian. But the voice is weak. The whole purpose of this structure is incubation. The way it works is that a group of male frogs surround the twenty or so eggs recently laid on the ground and fertilized. They guard that clutch for as long as three weeks. Then, when the embryos within begin to move around, each male flips out his tongue and picks up several eggs, sliding them back into the pouch. There the young remain throughout the larval stage, emerging as perfectly formed little froglets of about a half inch in size.

The small arrow-poison frogs of South America also act like devoted fathers. Here, the eggs are attached to the back of the male where the young remain after hatching in numbers of about twenty or so. As they grow larger and form a bulkier load, the male is forced to look for bigger and bigger holes in which to hide. They do not leave the father's protection until they are quite mature, at which time he immerses himself in water and allows them to swim free.

Some amphibian mothers achieve protection of their young by keeping them within their bodies as do human beings. Some caecilians remain within the mother's uterus, feeding from nutritive material that is somehow secreted in this area. Fire salamanders live within their mother's body for ten months, emerging in the water as almost completely metamorphosed amphibians. They have well-formed arms and legs, but there are still gills present to assist them in the watery life they lead until, as fully mature adults, they take to the land. Alpine salamanders have about fifty eggs reaching the oviduct of the mother, but only one or two actually form embryos. The yolks of all the others are used as food by those developing.

The length of time it takes for a young amphibian to develop into a fully mature specimen varies tremendously according to species. Some are quite adult in less than a year; others, like the bullfrog, take four or five years to develop completely. Some amphibians grow in size without making the change from aquatic to terrestrial form. This process, known as neoteny, can be seen in some salamanders which reach adulthood without losing their gills or other larval characteristics. Although they look like overgrown babies, they are capable of mating and having young.

This kind of growth usually occurs in species living their entire lives in cold, deep water.

The life span of an amphibian is also variable. Some species must live out their whole existence in a year, while others have a much longer period on earth. The record for longevity seems to be held by the giant salamander of Japan, which has been known to reach the ripe old age of fifty-five years.

CHAPTER FIFTEEN

Some Common Amphibians

Having reviewed the history of amphibians and examined the group as a whole, let us concentrate on some of those most frequently encountered in their natural habitats.

THE LEOPARD FROG
(*Rana pipiens*)

The leopard frog is one of the most beautiful of all frogs. It is also the one commonly found all over North America. There are several races found in different geographical areas. Each race has its own characteristic coloring and marking. Generally speaking, however, a leopard frog is an iridescent bronze, with an underlying base color of olive-green. Soft yellow "leopard" spots dot the back and head. The belly is ivory toned. The skin is quite smooth except for two folds that run down either side from the eye to the hips.

The more formal name for the leopard frog is *Rana pipiens*. *Rana* is the scientific name of the genus to which it belongs; *pipiens* denotes the species. The name of the family to which *Rana pipiens* belongs is the Ranidae.

The family Ranidae includes all those creatures known as "true" frogs. Other well-known members are carpenter frogs,

The beautiful leopard frog (*Rana pipiens*) is easily found throughout North America in any area well populated by grasshoppers.

pickerel frogs, and bullfrogs. There are representatives living on
every continent.

The genus *Rana* probably originated in Africa and from there
spread throughout the world. Most frogs of the genus *Rana* are
slim-bodied, long-legged amphibians, with pointed toes; those of
the rear feet are webbed. "True" frogs do not burrow, nor do
they emit evil smells from their glands. Their only defense lies

in escape. Therefore, they are built for speed. Leopard frogs are the best jumpers of the whole group, attaining distances of five feet or more in a single leap. They are alert to danger and will disappear quickly at your approach. All the Ranidae are diurnal (except during the mating season), as the insects they prey upon are day-living creatures. They have thin skins, so evaporation is something of a problem. Therefore, the "true" frogs live at the edges of ponds and streams and are frequently found floating in the shallow water.

The leopard frogs are more frequently encountered than other members of the family, for not only are they more common, but they travel greater distances from the water. You are likely to find them in meadows and orchards in the country, where they go to find the grasshoppers they so often eat.

Leopard frogs sleep away the winters in the muddy bottoms of their ponds, but they arise early. Only the spring peepers appear before them. You can hear their hoarse croakings in the evenings in strong contrast to the shrill song of the peepers. They have begun the chorus that announces that the time for mating has arrived.

This frog has four distinct sex calls: the song that brings the female to the pond; a warning call given when one male accidentally grabs another; a sound the male makes when he approaches a female; and the female's rejecting grunt if she is not ready or has already laid her eggs.

As the female enters the water, a nearby male will circle her while singing his approach song. If she does not reject him, he will jump on her back and clasp her around her shoulders. She carries him around on her back this way for a while until both are ready to assume the right position for egg-laying. For the female, this means spreading the thighs and putting the heels together. The male raises his knees and puts his feet on her thighs. Now the female begins to pump out the eggs, as the male, bringing his cloaca next to hers, fertilizes them with his sperm at the moment the eggs appear in the space between their legs.

The eggs, laid in masses of from four to five hundred, may be attached to sticks and reeds, or may simply float free on the water.

Life for the tadpole is fraught with danger. Many creatures make a diet of tadpoles and it will be lucky if it can escape all of them. Insect larvae, fish, turtles, and water birds will all be out hunting.

If the tadpole is able to avoid all his enemies, he will begin to metamorphose in about one month. Although the tail has grown until it reaches a length of about twice the size of the body, the hind legs are beginning to show. The front legs appear next. The head takes on a froglike appearance with appropriate eyes and mouth. Then, finally, the tail becomes absorbed.

Throughout the summer months, the spring breeding grounds of the leopard frogs abound with tiny froglets. They live in the shallow water among the weeds and wander about the nearby ground in search of their new food. Along with all the other transformations, a change of diet has also occurred. The froglets have become carnivorous and now live primarily on small insects. Young grasshoppers are a favorite food and spiders, beetles, and crickets are also eaten.

The young leopard frogs have long noses and slender bodies. The coloring is not quite the same as that of their parents. Sometimes they lack the characteristic spots and are instead a beautiful, shimmering metallic bronze or green all over.

Soon the young frogs will join the adults, feeding with them until the autumn frost sets in. Then, all will go together to the streams to sink down into hibernation. At the bottom, hidden away in the mud, they sleep, awaiting the early spring return to life and the calls to come and breed.

THE AMERICAN TOAD
(*Bufo americanus*)

American toads belong to the family known as "true toads," the Bufonidae. The Bufonidae, like the Ranidae or "true frogs," has several genera in the warmer parts of the world, but one main genus, *Bufo,* is found on every continent except Australia.

Unlike their cousins, the frogs, the true toads have fat bodies and short legs and are not very speedy travelers. To escape their enemies, they must rely on other characteristics. They blend in wonderfully with their surroundings; the brown warty skin looks just like the earth they sit upon. Whenever anyone approaches, they flatten out their bodies and lie perfectly still, so they are often unnoticed. If they should be seen, they roll over onto their backs and play dead. With all motion stopped (even breathing is suspended for a few moments), many enemies are fooled.

If this fails, the toad may burrow his way to safety. He is well equipped to do this, for there is hard skin on the hind feet and usually a sharp, horny spur used for digging. He can hollow out a hole very rapidly, backing in all the way until the earth falls in around him and affords him complete cover.

If, after all this, he is ferreted out anyway, he still has another protective method. All the so-called "warts" on a toad's body are really glands. The two largest ones, located behind the eyes, are known as the parotoid glands. From these comes a poisonous secretion which is irritating to mucous membranes. Any animal taking a toad into its mouth is likely to regret it. Human beings who have handled a toad must be careful to keep their hands away from their eyes and mouth until they have washed. There is no possibility, however, of getting warts from handling these amphibians.

The American Toad (*Bufo americanus*) is frequently encountered in gardens, where, because of his insect-hunting prowess, he makes a welcome guest.

Toads can live farther away from the water than frogs, for their skin is thicker and less susceptible to evaporation. For this reason, toads are more familiar than frogs to people living in the country, for they frequently inhabit our gardens. The toad you are most likely to meet in the eastern United States is the American toad.

American toads are squat animals with big heads. The females, who are larger than the males, can attain a length of 4½ inches. Their color varies from light to dark brown. Most, however, are a sort of reddish-brown with a few spots and blotches of lighter browns. The warts are frequently red or orange. Sometimes there is a light stripe right down the middle of the back. Unlike most animals, the female is much brighter in color than the male and her throat is a grayish-white while his is black.

On the head, over and behind the eyes, are kidney-shaped crests or ridges that are made by the bones of the head. There are four fingers on the hand and five webbed toes on the feet.

The toad's whole body is covered with many conspicuous warts, which some people find repulsive. The eyes of a toad, however, are breath takingly beautiful and have even inspired poetry. The pupil is a shiny black, while the iris is golden.

If you go out in the spring to collect amphibian eggs, you will notice another way in which the toads differ from the true frogs. Rather than the shapeless egg mass laid by Ranidae females, American toads lay eggs in long tubes of jelly, with the tiny black eggs lined up neatly in a single row. Each female produces from four to twelve thousand eggs each year. The jelly tubes are clear and transparent when first laid but soon become twisted and muddy from the debris at the bottom of the pond. The eggs take from five to twelve days to hatch, depending on the temperature.

The transformation from tadpole to adult is very similar to that of the leopard frogs. By mid-June thousands of tiny but perfect toads fill the ponds. Young toads go on land soon after transformation, as they cannot breathe in water once their lungs have fully developed. As they swarm up on the shores, they encounter their enemies. Snakes, hawks, owls, and ducks are all lying in wait and many thousands of the little creatures will be devoured.

The young toads that manage to survive their first summer burrow into the earth in the fields where they have been feeding. There, they sleep until the warm spring air rouses them. During the winter months they have grown to considerable size and have exchanged smooth skin for a tough, warty exterior. They are not yet ready for breeding, however. Sexual maturity is not reached until the age of three or four years. This is in keeping with the toad's longevity, for they are known to live to be more than thirty years of age.

Toads grow very rapidly. But their skin does not grow with them as ours does. When the old skin gets tight, the toad must shed it. (This skin shedding is typical of all amphibians.) During the summer months, when food is plentiful, the toad sheds about every three days. The process of shedding is smooth and quick, taking only about five minutes. The toad hunches up his back and bends his head down. The old skin splits right down the middle, from head to back, down the belly and across the chest from arm to arm. The toad pulls the loosened skin into his mouth. He will then eat it, and it has great food value. The skin is removed from the back end forward with the head skin being the last to go. The new skin is shiny and pretty, but within a few moments, it will be covered with earth, making the toad as well camouflaged as ever.

Toads act like homebodies. When a young toad is finally ready to mate, he will return to the pond in which he was hatched. The feeding place he has established while he was immature will remain his headquarters throughout his life. Any cool, moist place is a good home base. The toad lives in cellars, under porches, and in woodpiles. He comes out in the evenings to feed.

Any gardener must consider himself lucky if he has a toad policing his property, for the toad consumes many of those insects harmful to plants. With his limber, front-hinged tongue, he grabs locusts, beetles, lice, and caterpillars by the thousands.

Having stuffed himself with insects throughout the summer, the toad sleeps away the winter. Using his sharp spurs, he backshuffles his way into a deep burrow, snuggles in, and leaves the cold world above. When he awakes, if he is fully mature, he will be stirred to join others of his kind returning to the breeding pond. Once there, he will fill his vocal sac and begin to sing. The song of the toad is one of the prettiest in nature. It is a sweet trill that seems to come from many directions at once. The call sounds appealing to us—to the female toads, who do not sing themselves, it is irresistible. They swarm to the pond and there begin the mating process—the start of a new life cycle.

THE COMMON TREE FROG
(Hyla versicolor)

Tree frogs of the genus Hyla include some of the prettiest little frogs in the world. The family Hylidae is centered in tropical America. There are five genera now located in the United States. Species of the genus have spread to every other continent. Most members of the tree frog family have suction discs on the tips of their toes, with which they cling to any available surface. Their legs are usually long and thin, with thighs heavier than shanks.

Most frogs of the genus Hyla are tiny, usually under two inches long. In addition to the common tree frog, some of the better-known species are the spring peepers, the green tree frogs, and the squirrel tree frogs.

As you might guess from the scientific name of the common tree frog, its color is changeable. It might be white, gray, green, or brown. If it is in one of its lighter phases, you should be able to see a small star across the top of its shoulders and bands of darker color on its legs. When the overall color is dark, these markings blend in and are not visible. The belly is white. In the folds of the hind legs there are splotches of bright orange. Two white spots are on the face, one beneath each eye. Because its skin is rough and warty, the common tree frog is sometimes called a tree toad. For a tree frog, it is big; sometimes attaining a length of 2½ inches. The broad discs at the end of the fingers and toes secrete a substance that helps them to hang on anywhere. Common tree frogs can be seen, if you look closely, anywhere in the eastern half of the United States.

Common tree frogs come to the ponds to breed in the late spring. The male's call is a loud, birdlike trill that begins early in the afternoon and continues until long after dark. Tree frogs attach their eggs, either singly or in small groups, to the stems of water plants. These eggs are a light gray color on top and white below. They hatch very quickly, in just two or three days.

The tadpoles are not dark as in most other frogs, but bright yellow. They have orange eyes and a beautiful red tail. Within a very short time, about three weeks, the tadpoles are well developed and even have the hind legs beginning to show. Less than two months after hatching, the tadpoles have completely metamorphosed and are ready to leave the water. Although only about ½ inch long, they are ready to feed upon spiders, flies, and plant lice.

This small amphibian is usually found up in the crotch of a limb, where, because of its camouflaging colors, it can hardly be distinguished from the bark. On the tree can be found an extraordinary variety of foods. Flies, beetles, ants, and crickets are all likely to be in easy reach.

When hunting, the tree frog shows its great acrobatic skill. He has fine vision and can spot a small insect at a distance of more than two feet. He will take a long, flying leap at anything. He simply spreads his arms and legs straight out from his body and glides. On the way back, the fingers and toes are spread, for all he needs is a single toe hold to keep him secure. The disc cuts down the atmospheric pressure exerting suction, and the sticky secretion works like glue. The moist surface of his belly and legs will also help to hold him firm on any leaf or window.

Common tree frogs sing all through the summer months, particularly at times of dampness. For this reason, they are called rain frogs and are considered to be weather prophets, singing their loudest just before a storm.

RED-SPOTTED NEWT
(Notophthalmus viridescens)

The red-spotted newt, so common in the eastern United States, belongs to a family with almost all its members in the Old World. The family Salamandridae has only two genera in this country, one in the East and one in the West. The western newts (genus *Taricha*) are larger than the eastern species and not so colorful.

Eastern newts of the genus *Notophthalmus* are mostly aquatic except for a transitional stage of about two years when they are terrestrial. In some areas, however, this terrestrial stage is omitted and the newts are permanently aquatic.

The red-spotted newt can reach a size of five inches in length, but is usually from three to four inches long. As an adult, it has an olive-colored back and a yellow belly covered with fine black dots. Along each side is a straight row of scarlet dots circled with black. The tail is flattened for efficient swimming.

Red-spotted newts are fascinating to watch as they mature, for they go through many radical transformations. As larvae, they not only have gills as do the frogs and toads, but also balancers placed midway between their eyes and their gills. They are born with the front legs already "budded" and they have broad, fishlike tails.

The mature larvae have wedge-shaped bodies that are quite slim. Although both sets of legs are well developed, there are still gills, which now lie flattened along the back. There are small white dashes from the gills to the tail which indicate the presence of lateral-line organs.

By autumn, complete transformation has taken place. The gills are gone, as are the tail fins. We now see a recognizable newt. The color at this point is a sort of yellowish-brown and the characteristic spots on the sides are pink.

The next stage is unique. The young newt does not immediately assume the appearance and life pattern of its parents. In most areas of its range, there is an adolescent phase which is quite different. At this point, the newt becomes terrestrial. In a few localities where ground cover is not adequate or if there is a shortage of food on land, the adult state is reached immediately and the small amphibian remains aquatic.

But, if conditions are right, the spotted newt becomes a red eft. The skin becomes rough and thick. The overall color is a bright brick red with the side spots prominent. The tail is rounded. Red efts wander far from their pond and can be found deep in the moist woods where they feed on insects, spiders, and worms. For a year or so, the young newts continue to live in this manner. Then they make their way back to the pond. On the way there, or very shortly thereafter, they assume typical adult dress and begin their mature aquatic life.

The breeding season, which may extend from spring through autumn, demonstrates another interesting difference in appearance. For the male is quite unlike the female. He develops a broad fin on his tail and his cloaca is swollen and protrudes. Black horny growths appear on his inner thighs and on the tips of his toes. His hind legs are much stouter than his front legs.

Newts have a much more elaborate courtship than frogs and toads. The male begins by clasping the female under her throat with his hind legs. He then bends his body into an S and rubs his head against hers. At the same time, he brushes her with his constantly swaying tail. Sometimes he shakes her rather roughly. After hours of this ritual, the pair separates. The male then begins to deposit spermatophores on the bottom of the pond. These are white and vase-shaped. The bottom portion is gelatinous with a stiff, spinelike structure rising from it. At the top is the round portion which contains the sperm. Each time the male moves on to deposit another one, the female comes along behind him. She presses her cloaca over the newly placed spermatophore and the tiny sperm cells then travel upward into her body to fertilize her eggs. She appears to take in only as many spermatophores as are necessary for the eggs she has within her, since quite a few of the male's offerings are ignored.

The female lays her eggs one at a time and fastens them to leaves and stems of aquatic plants, away from swift currents. She holds the stem between her hind legs and pulls her thighs together, thus forcing out the eggs one at a time. Each egg is in a tiny envelope of jelly which sticks to the surface of the plant. A female can lay three hundred eggs at a time. The egg is brown at one end and light green at the other. Temperature is the deciding factor in hatching time. In warm weather, the larva may hatch in three weeks, but if it is cold, it may take five weeks.

Although adult newts breed only in the warmer part of the year, they are able to tolerate the cold very well and can sometimes be seen swimming in a pond beneath the ice-covered surface. If it is too cold, they will burrow into the mud at the bottom.

As adults, newts eat a large variety of meats. Worms, insects, and small frogs are all acceptable food. They themselves are relatively free from predators, for they are protected by a nasty-tasting skin secretion.

DUSKY SALAMANDER
(Desmognathus fuscus)

We have just discussed the newts: amphibians that spend most of their lives in the water, yet are dependent upon lungs for breathing. Dusky salamanders, like the rest of their family, the Plethodontidae, live practically all their lives on land and are lungless. Adults have no gills, either, but take in oxygen through their skins and the lining of mouth and throat.

The Plethodontidae is the largest family of salamanders in the world. One hundred and fifty live in the New World and there is one other in Europe. They are all small to medium in size, the tiniest measuring a little over one inch and the biggest about eight inches. Such well-known forms as the spring salamander, the red-backed salamander, and the red salamander are all members of this group.

Dusky salamanders are the most common salamanders in the eastern part of the United States. Although there are many of them living near brooks and streams, they are not easy to see. They hide in crevices and under stones throughout the day and only come out after dark. Sometimes on rainy days, they do venture forth, but even if you should see one then, you would be unlikely to catch it. It is very alert and scurries away swiftly. If you succeed in grasping one, you probably won't be able to hold onto it, for it twists very vigorously and will even bite if necessary.

The dusky is aptly named, for it is rather drab in color. The adults are brownish-black above and gray below. There is an irregular row of black spots down each side of the back and a white line from eye to jaw. The larvae are brown with two rows of light spots.

The adults are rather stoutly built with hind legs longer and heavier than the forelegs. The tongue is attached at the front of the mouth and is loose at the back and sides. Although the lower jaw is hinged and attached in the same way as that of other salamanders, it is unable to move very much. The jaw is held rigid when the dusky eats and the upper jaw does all the work. This makes the entire top of the head move with each bite of food. The lower jaw is handy as a wedge when the salamander wants to dig in under a stone.

Most amphibians share a desire to be in contact with the sides of any hiding place they occupy. This habit is known as thigmotaxis. It is especially developed in the duskies, which have been found wedged into discarded glass bottles, peacefully sleeping (with heads turned toward the mouth of the bottle) in broad sunlight on the surface of the ground.

Courtship between duskies is more romantic-looking than in other amphibians. Because the male has a gland on his chin which secretes a substance irresistible to the female, he rubs noses with her. This "kiss" stimulates the female to follow behind him, picking up the spermatophores he has just deposited.

Fifteen or twenty cream-colored eggs, laid in two small grape-like clusters, are the result of this mating. The female retires to a small nest under leaves or stones. This nest is large enough to include mother as well as eggs, for, unlike most amphibians, duskies stay with their eggs. The mother lies with her body twisted so that it is in contact with all her eggs.

Each egg is only about ⅛ inch in diameter, but has three protective envelopes of gelatin, bringing the total size to about $1\frac{3}{16}$ inch. In about eight weeks, the eggs hatch, the larvae measuring about ⅝ inch long.

The larvae, very surprisingly for amphibians, are not quite ready for aquatic life when born. Although they have gills, they remain on land, sometimes for as long as fifteen days, before finally entering the water. Once there, they will remain aquatic for about nine months, making the transformation to adult form in the spring. With the coming of the warmer weather, the duskies head for land once again, there to breed and spend the remainder of their lives.

Dusky salamanders congregate in large groups and can be seen piled on top of each other in dark, damp nests during the hot daylight hours. At night, they come out to hunt, looking for the worms, slugs, and insects they particularly relish. In turn, they are hunted out by snakes and frogs.

THE MUD PUPPY
(Necturus maculosus)

Mud puppies, sometimes called water dogs, belong to a very small family, the Proteidae, which includes only two genera. One, *Proteus,* lives only in southern Europe, while *Necturus* is found in ponds and lakes in Canada and the eastern half of the United States. The animals of this family never metamorphose, but remain in larval form throughout their lives. Although they grow larger (some reach a length of nineteen inches) and are able to mate, they retain all their infant characteristics. There are large gills and open gill slits. No eyelids develop. They do have front and hind legs, although these are not too obvious at first glance. Each foot has just four toes, a characteristic which sets them apart from other aquatic salamanders.

The most common of the two species of *Necturus* is the mud puppy, *N. maculosus*. Mud puppies are flat-bodied salamanders with big, round heads. The gills at the sides of the neck look like floppy ears. It is easy to see why they were given their common name, for they do look like small dogs scurrying along the muddy pond bottoms. Perhaps it was their appearance that gave rise to the myth that these salamanders bark. They do not. Like most salamanders, they have very small voices, scarcely more than a squeak.

The mud puppy has a soft brown color speckled with a few black spots on its sides and back. The body is streamlined and the tail is wide for more efficient swimming, as these amphibians never leave the water. They are difficult to observe in their natural habitat, for they are active mostly at night and spend the days hiding under rocks or debris. The color works as camouflage in the stream bottoms when the mud puppy does move around in search of food.

If the water in which a mud puppy lives is stagnant, you will stand a better chance of catching sight of it. For then the gills are expanded in an effort to gain more oxygen. The gills become bright red then, and wave back and forth through the water. In clear, cool water, the gills remain dark and are held close against the head. Mud puppies are fortunate in having lungs as well as gills and are also able to practice skin breathing. In this way, should some injury befall the spectacular gills, the animal can go on breathing.

From their hidden positions in the water, mud puppies are able to obtain a large variety of edibles. They dine upon snails, crayfish, insect larvae, small fishes, and the eggs of frogs and fish. In some areas, they eat so many fish eggs that the fishermen consider them to be a nuisance.

Autumn is the season for mating among mud puppies, although the female does not lay her eggs until the spring. Courtship continues for some time, with the male swimming over and under the female until she willingly picks up his spermatophores. These the female retains within her body until she lays her eggs. Occasionally a pair of mud puppies will remain together for some time after mating takes place.

When the female lays her eggs, she attaches them singly to the underpart of a stone or log. Each is a small, light yellow circle about ¼ inch in diameter. If the water is warm, they may hatch in about five weeks; otherwise nine weeks will be necessary. During that time, the female stays within the nest cavity. This is probably not due to any great maternal protective instinct, however, as many of her eggs are frequently eaten during this period by creatures smaller than herself without causing her any great concern. Most likely, it is the secluded spot itself which draws her, rather than her potential offspring.

The young, when first hatched, are only about one inch long. Their front legs and fingers are well developed, but the hind legs point backward and have no toes yet. There is a broad, dark stripe down the middle of the back that runs from snout to tail. There is also a narrow yellow stripe on each side, from the gills back. In time the young mud puppy darkens to look like its parents, and grows steadily larger. By the time it is five years old, it has reached a length of eight inches and is ready for mating. The customary development of eyelids, however, and loss of gills never takes place. Jacobson's organ, used for testing objects in the mouth for edibility, is completely lacking.

Nevertheless, the mud puppy is tough and can be found active in all seasons. Even the coldest winter day will find a mud puppy walking slowly along the bottom under a film of ice. Although usually lazy in its movements, a mud puppy is capable of a good deal of speedy swimming if alarmed. The legs, then, are held close to the sides, while the broad tail does the job of propelling the animal rapidly through the water.

If the mud puppy's great success is due in part to its toughness, it is also partly due to its caution. If a mud puppy encounters a new form of food, for instance, it will swim for all it is worth in the opposite direction; the desire for safety overcoming its enormous appetite.

CHAPTER SIXTEEN

Your Own Amphibian

Reading a biography can give you a great deal of information about a man. You can learn about his ancestors, his home environment, and his way of life. You can even get an idea of the way he looks. But you will not know the man. The same is true of an animal. Through books you can find out about an animal's history, biology, and its living habits. But you will not understand that animal until you actually go out and meet it.

Meeting an amphibian is a relatively simple matter. You seek him out in places where he is likely to live at a time he is likely to be in evidence. The techniques for finding and observing amphibians are easy and you do not need any special equipment.

Amphibians can be found in every state in the United States. They do not live in the cities, for these are not likely to provide adequate living conditions. It is necessary to go a little way out to the country. There they will be in any moist, quiet situation.

Before you leave on your expedition, stop and think for a moment. Just which kind of amphibian will you be searching for? Then use the information you have gathered to pick a suitable location in which to hunt. Is it an appropriate season for observing amphibians? Dry, hot days are likely to find all your potential aquaintances hiding underground or deep in the ponds. Cold winter days are suitable only for a few, very hardy species. Is the creature you are after lively during the day or does he put in an appearance only after dusk?

Once you have decided what to look for and where and when to find it, you will have to give a little thought to your personal needs while on the trip. Be sure to dress appropriately. Old, comfortable clothes are the best. Since most amphibians are at their best in damp weather, you had better plan to wear a raincoat. Early morning and late evening are likely to be chilly even during the summer, so if you plan to be out at those hours, wear a sweater. Be sure to wear comfortable shoes. You are not going to be able to drive right up to an amphibian to say hello. Some walking, perhaps a great deal of walking, is going to be necessary. If you are comfortable in water-resistant boots, wear them, for you will be on damp ground. Otherwise try roomy shoes that allow you maximum flexibility.

If you are planning an all-day trip, you had better provide yourself with some food. Take small, simple things, easy to carry in your pockets. Sandwiches, fruits, and nuts are all good. Bring along a canteen, for the pond you visit may not provide drinkable water.

You may be searching in the marshes for a favorite amphibian. If so, be sure to bring along some insect repellent. Mosquitoes can make a field trip a real misery.

Many amphibians are most easily observed at night. To see them, you will need a flashlight. Usually if you stand very still, the light will not bother them. You can shine it directly on your discovery and remain quiet. He will go right on about his business.

Once you have thought about your trip and are dressed and ready to go, get there as quickly as you can. Then slow down. Nobody ever discovered any wildlife by rushing. Remember that it may take you some time to find your quarry and if your pace is leisurely, you are less likely to tire.

Shouting and stomping will frighten away any little amphib-

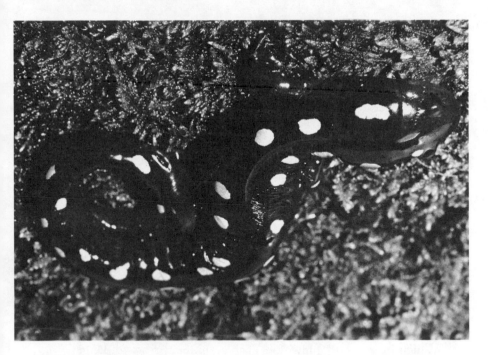

The spotted salamander (*Ambystoma maculatum*), a common amphibian found under logs and stones in the eastern and central U.S.

ian. Be quiet as you walk. Try not to brush against twigs or branches. Don't talk.

If you are going to meet an amphibian, you will have to find it first. Look carefully as you walk along. Get into the habit of turning over promising-looking rotten logs and moist rocks, without however destroying potential homes for many small animals. Listen for any possible calls.

Bring along a notebook, so you can quickly jot down information you will want later. If you make notes on each trip—when and where you went, what the weather was like, what species you saw—you will soon have a very good idea of how to plan subsequent trips for the utmost satisfaction.

When you get home from your trip, write yourself a detailed report from your notes. Include everything you have observed. Which species did you see? Was it breeding season? If so, make sure you write about any courtship activities you were able to witness. Also, what about actual mating? Were you able to find any eggs? Describe them. How were they attached? How many were there? If you are out in early summer, you will be lucky enough to see tadpoles and newly transformed adults. Note the differences between them and their parents. Find out what they eat. List everything you are able to observe about their daily habits. What are the effects of various weather conditions on a species? Have you noticed different sorts of amphibians in distinct natural situations? Which have you seen in meadows? Which in marshes? How does each amphibian react to danger?

Each trip you make will add more to your fund of information. Although it may be a little difficult at the beginning, after a few trips you will find yourself becoming more expert. Your work will be doubly rewarding. First, and most important, you will have established a real relationship with a charming group of animals. It will not be long before you will have figured out how to get a frog to eat from your hand, for instance. In addition to the warm feeling you will get from your friendship with amphibians, you may also find yourself the discoverer of a brand-new set of facts. For amphibians have been much neglected by scientists and very little is known about the habits of many species. Imagine the satisfaction you would feel at being the sole possessor of new knowledge about a favorite animal.

Visiting amphibians in their own natural homes is a delightful recreation. But perhaps you will decide to study one kind very seriously and at your leisure. Or you will simply fall in love with an amphibian and want it near you always. In either case, you are going to make a drastic change from objective observer to responsible owner. You must take your responsibility very seriously, for another life is involved. You are going to remove a living creature from its own choice of habitat to one of your own making.

Before you take an animal away from its natural environment, be prepared with a good substitute home. Since you have been watching carefully during your field trips, you will know what sort of conditions your creature has been accustomed to. You must try to duplicate them.

If you are interested in a serious study of amphibians, surely the best way to begin is with the animal's beginning—the egg. There are two ways to collect eggs. One is simply to go to the right pond during the breeding season and secure two adults about to mate. With frogs and toads, this is a relatively simple task. The male's song announces the time and place. So many individuals are there, that it will not take long to spot one male clasped onto a female's back in preliminary mating position. Because both animals are preoccupied with the task at hand, they do not exercise their usual caution with approaching strangers. Indeed, they will not even notice your presence.

Walk quietly up to the edge of the pond. Then begin to wade in slowly for a few feet. When you have located your prey through sound and then flashlight beam, catch them in your hand (or use a net if you prefer), and dump them into a canvas bag for transporting. Fill a gallon jar with water from the pond and add a few of the water plants. As soon as you get home, place the pair into the jar or an aquarium full of their own pond water and plants. There is an excellent chance that they will go right on with their mating. You will then have their fertilized eggs in your possession. Keep only a few of them. Scoop out the rest in some of the water and put their parents back in the bag. Return them all to the pond where you found them.

The most direct way to collect eggs is simply to find out where they have been laid and take a few. Most salamanders attach their eggs to water plants. Frog eggs are frequently found in gelatinous masses, floating on the surface of a pond, while those of toads are in long, beadlike strings at the bottom. If you have been doing your nature observing efficiently, you will know just where to look for the kind of egg you want.

Once you have some amphibian eggs in your own home, you can sit back and watch the action. The next few days will be fascinating. You need do nothing for the eggs. Their needs are met with the water and plants you have already provided. This would be a good time to prepare a home for the prospective larvae.

While the tadpoles are little, you can go on keeping them in your jar. If you are going to keep a lot of them, however, you will need a larger home. The aquarium tank is probably your best bet. In order to provide enough oxygen for your amphibians, you need a large surface of water exposed to the air. It is better to have a wide, shallow tank than a deep, narrow one. If you intend to buy a tank in a pet store, look for one with a metal frame, as it is sturdier than the all-glass type. With a large number of tadpoles, you will do better with several small tanks rather than one large tank.

Small tanks are easy to make and you might prefer that to buying them. You will need six panes of glass—four of them 8″×10″ and two 8″×8″. You will also need a roll of 2″ adhesive tape. Fasten the four side pieces together with the adhesive tape (two of the 8×10's and two 8×8's). Then attach the bottom with more tape. Add a second layer of tape to the bottom and line the edges of the top of the case with tape. Use the sixth piece of glass as a lid. You need not attach it, but should line the edges of it with tape. When you have finished putting it together, you might like to paint the tape a cheerful color. The inside corners should be puttied with aquarium cement. If you intend to move your tank around frequently, set it on a wooden base, slightly larger than the tank.

Whether you buy your aquarium or build it, you must test it for watertightness before using it. Fill it with water and let it stand overnight. If, in the morning, you find that it has leaked, you will need to repair it with cement.

When you are looking for a good permanent position for the tank, keep in mind that the temperature should be constant (about 60° is ideal for amphibians, so avoid radiators). Steady sunlight is important, so a position not too distant from a window with a good northern exposure is ideal. You can solve any lighting problem with electricity. An electric bulb or an aquarium reflector can be placed above the tank.

Tadpoles are easy to feed. You can simply scoop out some algae from any stagnant pond. This will satisfy their needs until their mouths are transformed and working. Frog and toad larvae are vegetarians and you can feed them with small quantities of cooked lettuce. All tadpoles do well on corn meal. This is probably the simplest of all foods, for you have only to sprinkle a little in the water each day. Since tadpoles are natural scavengers, they will clean up their own tank, if not overfed. If you see bits of food remaining by the next feeding, however, you must get it out before it has time to foul the water. A small dip tube works well in removing any debris. Just put your finger over one end of the tube and lower the other end to the bottom of the tank. Raise your finger and the water with the debris will fill the tube. Put your finger back over the open end and lift the tube and its contents out for dumping.

Salamander larvae will feed on corn meal, too, but the best food is insects and insect larvae. In order to keep a steady supply, you may want to raise some yourself. Aquatic insects can be raised in a glass jar. Put a layer of sand on the bottom of the jar and fill with pond water. Add a small cutting from a water plant, with part of the plant above water level. Cover the jar with a piece of screening. If you have vegetarian insects, that is all they will need. If you are raising meat-eaters, you will have to add small insect life that you scoop from ponds with a dip net.

A meat bone added to a salamander larvae tank will provide a great occasional treat.

If the sides of your tank become caked with green slime and the water looks green as well, don't worry about it too much. This is just algae growing. It won't hurt your tadpoles at all. It might make it difficult for you to view, however, so you will probably decide to get rid of it. Since it is sunlight that causes algae to grow, the simplest solution is to move the tank to a somewhat darker situation. To hurry the clearing procedure, you might also want to scrape the sides with a razor blade. To keep it clean and neat, add a few pond snails to your tank. They will multiply in time, but don't worry—your amphibians will soon mature to the stage where snail meat tastes good.

Careful selection of a position for your aquarium, the addition of the right sort of plants, and scrupulous cleaning of debris pays a dividend. You will never have to change the water. The glass top will keep evaporation down. Just lift it slightly (a matchbook under one corner is sufficient) to allow air to enter. Add a little water occasionally to keep the level constant, but do not use tap water, unless you have set it aside for twenty-four hours to allow sufficient time for the chlorine to disappear. You

Your terrarium should provide a home similar to your pet's native habitat.

can buy anti-chlorine mixture at your pet store for immediate decontamination.

In time, your tadpoles will begin their fascinating process of metamorphosis. You will need to prepare for this. Put in a flat rock that projects just above water level, or float a piece of wood on top of the water. If tadpoles are forced to remain in the water at the time their lungs take on the job of breathing, they may drown. Once they have come out of the water, you will have to transfer those that are land-living.

Making a permanent home for adult amphibians is the real test of your ability as a naturalist. You must remember where you saw adults of this species in the wild and do your utmost to duplicate those conditions.

If your pet is one of the woodland amphibians (a toad, for instance), you can plan a home that will be comfortable for him and beautiful for anyone observing. Go back to the woods where you saw others of his kind. Take with you a sturdy box and a few plastic bags. A newspaper is also handy. You will need digging tools—a small spade and your pocketknife should do nicely. Look first for some nice clumps of moss. Take them up carefully in long sheets. Put them down in the bottom of the box and cover them with some newspaper.

Now look around for some pretty, small plants. Use your trowel to dig beneath them and make sure you take the whole root along with some of the earth surrounding it. Place each plant in some newspaper and wrap it gently. Put the plants, individually wrapped, on top of the moss. Don't try to transplant anything exotic. Some of the prettiest plants are also the hardiest and these are the ones to use. Pack some nice-looking pieces of bark and a few small rocks. Use the paper bags for carrying plenty of the good, rich leaf mold under your feet.

Hurry home and be ready to plant immediately. The bottom of your tank should be covered with a two-inch layer of gravel or pebbles, mixed with a few bits of charcoal. Now add two inches of leaf mold. This should be moistened enough so that it will form a ball in your hand when you squeeze it. Then add your rocks, placing them in interesting positions in the tank. Arrange your plants as naturally as you can, placing the taller ones nearer the back. Finally, take your carefully preserved sheets of moss and set them down like a carpet around the base of your plants. Tap the moss down very gently. Add any sticks, pebbles, and bark you feel will enhance the effect.

Moisten the planted tank evenly (a small sprinkling can works best) and place it in a cool spot. Keep it shaded, as the woods are. If you keep the glass cover on the tank, you will not need to do any further watering. If you should notice a lot of moisture on the sides, use a matchstick under the cover. This will raise it just enough to allow the excess moisture to evaporate. Remove the stick when the moisture has disappeared.

Suppose your amphibian is one of the many that makes its home in the swamps. You will then want to provide a bog terrarium.

The first thing to do is to make sure your tank is completely watertight. Then provide for two separate areas—one will be land and the other water. Get a piece of glass about half as high as the sides of the tank and place it as a divider between the two sections. You can fasten it in place with a little aquarium cement. Proceed with the land side as you would for a woodland terrarium. Two inches of gravel, mixed with charcoal for sweetening, is your bottom layer. Dig up some sphagnum moss from the nearest marsh to provide a three-inch layer that comes next. Get it very wet.

While you are out digging bog plants for the terrarium, be sure to take along plenty of rich soil from around them for the third layer of the tank. Note the depth of the plant roots as you dig, so that you can transplant them properly. You can add a few small rocks or a piece of rotting tree branch to the top.

Over on the water side, you will need to provide a bank for your creature to use in moving from one side to the other. Pile some earth and pebbles against the glass partition. Fill the rest with marsh water and a few aquatic plants and you will have duplicated the natural habitat of most common amphibians.

All amphibians need a bit of privacy, so be sure to provide a hiding place of some sort. A little cave made of rocks would be fine. A flowerpot, placed sideways, works just as well.

Burrowing animals, which need a lot of privacy, do not make the best pets. But if you have an interest in that sort of amphibian, you can keep it in a large glass jar. Wrap some black paper around the sides. Fill the jar with sandy soil. When you have put the animal inside, cover the jar and leave it alone for a time. When the burrower has had a chance to get used to its new surroundings, you may remove the black paper and see what he is doing. Be sure to replace the paper after each observation, or your pet will be most uncomfortable.

Some amphibians remain aquatic all their lives. Use the same sort of arrangement as you would for tadpoles, not neglecting the floating perch. An aquatic situation is a little harder to keep clean, so don't put in a lot of accessories. The less cluttered the tank, the easier it is to clean.

In keeping amphibian pets, there are several important considerations. First of all, be sure you do not overcrowd your tank. Two or three occupants to a medium-sized tank is enough. Make sure you include only animals of the same size or else the largest is likely to have the smaller ones for dinner. Use your space wisely. Different kinds of amphibians in one tank, rather than several of one habit, make for more room and greater interest. For instance, you can put tree frogs into the same tank in which you have toads. The tree frogs will stay up in the plants, while the toads squat on the ground.

Don't overfeed. Remember, however, that even the tiniest tadpole will grow to be a large adult with an insatiable appetite for insects. If it is going to be difficult for you to find enough of these, then keep away from the larger species.

You can eliminate the feeding problem by growing your own food. Earthworms are a big hit with many adult amphibians. You can start an earthworm culture in a wooden crate. Fill it with about one inch of moist soil. Buy or dig up as many earthworms as you can. The box will hold well over a hundred. Place the worms on the soil and cover them with a layer of rotting leaves. Feed them with corn meal, breadcrumbs, or cooked vegetables once or twice a week. Be sure to keep the soil moist but not wet. You can cut down on evaporation by covering the container. A sheet of glass or an old piece of heavy cloth will do nicely. Keep the box in a cool, shaded indoor place. (The basement is ideal.) You can also buy earthworms at many pet stores and bait shops.

White worms are fine for smaller amphibians. You can buy some at a pet store and let them propagate. Set them into the same sort of situation suggested for raising earthworms, but add cooked vegetables and meat rather than rotting leaves. White worms (*Enchytraeus*) are much too small to be picked up individually for feeding. Simply scoop up a clump of an appropriate size when you need them.

Mealworms are another favorite amphibian food. These are actually the larvae of certain beetles and not true worms at all. You can buy a culture from a nearby pet store. Fill a glass jar with bran and crumple a paper towel on top of the bran. On the paper, place a chunk of apple or potato. Now dump in your culture, which should include adults, eggs, and larvae. Cover the jar with window screening and leave it in a warm place. When the apple or potato dries out, replace it. Mealworms are inexpensive and easily available, so you may not want to go to the trouble of raising them. If you are going to buy them from the pet store for feeding, be sure not to waste your money by getting more than a few days' supply. Do not feed your pets exclusively on mealworms, for they are constipating.

Perhaps the healthiest food for amphibians is crickets. Most pet stores sell them. You could raise them yourself. Start with a glass jar or aquarium tank. Put down a two-inch layer of soil and cover with some screening. Add a small water dish. Feed the crickets moistened bread, mashed potatoes, and lettuce. Sprinkle the crickets with some powdered vitamins for a truly nourishing meal.

Fruit flies are good food for many tiny amphibians, tree frogs particularly. You can gather fruit flies easily by leaving a little decaying fruit in a bottle near the window. Scientists have developed a strain without wings for easy care at home. You can buy a culture in some pet stores or through biological supply houses. The same source will supply the medium on which they feed. Put some of this into a wide-mouthed jar. Add a crumpled paper towel and a few fruit flies. Then plug the bottle up with some cotton. In about two weeks, you will have more fruit flies than you ever dreamed possible.

Small fish make good food for aquatic types. You can find minnows being sold at many bait shops and guppies in all pet stores: Guppies are easy to raise at home and multiply faster than your amphibians can eat. Just buy a pair (you can recognize the males by their smaller size and bigger tail), and put them in a small tank filled with dechlorinated water and a plant or two. You do not really need any special equipment, but if you want quick results, buy an aquarium heater and a light and feed them lots of fish flakes. In a short time, you will see innumerable tiny guppies near the bottom of the tank. If you take just a few at a time, soon the babies will have babies, etc., etc. You will have a constant supply of food as well as another pleasant and instructive pet community.

If you are looking for an easy supply of food for your tadpoles, you can buy infusoria tablets at your local pet store. Infusoria is a name given to many different kinds of microscopic plants and animal cells appetizing to young frogs and toads. The tablets sold at stores can be dropped directly into the water in your tank. (One a day is more than adequate for a medium-sized tank with several larvae.) As the tablet dissolves, food is released for the infusoria, which will then rapidly multiply.

Pet stores carry other foods acceptable to many amphibians. Tubifex worms are available almost everywhere and are eaten by many aquatic salamanders. These worms resemble tiny wiggling earthworms that stay clumped together in water. Do not buy more than three or four days' supply, for the worms will not live longer than that and the salamander is not interested in dead worms. Put in just enough to satisfy your pet at one meal. Too many in the tank will foul the water. The worms can be kept in a closed container in the refrigerator between feedings.

Freeze-dried tubifex worms are packaged in small cubes. You can break off an appropriate-sized piece and throw it into the water in your tank. As the cube dissolves, the tiny dead worms separate and float free. Many salamanders and newts will dine on these worms. Some will also accept dried tropical fish food.

During the warm seasons of the year, many insects are available to you. You have simply to step outdoors and catch them. Beetles, moths, flies, grasshoppers, and dragonflies all make good eating. Most household pests can be put to use as amphibian fodder. Just dump into your tank any houseflies, moths, or roaches you encounter and you will have solved two problems simultaneously. If you have a plant covered with plant lice, just put the pot into the terrarium and watch your pet do a clean job on the plant.

Of course, it is best to feed any pet with the food it would find in nature. But sometimes this is inconvenient or even impossible. If you are very patient you can teach an amphibian to accept other food. Lean meat is nourishing for most amphibians. Frogs and toads accept only moving food, however, so you must make it move. Take a small piece of meat and tie it to the end of a long line of string. Dangle it right in front of your pet's eyes and let him jump up and catch it. Repeat until his appetite is sated. Be careful not to stand where you throw a shadow over your pet or jiggle too violently, for he will be too frightened to eat.

It is important to keep your pet's diet varied. Do not limit him to one or two foods, as it may lead to digestive disorders.

A few good foods are listed below:

THE SPOTTED SALAMANDER—small crustaceans and tubifex worms.

NEWTS—lean beef. They will also accept small bits of fish and liver.

CRICKET FROGS—fruit flies and small mealworms.

THE GREEN TREE FROG—houseflies.

BULLFROGS have enormous appetites and will eat anything that moves. Always keep a bullfrog in solitary confinement.

MUD PUPPIES need one or two big feedings weekly—raw beefsteak, strips of beef liver, or hunks of fresh fish as a substitute for the foods they naturally eat.

Earthworms are suitable for almost all amphibians.

You should be able to prevent most amphibian diseases with proper care. Of particular importance are: a clean, well-planned tank with a cool, constant temperature; uncrowded conditions within the tank; a varied diet in appropriate quantities. (Overfeeding is more harmful than underfeeding.)

There is always some danger of illness, however, even when you have been very careful. If one of your pets is afflicted, you are going to have to make some serious decisions. If you have several animals in one tank, you must separate the one that is diseased as soon as you observe the first symptoms. Most amphibian ailments are contagious and will spread throughout the entire tank. Also, if you want to try to cure your sick pet, lots of special attention must be devoted to the job and that is easier if he is separately housed. Be forewarned, though. Many amphibian ailments are almost impossible to cure in a terrarium situation.

The kindest and least frustrating course to follow is to return your sick pet to his natural environment. This is also true with the problem-eater. If, after several days, an amphibian refuses food, return him to the spot where you found him. No one wants to watch a pet deliberately starve himself to death.

Several of the most common amphibian ailments are listed below, primarily to enable you to recognize the symptoms. Methods of treatment are also given, although cure is always doubtful.

Salamanders have extremely delicate skin. It is easily damaged and this leads to very serious illnesses. Be careful to avoid scratching or bruising when transporting your pet. Be sure not to put two or more aggressive males into the same tank, for skin injuries incurred during a battle can be fatal.

If you notice patches of white fuzz on your salamander, you will know that his skin has been hurt and a fungus infection has started. This fungus is highly contagious and will spread quickly to contaminate the other occupants of the tank if you do not take immediate steps to prevent this. Separate the sick animal from the others. Put him in one tank and the others in another. The tank in which they have been living must be completely cleaned and sterilized before reusing. Everything—gravel, plants, and rocks—must be removed and carefully washed. The tank itself must be thoroughly scoured before it is safe to place another amphibian into it.

A pet store proprietor might suggest potassium permanganate for fungus infections. This is definitely not a remedy for amphibians. Many people believe that dipping the diseased animal

Salamanders have very delicate skin. Great care must be exercised not to bruise or scratch your pet or serious disease may follow. Shown here is a northwestern salamander (*Ambystoma gracile*).

into a salt-water solution will help, but it will not. The salamander with the fungus infection should be placed in a situation with running water. Should this prove difficult in your home, be sure to change the water in the tank at frequent intervals through the day.

Some antibiotics have been used successfully in treating salamander skin diseases. Your local veterinarian can prescribe the right kinds. You must also find out from him the correct dosage for your pet (it is determined by the animal's weight), for it will be up to you to administer the medication. Do not, under any circumstances, allow your amphibian to receive injections.

Salamander "leprosy" is the name given to a horrible disease with symptoms resembling those of human leprosy. The animal appears swollen with bloody splotches beneath the skin. The skin turns dull, shrinks, and then peels. The peeled areas seep moisture. The tips of the tail and the digits begin to rot. The salamander has no appetite.

This unsightly condition appears to be due to overcrowding and generally unclean, overly dry terrarium conditions. Potassium permanganate and sulfa powders are not effective. The disease is almost hopeless. But antibiotics are sometimes helpful and should be tried if you are fond of your pet. You must also place him in a clean, empty tank with a lid. Do not put any gravel on the bottom of the aquarium. Add just a half inch of water and a small rock for climbing. Slant your tank slightly by putting a matchbook under one end. Spray it daily with a little clean dechlorinated water.

Sometimes swellings under the skin can be caused by heart and kidney diseases. They might even be a symptom of tubercular disorder. If so, you can offer a little relief by puncturing the swollen areas and draining the fluid.

Skin swellings in salamanders can be the result of constipation. Watch your pet carefully to see if he is eliminating regularly. When you are sure that constipation is the source of the problem, force feed cod liver oil. Do not offer any food until the animal has resumed normal elimination. Gently massage the swollen area.

Should your salamander begin to demonstrate difficulty in

swallowing, you will know that he has a sore throat. Put him into a low-water situation or lay him on a little clump of moss. Allow him to rest quietly in isolation until he has recovered.

Eye and lid diseases are frequent and always quite noticeable. The affected area looks sore and swollen. Place the afflicted animal in an antibiotic solution for an almost sure cure. Keep spraying him with fresh water.

Roundworms are parasites that can cause salamanders a lot of discomfort. They are quite noticeable in the stool. If your animal has begun to lose weight rapidly in spite of feeding well, check carefully for any small white worms crawling in his excrement. If they are there, remove all the gravel in the tank immediately. You must either disinfect the old gravel with boiling salt water or get some new gravel. Change the water frequently, force feed some cod liver oil, and hope for the best.

Adult males frequently become belligerent toward one another in captivity. Sometimes they fight so ferociously that they severely damage legs and tails. If your pets suffer such wounds, it is wise to amputate the affected parts. The tails will regenerate (grow back) and a missing leg will scarcely be noticed by your pet.

One of the most serious illnesses to which frogs and toads are prone occurs when they are very young. This is rickets, a disease of the bones that troubles many rapidly growing young creatures, including humans. You can prevent this by offering lots of vitamins. This will be an easy matter if crickets are the main source of food. You simply sprinkle your culture with a liberal dose of a powdered vitamin preparation at frequent intervals. Bone meal is good too. It won't bother the crickets—they'll simply be covered with powder—and your young pets will be protected without knowing it.

Frogs and toads also suffer from roundworms. Detection is easier than with salamanders, for one of the first symptoms is a yellowing of the iris. Use the same treatment recommended for salamanders.

Occasionally, you will notice a toad with a nose that appears to be rotting. Some blowfly has managed to lay its eggs there and the larvae have hatched. You should drip a disinfectant (like Lysol) on the larvae and try to remove them with tweezers.

Frogs also get "leprosy" and need the same isolation and treatment recommended for salamanders.

Aquatic frogs can develop cramps and even paralysis if the tank is allowed to remain dirty. Hurry up and clean it.

Paralysis can also be caused by a lack of calcium. Douse some crickets with powdered calcium or bone meal and add a dash of vitamins A and D, while you are about it.

Tree frogs are frequently troubled by constipation. An unfortunate symptom is an everted rectum. (It sticks out rather than remaining inward.) Feed your pet plenty of cod liver oil. The rectum may or may not return to its normal position when the condition has been relieved.

One of the most frequent diseases of aquatic frogs is "red leg." It is caused by an airborne bacterium and can happen anywhere. As suggested by the name of the disease, the major symptom is a red flush that appears on the hind legs. It also colors most of the underparts of the afflicted animal. The redness is caused by the breaking up of blood vessels just beneath the skin. The kidneys are affected and cannot properly eliminate all the fluid taken in the skin. The body becomes bloated. The condition is very serious, but can often be checked with antibiotics.

The pickerel frog (*Rana palustris*) has a skin secretion that is absolutely fatal to all other frogs. There is no cure. Just be sure to keep this frog in a separate tank.

Administering medicine to a sick amphibian is a little complicated. You must be sure not to injure him more with the treatment than he has been with the illness. The best method is to put the prescribed dosage into an eyedropper. You can buy one that is marked along the sides for proper measuring. Attach the end of the eyedropper to a thin rubber tube. The insulation referred to as "rubber spaghetti" that covers electric wires, works well for this purpose. Slice the end of the tube at an angle. Then gently slip the tube deep into the animal's throat and squeeze the bulb of the eyedropper.

Frogs can get very nervous in captivity. They may fling themselves against the sides and lid of the tank. In so doing, they frequently injure themselves. Eye wounds can be treated with antibiotics dropped directly into the eye. Bruised noses just have to heal by themselves. If these nervous habits continue after the animal has been in your home for several days, it is kind to release him.

After you have kept some of the local kinds of amphibians, you may want to try your hand at some more exotic species. Pet stores carry a dazzling variety of imported frogs and salamanders. Some are very beautiful. Many have fascinating living habits. When you consider yourself an expert, buy one. Do not do so before you have considerable experience, for if you are unsuccessful, or find you haven't the time to devote to your hobby, you will not be able to release the animal. If you put an amphibian native to one area into an alien environment, you are almost certainly condemning him to death and may be making serious problems for the local inhabitants besides.

Before buying an amphibian from another part of the world, check carefully with the pet store owner as to its needs and home conditions. Use your discretion when listening to the answers. Many pet store owners are knowledgeable and sincere, but some do not know the answers and others will not tell anything

Zetek's frog (*Atelopus zeteki*), a native of Central and South America has black spots dramatically opposed to its golden-yellow back.

that might hinder a sale. This is when your own experience and common sense will help. Do a little extra reading about the area from which the amphibian was taken and find out what the climate is and what kinds of food he is likely to have found. If it can't be duplicated by you, think of a logical substitute.

Check to be sure the animal you select is healthy. Pick the fattest, most active animal in the tank. Make sure the eyes are clear and shiny. The body should be perfect with well-formed tail and limbs and a full complement of toes. Be particularly critical of the skin. Any trace of white fuzz eliminates not only the animal that carries it, but the others in that tank.

When you have your amphibian home, you may find that he is unwilling to eat. This is not an unusual circumstance with exotic amphibians. Allow him a few days to become adjusted to his new surroundings. Then, if he is still refusing food, you will have to force-feed him. Use some raw, lean beef and ground-up insects mixed into a solution of cod liver oil. Feed with the medicine eyedropper described above. After a while your pet should begin to take food by himself.

PART III

Reptiles as Pets

INTRODUCTION

Whenever anybody says "reptile" he usually is thinking of a snake. Many people, whenever they think of snakes, are afraid. People have been afraid of snakes for thousands of years. Sometimes it seems that the only people who do not fear them are small boys—and even some of them dislike snakes.

This is really too bad. Snakes are not evil. In fact, they are among the most useful and valuable animals living today. And they are very interesting!

When we speak of the natural food of animals, we mean food that those kinds of animals like best to eat. The natural food of many snakes is rats, mice, and other destructive rodents.

Farmers used to chop up every snake they saw with a hoe just because it was a snake. Out of fear, they would say, "There's a snake, kill it!" In the past few years, much has been learned about snakes and other reptiles. Now farmers are not in such a hurry to kill the animals that may help keep their barns free of pests.

Many farmers now like to see a snake in the barn. Some of them have even bought snakes and let them loose on their farms in order to help keep the rats and mice under control. The best snakes for this work are bull snakes, corn snakes, rat snakes, chicken snakes, king snakes, and milk snakes. King snakes and milk snakes are different members of the same group. Rat snakes, corn snakes, and chicken snakes are all members of another group. The bull snake belongs to yet another group. All of these animals should be left alone when they are found, because each year every specimen will eat a very great number of rats and mice.

Some snakes are poisonous and can kill people by biting them. Obviously, poisonous snakes should not be kept as pets, except in a zoo or by experienced *herpetologists*. A herpetologist is a person who studies reptiles. The name comes from *herpes,* which is a Greek word meaning "to creep," even though not all reptiles creep.

Snakes are not the only reptiles. Turtles, lizards, and crocodilians are also reptiles. Frogs and toads are not reptiles. They are *amphibians.* Amphibians are animals which must return to water in order to breed and lay their eggs.

Only two species of lizard are poisonous. There is only one species in the United States and one in Mexico. Turtles and lizards are not poisonous, and neither are crocodilians.

Turtles, crocodilians, and lizards can bite. Some of them bite hard, and will tear your skin. Some non-poisonous snakes can bite, too, and some of the large ones can hurt. The bites are not dangerous unless they become infected. Any time you are bitten by a reptile, you should dab some disinfectant on the bite and cover it with a bandage to keep it clean.

Most animals bite only from fear and in self-protection. If they are handled gently, as if they have nothing to be afraid of, they will stop trying to bite every time you pick them up.

Nearly all animals will try to bite if they are ready to have their young, or already have had them. But snakes and other reptiles are different. They do not protect their young or eggs. They might even eat them if the babies cannot escape fast enough! Reptiles do not have any *maternal instinct,* which means that they do not take care of their young. They lay their eggs in a sand pile, or under a log, and leave them alone to hatch. A few snakes and lizards curl up around their eggs, but they are not protecting them. If the animal is disturbed, it will leave the eggs. The only group of reptiles that shows some maternal behavior are the crocodilians.

Unless you know about an animal, you should never try to keep it as a pet. If you find an unusual reptile in the pet shop and the clerk does not know the real name of it, or what it eats, or how warm it should be kept, it would be better to leave it there and not try to take it home. Without proper care it will die very soon. Many thousands of reptiles die every year because the people who sell them and the people who buy them do not know how to keep them. In this book I am going to try to tell you about many different kinds of reptiles and how to keep them at home. Different reptiles need different conditions to remain healthy. Some need warmth. Others must be kept really hot. Still others will die unless they are kept cool. Some of them cannot drink water from a dish. These kinds of reptiles die very quickly after they are brought home.

Some reptiles are *nocturnal*. This means that they are active only at night, which is the only time you will really see how they go about their lives. Other reptiles are *diurnal,* or active in the daytime. Still a third group are *crepuscular*. This group is active in the early light of dawn and the dim light of evening. Many desert reptiles are crepuscular. This way they avoid the great heat of the daytime and the cold of the night.

Knowing about all these things makes it easier to take care of the little animals.

Many reptiles are *solitary*. They like to be alone, and cannot be kept in a cage with other reptiles. They will either fight their companion or huddle in a corner. Usually, two males cannot be kept together, because they will fight. Large specimens should never be kept with small specimens. The big ones will often eat the little ones—even if they are the same kind, and even if the small ones are offspring of the big ones!

If you know these things when you get your pet turtle, snake, or lizard, you will stand a better chance of keeping it as a pet. If you do not know things about the animals, then you do not have pets, just captive reptiles. They will suffer for a while and then die. Reptiles cannot tell you when they are suffering. There isn't any way you can tell, either, until suddenly they die. The trouble is that they do not die suddenly, but suffer for a long, long time first.

CHAPTER SEVENTEEN

A Little About Reptiles

In the beginning, animal life on earth was probably *protozoan*. Protozoan is a name made up of two Greek combining words: proto- meaning "first" and -zoa meaning "animal." After millions of years of evolution, larger animals developed, still living in the seas and warm fresh waters. Many of these animals laid eggs, but the eggs were soft and jellylike and had to remain under water all the time to keep from drying out.

The animals themselves could leave the water for short periods to find food or to walk about on land. They had to stay near the water, though, because if their skins dried out, they would die. They had to go back into the water in order to breed and lay their eggs. These animals were called *amphibians*, and there are still some amphibians living today. Toads and frogs are amphibians. So are salamanders.

All amphibians have two things in common. All must return to the water to lay their eggs, and the young sometimes do not look like the adults, but go through a larval stage in the water. After a time, they undergo a very big change in habit and shape. This change is called *metamorphosis* and means "a change of shape." After metamorphosis, the amphibians then leave the water and live on land.

Reptiles are different from amphibians in their breeding habits. Reptiles usually lay eggs, but some species give live birth by retaining their eggs inside the body until they are ready to hatch. If they give birth to live young, they are called *ovoviviparous* reptiles. If they are the egg-laying kind, they are *oviparous* reptiles. The shells of reptile eggs are tough and rubbery. They are not brittle like a hen's egg, but soft and flexible.

If reptiles had not developed this kind of egg, there would not be any people on earth today. It was the ability to lay eggs that did not dry out that first made it possible for vertebrates to come out of the water, and for life to start developing on the land parts of the world. Even so, the eggs of reptiles will dry out if they are not kept a little bit moist. If reptile eggs are kept in water, the moisture will go right through the shell and the *embryo* developing inside will drown. But they must not be exposed to the dry air for long periods of time, either.

No snake has real legs any more. Millions of years ago some snakes did have legs, but they gradually became useless. Some of the boas have two little stubs sticking out of the rear part of their bodies, but that is all that is left of their legs.

Snakes travel in several different ways. The usual way a snake gets around is by *undulating* its body. This means looping its long body from side to side, pushing against small stones, twigs, clumps of grass, and other things on the ground. As long as there is anything to push against, the snake can let its body flow around the stone or twig until it reaches another point to push against. It does this so rapidly that the snake doesn't seem to touch anything but just pours along the ground.

Another way the snake can move is by using the scales (called *scutes*) on its belly. Inside the snake's skin its ribs are attached to the ends of the scutes. A snake can move its ribs independently. Starting at the head, it can raise a pair of ribs and the scute attached to it, then push back against the ground with the scute. Each scute and pair of ribs follows the first one in a ripple down the body of the snake. The animal can move quite rapidly along the uneven ground by this method, but it usually undulates at the same time to gain speed—especially if it is running away from an enemy.

It is easier to tell the snake's body from its tail than you might think. On the belly side of every snake is an opening. This is sometimes called the vent. Its real name is a *cloaca* which is a Latin word meaning "sewer." A snake uses this opening for several purposes. It gets rid of its body wastes, lays its eggs, and mates through the cloaca. The same opening serves all these functions for the animal. A snake's body stops at the cloaca. Beyond this point is the tail. A large scale usually covers the vent, and in some snakes this scale is divided into two halves instead of being one large plate. The type of scale covering the vent (together with other markings) is used to identify different species of snakes. This scale is often referred to as an anal plate.

The scales on snakes' bodies differ, too. Some of them are very smooth and shiny. Others have a ridge running across them. It is said that these scales are *keeled,* because the ridges look like the keel on a boat. Water snakes generally have keeled scales. King snakes generally have smooth scales.

Snakes that live in places full of brush and twigs are often striped down the back. This helps them to hide among the sticks and shadows of twigs. Those that live on forest floors where there are fallen leaves and decaying underbrush often have spots or blotches down their backs. If this kind of snake stays still on a pile of leaves, it is almost impossible to see. The spots and blotches look like spots of sunlight on a dark pile of leaves.

Snakes that live in burrows and underground generally have skins that are plain color without any markings at all. They do not need anything to help them hide from their enemies.

Coral snakes are exceptions to this rule. They are very

Hybrid Pine Snake. *Pituophis melanoleucus*. The blotches on the skin of this snake tells you that it lives in the sun-speckled forest rather than in the grass.

brightly colored. In fact, they are gaudy and stand out very clearly from their surroundings. This, too, is a way of protecting them from their enemies. Their brightly colored skins tell their enemies that they are dangerous, and that it is better to leave them alone. Coral snakes are very poisonous and their bite can be fatal. Some harmless snakes are colored like the coral snakes. This helps the harmless snakes escape their enemies because the enemies think they are looking at a dangerous snake instead of one that is good to eat.

Since a snake has no eyelids, it cannot close its eyes at all. A snake's eyes are covered with a clear scale to protect them. The tongue of a snake is forked or double at the tip. It is kept in a tube in the bottom of the mouth. Generally there is a small opening at the lower front part of the jaw so the snake can stick out its tongue without opening its mouth.

Very often, as it crawls along, the snake sticks its tongue out and waves it up and down, then pulls it back into its mouth. In the tube that holds the tongue are special parts called Jacobson's organs. The tongue rubs across these organs when it is pulled into the mouth. Particles of air stick to the tongue when the animal moves it up and down. In this way, the snake can sense its food or enemies. It is not really either tasting or smelling, but scientists think it is a little bit of both. This is a special sense that we do not have. The tongue of a snake is perfectly harmless. No snake can hurt anything at all with it. And the snake is deaf, as it has no eardrums.

As snakes and other reptiles feed and grow larger, their skins become too small for their bodies, so they have to shed them. Most of the time a snake sheds its skin in one piece. Even the skin over the eyes is shed. For a day or two before shedding the snake is almost blind, because the old skin loosens over the eyes and becomes milky in color. During this time even very tame snakes are very much afraid, since they are almost helpless. At this time you should leave them alone as much as possible.

After the entire old skin is loose, the snake will catch its lips on a pebble or bark or other rough anchor. It will pull its lips and head out of the skin, then crawl right out of the entire skin

—turning the old skin inside out as it goes. After shedding, the snake is very bright with colors that stand out. Some of the highly colored ones can be very beautiful then. The number of times a snake sheds its skin in a year depends on the amount of food it is able to eat, and on how fast it grows.

A snake can eat food many times larger than itself. The jaws of a snake come apart at the joints. The upper jaws can snap apart from the lower jaws, and the right sides separate from the left sides. The only thing holding the jaws together then is the skin, which can stretch like rubber.

The teeth of most snakes that have them curve backward in the jaw. When food is caught, these curved teeth can hold it firmly while the snake eats. Many snakes eat their food alive. They grasp hold of the prey and start to "walk" their jaws back and forth, gripping the prey with their curved teeth each time they push their jaws forward. The food slides easily down the throat of the snake, and it almost looks as though the prey crawls down by itself! Snakes that eat things like frogs, fish, toads, and insects usually have short teeth, while the teeth of snakes that eat rats, mice, and other furred or feathered animals are usually much longer. This is because the teeth of these snakes must reach through the fur or feathers in order to hold the prey while it is being eaten.

Snakes like the king snake, the rat snake, and pythons are called *constrictors*. This kind of snake catches its prey in its mouth, holding it with its teeth while it wraps its body around the prey and squeezes it until it is dead. Then it loosens its body and eats the prey.

It is not true that a constrictor cracks the bones of its prey and kneads the animal until it is soft before eating it. What the snakes does is hold the animal so tightly that it cannot breathe. Each time the animal tries to take a breath the snake tightens its hold a little bit more, until finally the prey is smothered. When a constrictor catches an animal the action is so fast that you can hardly see what happens. One minute a mouse or rat will be near the snake and the next instant the snake will be wrapped around the prey—squeezing it to death. Most of the time the rat or mouse hasn't even time to squeak!

Lizards are very different from snakes. They usually have eyelids and can close their eyes. Many of them have a clear spot in the middle of the eyelid and can see through this spot with the lids shut. The eyelids of lizards close from the bottom up instead of from the top down the way human eyes do. Most lizards have legs, some of them very long, and they can be very fast runners. Some of the desert lizards can stand up and run on their hind legs, looking like small dinosaurs. One kind—the basilisk—can run so fast on its hind legs that it can actually run over the top of water for a short distance without sinking! Of course, if it slows down or stops, it sinks right away, but it can swim well, so this does not seem to bother it at all.

When a lizard sheds its skin, it usually comes off in patches instead of in one piece, like a snake's. A lizard almost always eats its skin after shedding. This is a protective device. If the lizard leaves its skin lying around where it was shed, enemies can see that it lives nearby and can hunt it down.

Unlike snakes, most lizards have ears and most of them can hear very well. Usually there is an opening behind each eye that leads to the eardrum, but in some the eardrum (or *tympanum*) is flush with the skin as in frogs and toads.

Lizards usually have very sharp claws, which help them climb. Some of them live in trees most of the time, coming down to the ground only to lay their eggs. They can climb walls and curtains so fast that it is very hard to catch them if they get away from you. Many lizards live near water and go into it very often. The big iguanas of Central America and South America live in the trees on the riverbanks. When danger approaches they drop into the water. This makes it even harder to catch them.

Many lizards have the ability to drop their tails when attacked by an enemy. Their tails are divided into sections so they will snap off without much pain or bleeding. When an enemy pounces on the lizard, more often than not it is left with a wiggling part of tail while the body of the lizard scampers away. The tail jumps around for a long time after breaking off of the lizard. This is to keep the enemy occupied long enough for the lizard to make its escape. Animals that drop their tails like this can grow new tails, but usually the new ones are not so long or so pretty as the old ones. Sometimes the new tails grow in crooked or forked, or even double or triple. Lizards with two or three tails have been seen.

A surprising number of lizards have no legs at all. Among them are the ones that are called "glass snakes" in the southern part of this country where they live. Usually glass snakes do not make good pets because they frighten too easily and are hard to feed. Whenever you see a smooth, shiny snake flowing through the grass and weeds, look closely at it if you can. If it has eyelids and can close its eyes, and has ear openings on each side of its head, then it is a legless lizard and not a snake at all. The bodies of these animals are rounder than a snake's body, and much firmer. There are usually stripes running down the sides and back.

A skink is a kind of lizard that is very timid and usually is active only at night. It stays under fallen logs and stones, and among the dry leaves in the forests. The skink is usually smooth and shiny-looking and very fast. It also drops its tail easily and bites when it is caught, but cannot do much damage. Some of the skinks are very brightly colored and are among the most beautiful of the lizards. They almost all have eyelids. When skinks run about they wiggle their bodies like snakes. The skinks (and some geckos) seem to wiggle more than other lizards. Skinks generally have more pointed heads and jaws than other lizards. And several kinds of skinks grow to be almost two feet long. These giants are not found in this country, but come from Australia.

Geckos are lizards with some interesting habits. They can walk almost any place and anywhere. Many of this group have toes covered with very tiny stiff hairs. The toes are flexible and bend both backward and forward. Geckos do not have suction pads on their feet as many people think. When a gecko runs or walks he puts his feet down with the toes curled backward, then flattens them out so the hairs grip the surface he is walking on. When he lifts his feet he first must curl his toes up to release the hairs. These animals can walk right up a windowpane by gripping the uneven surface of the glass with the hairs on their toes! They can run across a ceiling just as easily as across the floor.

Some geckos have eyelids and others do not. Geckos have a funny way of cleaning their eyeballs. They do this by licking them with their tongue! Most geckos are night animals with vertical pupils in their eyes; but some of them are active both during the day and at night. The eyes of these kinds of geckos have a special kind of iris. The pupil is vertical, but instead of being straight like that of the night gecko, it is wavy. When the gecko is in the bright light of day, and the iris is tightly closed, three or four little pinholes are left open by the wavy line, so the animal can see very well without being blinded by the light. Many geckos have very beautiful eyes. They are silver, gold, or brightly colored. Sometimes they are two colors.

Unlike many lizards and snakes, which can only hiss, the gecko has a voice. It is not a true voice; the noise is made by pulling air into or blowing it out of the lungs. Some geckos can cheep or squeak, and the tokay gecko barks like a small dog. When geckos are well fed, warm enough, and contented, they will cheep throughout the night.

There are a great many different kinds of turtles. Not all of them are good as pets, but most of them live for a long time. Turtles are among the longest-lived animals on earth.

There are some turtles that live on land all the time and do not need water. There are others that must live in the water all the time. Then there are turtles that live on land but need water to swim in. Some of them will not feed unless they eat under water. Of course, the turtles that live on land are the easiest kinds to keep. Some turtles eat vegetables and fruit as well as meat, but others need meat all the time.

CHAPTER EIGHTEEN

How to Collect Reptiles and Where to Buy Them

Many reptiles that make good pets can be found in the woods and fields near where you live. If you live in big cities like New York or Chicago or San Francisco, then you have to go outside the city to find animals. A streetcar or a bus can take you to the edge of the city and you can look in the fields and woods nearby for your specimens.

If you go to camp during school vacation you have a very good chance of finding a reptile or two to take back home with you as a pet. Most reptiles do not come near houses or places where there are a lot of people, but some snakes and a few lizards do. If you can go to a farm for a collecting trip or a visit, you may find corn snakes, milk snakes, rat snakes, chicken snakes, and king snakes around the barns.

As you look in the fields for snakes, lizards, or other reptiles, don't forget to look in the low trees and bushes too. Many snakes can climb very well. A few of them make their homes in trees all the time and feed on birds and other animals that also live or roost in trees. Many snakes will use trees for hiding places. Rat snakes like to climb trees and go under loose bark at night. Then they stay there until the bark is warmed by the sun the next day. If you go snake hunting in the morning, be sure to pull away large pieces of loose bark on a tree. You may find a sleeping snake under it.

Hardware stores sell three-pronged cultivators. These are tools with long handles and three hooks on the bottom end. They make perfect reptile-hunting tools, and you should have one if you go out to hunt. Use it to turn over small logs and flat stones. Under them you are apt to find small snakes, lizards, and even turtles, which sometimes like to sleep under a flat rock that is warmed by the sunshine. In the early summer you can often find reptile eggs under the rocks, too.

You should never go looking for reptiles in the woods alone. Always take someone with you—your father, an older brother, or a friend. This is especially important if you live or hunt where poisonous snakes are known to be found. You just might be bitten by one, and your friend could help you or go for other help if he was unable to do anything himself. The chance of being bitten by a poisonous snake is very small, but it is there, and you should think about that. No chances should be taken in the woods in places where copperheads and rattlesnakes live. Never pull a log or stone with your hands. There just might be a copperhead resting underneath it. Always use your snake hook or cultivator to do the actual pulling, and always pull a rock over so you are out of the way when it falls. That way, it will not fall on your foot and hold you fast while anything underneath escapes. It just might hurt your foot, too.

Another good reason to have someone with you is that your companion can help you look for specimens. One person can pull over the log or rock and the other person can be ready to catch anything that might be underneath. But be sure that the person who is catching knows a dangerous animal when he sees one. About the only dangerous animals you might find would be copperheads and rattlesnakes, unless you live in the South and Southwest, when you could also possibly find a gila monster or coral snakes. Water moccasins are generally found not in the woods but near streams, rivers, lakes, and ponds. When you are hunting in those places, look out for them. Coral snakes usually are not easy to find. They live in burrows in the ground and seldom come out. After a rain they may be out under stones or logs, because their burrows have filled with water and they are forced to the surface. Sometimes a farmer will plow up a coral snake.

Rattlesnakes and water moccasins almost always try to escape when you come upon them in their homes. Most of the time they will slide away from you so that you will not even know they were there. Coral snakes stay in their burrows. But copperheads do not run very far. They curl up on the other side of a fallen log, under a pile of dry leaves, under a stone or piece of flat bark, and try to hide. They just sit still and you may not see them. If you step over the log you might just step right on top of one. If you do this, and you are not stepping on the snake's head, it can turn around and bite you. Always look carefully before you step over a log. It is even better not to step over the log, but to go around it to the other side. That is why it is a very good thing to look where you put your feet in the woods.

Do not step on piles of leaves or on top of pieces of fallen bark, wood, or old cardboard boxes or anything that is loose and on top of the ground. Unless you can remember to do these things it is better not to go into the woods to collect reptiles at all, but get them from a pet store.

You may find skinks out feeding in the woods. They live under logs and stones and come out to search for food among the dry leaves on the forest floor. When you hear a rustle among the leaves, remain very still. If it is a skink, you may see it after a few minutes. It will be very still itself, and it may take you several minutes to spot the animal, because it is so well hidden among the leaves. The skinks are among the fastest of all the reptiles. They drop their tails very easily, so try not to grab one by the tail. If you do, it is better to let go and allow the animal to escape than to have it lose its tail.

Many reptiles are nocturnal. Some lizards and a number of snakes only go out at night. You might think a certain reptile is very rare because not very many of them have been found. For example, the leaf-nosed snake was thought to be one of the rarest snakes in the world because only one or two specimens were ever found. Actually it is very common. The reason not many were found was that the snake is nocturnal and only comes out at certain times during the night. When this was discovered, it was found that anybody could catch as many leaf-nosed snakes as he wanted. Now you can catch them easily at night along the road, or you can buy them from snake dealers for as little as two or three dollars!

When you find a snake, the best way to catch it is to hold it to the ground with your snake hook just behind the head. Hold it only tightly enough to keep it from running away. Too much pressure will hurt the snake, and you may even damage it severely if you are not careful. After pinning the snake to the ground with your snake hook, reach down and take hold just behind the head, and pick it up. The snake may wind itself all around your arm, but that will not hurt. Do not choke the animal. Remember that it has to breathe, so hold it just firmly enough to keep it from sliding through your hand.

The easiest way to put it into the snake sack is tail first, pushing the hand that holds the snake way down into the sack. Let go and pull your arm out of the sack quickly, and the snake is caught! Tie the neck of the sack securely in *two* places. This is not to keep the snake from escaping. If it were tied securely in one place the animal could not get away. Tying the sack in two places is to make a handle for you to carry the sack with the snake inside, without the chance of being bitten through the sack. Remember that the snake cannot hurt you very much, even if it is big enough to bite. The bite of a snake is clean and not very painful. The teeth are so sharp that they stick into you like a needle.

While I strongly recommend that you do not try to catch any poisonous snakes or lizards or try to keep them as pets, I suppose some of you will do so anyway. The double tie on the snake sack is then a perfect precaution against being bitten, but also remember that if you allow the sack to brush against your leg while carrying it, you just might be bitten there. Also remember not to throw the sack over your shoulder to carry it, unless you happen to be wearing a suit of armor. Poisonous snakes are best put into individual sacks, then these should be placed into a carrying box or basket of some kind. This will insure you against being bitten, at least while you are carrying them home.

Catching lizards is a little harder than catching new snakes because lizards are so much faster than snakes and can hide more easily. Also, lizards can run right up a tree or a fence post or a wall and disappear before your very eyes! A good time of day to catch lizards is in the middle of the afternoon. And a good way to catch them is with a thread noose. Take a piece of buttonhole thread about a foot long and tie a loop in one end around a large nail. Make sure you tie the loop with a knot that will not slip and tighten up when you use the noose.

Cut the short end of the thread off close to the knot and slip the loop off the nail. Then put the long end of the thread through the loop to make a noose like a lasso. Tie the free end of the thread onto the end of a four- or five-foot pole. A bamboo fishing pole is perfect for this purpose. You now have a lizard noose, and you should be able to catch many animals with it.

A lizard will run a short distance when you come near, then

stop and watch to see what danger is around. When it stops you can reach out slowly with the pole and dangle the noose in front of the lizard's head. Usually the animal will look at the noose but not run away from it. Slowly move the noose over the head of the reptile and as soon as it is around the neck, give a short quick jerk and you have your animal caught fast. Well, it is not caught *too* fast, because it can squirm and wiggle and slip out of the noose if you let it. But it *is* caught fast enough to let you swing it to your hands and catch hold of it to remove the noose and pop it into the catching bag. Lizards may bite when they are first caught because they have been frightened. After they are tamed they do not bite so much, but some species never get that tame. They are always afraid.

Catching lizards in the desert is different from catching them in the fields and woods. The desert lizards bury themselves under the sand and hide there. If you find any, watch them run and note where they dig under the sand. Then walk easily to the spot, reach down, and grab a handful of sand. You should have a handful of lizard too. Do not be surprised if the lizard has a mouthful of you! If it bites your hand, try not to pull your hand out of its mouth. If you do, you may possibly break its jaws. The lizard will bite for a time and then let go. Usually the bite will not even break the skin, but will just feel like a hard pinch.

When frightened, a desert lizard will try to escape to the nearest shrub or cactus. It will run up into the bush and flatten its body along the stems. When it does this, it seems to disappear. You can keep your eyes on it as it runs to the bush, then walk up and look right at it without seeing it. If there are holes around the bottom of a bush, the lizard will probably run into one of them. It is very hard to dig it out if the hole is more than a few inches deep.

Many desert lizards will run up a low sand dune and over the top. By the time you get to the top the animal is gone. It probably ran part way down the other side and buried itself in the sand.

When you go hunting desert animals, take along a friend who can help you. When you come to a place where you see a lizard, let the friend stand at the top of a dune while you scare the lizard out. When it runs up the side of the dune, your friend can sweep loose sand down the bank in front of the lizard. The animal will keep running on the loose sand, but not get anywhere, and you can run up behind him and grab him. Catching desert lizards can be an exciting thing, and lots of fun, even if you do not bag any.

However, most of the animals that live in the desert are found only at night. They sleep during the heat of the day and come out when it is cool—in the evening and at dawn. Almost all of them are out at dawn to drink the dew on leaves and rocks. Desert animals drink when the dew or ground water rises in the early dawn. In fact, when captured, many of these lizards will not drink from a dish at all and will die of thirst in their cages. You must spray the leaves of a plant with water for them to lap up.

If it is impossible for you to go out to catch your pets, the only thing left to do is buy them in a pet store. Every city has at least one pet store, and most have several. Even in small towns there is often someone who sells animals. If the pet store does not have the kind of reptiles you want, it can get them for you. Most reptiles are fairly cheap, but some of the very rare ones can cost a lot. Snakes are the most common reptiles sold in pet stores, lizards are next, and then come turtles. Pet stores often have animals from foreign countries that would be very hard to obtain otherwise. Some of the animals from tropical countries are much more colorful than those found in this country. We have some very pretty snakes in the United States, but the tropical lizards are more highly colored and larger than the ones that live here.

Iguanas from Central America are quite common in pet stores and very reasonable in price. Most of those sold are very young babies, but often you can get some large enough so you can tell the sexes. So get a pair. Iguanas live a long time in captivity if they are cared for properly, and will become quite tame. Iguanas often can be let free in the house. They will walk around, climb up the drapes, and sit in the sun on the window sills. They will take bits of food from your hands when you go up to them. Of course, if your parents have delicate plants in the room, the iguanas might break them when they climb on them. This is not deliberate, but the animals are too heavy for such plants. They also might nibble a leaf or two, since their natural food is plants and fruits.

These lizards may get to be six feet long from the nose to the end of the tail! After they get too big for you to keep easily, you may have to sell them to someone who has more room for them. Sometimes you can donate specimens like that to small zoos or to schools. In Central and South America the people eat iguanas. The meat is supposed to taste like chicken.

The other most common lizard sold in pet stores is the little green one from the southeastern United States. It is called a chameleon, but this is not its proper name. It is not even closely related to the true chameleons which are all African species. The one our pet stores sell is an *anole*. The reason people keep calling it a chameleon is because the anole can change color from brown to green. A true chameleon changes color too, but it has more colors than the anole.

You will probably be able to buy baby "alligators" in the pet stores. These are not real alligators, either. They are *Caymans*. Sometimes the name is spelled *Caiman*. The only trouble with caymans is that they almost always have nasty tempers and never get tame enough to handle and have fun with. Also, most of them die because they are not fed the proper food or kept at the proper temperature.

The little baby turtles you see sold for fifty cents or so are baby *slider* turtles. These are also called *red-eared* turtles, because most of them have a pretty red mark on each side of the head. When they get old they lose this pretty marking and get a lot of black stripes instead. They grow to be about six or eight inches long across the shell. Most of the food sold in pet stores for these little turtles will not keep them alive. The very worst food you can buy for them is dried ant eggs. If you feed your pet turtles dried ant eggs, the chances are that the turtles will become blind, the shells will swell or soften, and the animals will die. No matter what the pet store man tells you, dried ant eggs are poison to little turtles.

Once in a while a pet store in the bigger cities will import animals from Africa. Then you can find wonderful rare things like the Madagascan day geckos, which some people consider to be the most beautiful lizards in the world. They are bright green with orange or red marking on the back.

Tokay geckos from Malaysia are also beautiful. Some of them can be tamed, but most of them will bite you every time you pick them up. The trouble is they don't just bite you and forget about it. They keep on biting you as long as you hold them. They have really nasty dispositions. But they are so pretty and unusual that it is nice to have one. Most of the time they will feed by themselves, but some of them will not eat unless you feed them. The way to do this is to hold the gecko in your hand and wait until he tries to bite, then drop mealworms down his mouth. He has a very big mouth, so you can drop the worms in without missing. A tokay gecko will eat twenty-five or thirty mealworms for each meal.

The most important thing to do when buying reptiles from a pet store is to find out what the animals eat *before* you buy them. If they do not feed well, or if the clerk does not know what they eat, it is better not to buy the animal, no matter how beautiful it is, because you will not be able to keep it alive very long. If a store has a really nice animal that you want, call your zoo. Ask them if they can tell you the food and the temperature the animal needs. If you can supply these needs, then you have a good chance of keeping it contented and alive.

The many different kinds of African chameleons are wonderful to watch. But one trouble with them is that they do not live very long. Many zoos have them most of the time, but the longest they can be kept alive is about eighteen months. Perhaps the lizards are short-lived in the wild, too. Anyhow, they do not live much longer than a year or so in captivity, but while they do live they are among the most interesting pets you can possibly find. For one thing, they are not always so afraid of you that you cannot pick them up. As a matter of fact, the trouble is not picking them up but putting them down. They are difficult to get off your finger. Their feet are like tongs and they seem to want to walk only to a higher object. They rarely walk *down* off your hand.

The heads of these animals come in all shapes. Some of them have big ridges and others have horns. There are some with one horn, two horns, three horns and even four horns on their noses! The three-horned ones look like a dinosaur called Triceratops, which lived millions of years ago.

While importing all these exotic animals from tropical countries, the pet stores may also import diseased reptiles. You should examine your animals carefully before you buy them to make sure they are healthy. Of course, if they have an internal disease you cannot tell unless the animal dies. But some diseases can be seen when a reptile is examined. Actually they are not diseases but parasites. Mites are often found on snakes and lizards. These are *arachnids* (spiders are arachnids, and so are scorpions). Some of the mites are very tiny and cannot be seen very well unless you look at the animal under a magnifying glass. If, on examination, you see these tiny parasites crawling on the animal, don't buy it. Also, make sure none of the mites come off on your hands to be put onto the next specimen you look at.

Lizards store fat in their tails. The reason for this is that, when they have a hard time finding food, they will not starve. Look at the tail of any gecko or lizard you want to buy. If it is nice and fat, the animal should be in good condition. If the tail is very skinny, it has been starved. If you starve a reptile too long, it will be unable to eat when you give it food and will die in a short time.

The next thing to look at is the skin. If the animal is fat and healthy the skin will be filled out nicely, except where it is supposed to be folded. If the skin hangs in folds and patches on the animal, it may very likely be sick.

Look carefully at the eyes of young turtles. If they are very puffy and the animal keeps them closed most of the time, you should not buy it. The chances are that the turtles have been fed on ant eggs and are going blind as a direct result of this bad food. Young turtles should be frisky and scamper all around their tank. When you see a little fellow acting like this, there is good reason to think that it is healthy and contented, and that it will feed and remain healthy as long as you take proper care of it.

Look at the skins of snakes to see if they are full of blisters and small swellings. These are generally indications of infection from ticks. Sometimes the snake will be cured when it sheds its skin. More often it will not, though, and it is not worth taking a chance.

As long as you are selecting an animal for a pet, you should take every precaution to get a healthy one to begin with. There is no sense in starting out with a specimen that is sick when you take it home.

CHAPTER NINETEEN

How to Determine
a Reptile's Health

It is a good thing to know about different reptile diseases, just in case your new pet had one you did not know about when you bought it, or contracted one after you got it home. And, though humans rarely catch these diseases, it is important to identify them. There is, however, one disease that may spread to people —salmonella. This is a bad sickness. It is sometimes given to people by pet turtles. This was not known until recently, but it has been found that small turtles (and big ones too) can carry the disease without being sick themselves. When this happens, the animal is called a carrier.

Baby turtles also frequently die from a *dietary deficiency*. This means that they are not getting the proper vitamins, minerals, and other things in their food. Such is the case when the turtle is fed dried ant eggs. It takes the turtle a long time to die, which means that it had to suffer. If your turtle shows any distress in its eyes you should make sure that you are feeding it properly. Sometimes the blindness can be treated with ultraviolet rays but the turtle does not often recover.

It is too bad that reptiles do not show signs of being sick until they die or are ready to die. Mammals and birds show some sign of not feeling well, but not reptiles. So there is no sure way to tell whether your animal is sick when you buy it. If it dies in a short time, there is a very good chance that it was sick and nearly ready to die when you bought it.

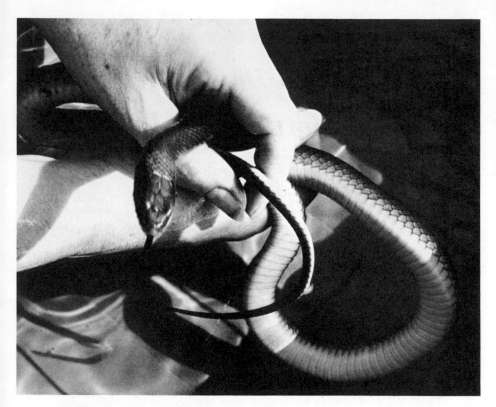

If your specimen is infected with mites, the best way to remove them is to hold the snake under water for several minutes. Bring its head out frequently so you do not drown him. The mites will leave the snake and drown in the water.

Mites are different. These can be seen most of the time. Usually a snake or lizard does not have mites in the wild. It will have got them after it was put in the wholesale dealer's cages or in the pet store. Many thousands of animals pass through these places each year. Some of them are bound to have mites. The tiny creatures jump off the animals and live in the cages until new animals are put in with them.

A headband magnifier is very good for detecting mites, because it leaves your hands free to hold the animal. The magnifiers come in different strengths. A good one to use for looking at animals is 10 power. Hold the lizard or snake in your hands so you can look it all over. Watch for a long time, especially at any fold in the skin. If mites are there, you will see one or more run out from under a scale and dart under another. If you see one, you may be sure there are more.

If you find mites on the skin of a reptile, put it in lukewarm water for ten to fifteen minutes at a time. Do this twice a day for two days, then once a day for a week. Then wait for three or four days and repeat the treatment. Most reptiles like water and will not struggle too much after they have been put in. Snakes will wiggle about a lot at first, then dunk themselves for a while.

You must be certain that all of the animal is under the water except the nose. The mites will drown and fall off. Remember, though, that some of them will be safe under the scales where the water will not reach, and these will not be killed. This is the reason for two baths daily for a time.

There will be eggs under the scales, too. They will not drown, but will hatch in several days. If you bathed the animal for only a few days and then left it alone, the eggs would hatch and the mites would run all over the animal again. This is why you must wait a few days and then give another week of dunking. If you do this for a month, you are pretty sure of getting rid of all the mites.

Many pet stores sell a product called Dri-Die 67. This is a powder that kills reptile mites. It would be a good idea to use the powder each day between the baths. The powder will kill any mites that did not drown when you held the reptile under water.

A good precaution to take if your animals have mites is to administer eye drops every day for a month or two. The drops can be bought in a drugstore. What you need is a .75% solution of sodium fluoride in water. This is *point* 75%, not just 75%, which would be a hundred times too strong! You might have to have your family doctor give you a prescription for the drops. He will probably do this if you tell him what you want it for.

The solution can be used to wipe the reptile's skin, too, as long as you take care not to get it in the mouth. If you see a mite duck under a scale, a drop of sodium fluoride solution can be put on that scale and the edge of the scale lifted with a pair of sharp tweezers or a toothpick to let the liquid run underneath. Just putting the solution on the scale will not do any good, because the air trapped under the scale will keep the solution from running under.

Baby iguanas need vitamins. Children's vitamins are good. A drop or two put on small pieces of lettuce will be eaten by the iguana. This should be given them every day, or at least every other day. When they get older and eat a lot of different things, the vitamins are not so important, but for the first two to three years they should have them.

Sometimes snakes will have a lot of blisters on their skins. The scales will stand up at the spot where the blisters are. Try soaking the snake in lukewarm water for ten minutes each day, and after soaking let it slide through a paper towel to dry off. Then rub a little antibiotic ointment into the blister. Neosporin or a similar preparation is good to try. The druggist will tell you of a substitute if he does not have Neosporin.

Some snakes get diseases that other snakes do not contract. The giant snakes like pythons, anacondas, and large boa con-

strictors might get a disease of the mouth. Mr. Raymond Ditmars, in his book *Reptiles of the World,* thinks that this disease
occurs because the snake does not have enough exercise and
does not feed when it is first kept captive. He says that the
snake's mouth becomes stagnant and bacteria start to grow in it.
Then the snake can suffer a small bruise or cut when it strikes
at hard objects in the cage, or at its keeper, and the cut becomes
infected.

Whatever the cause of the disease, unless it is caught very
promptly and stopped, the snake will die. Mr. Ditmars suggests
using Listerine. One part Listerine to two parts of boiled water
should be swabbed in the snake's mouth once or twice each day.
If the disease spreads, there is nothing much you can do about
it. If it gets very bad, put the poor sufferer out of its misery.

The very exotic Thailand water snakes that are being imported to this country often arrive with an internal disease
caused by an amoeba—a one-celled animal. The snake will die
if it has the disease. There is no way you can tell whether it is
present until the snake dies. The only bad thing about it is that
this disease is very *contagious.* That means that, if you touch the
water snake and then your other specimens, all will get it. You
will not become sick, because the disease does not attack human
beings. But all your other snakes and reptiles may contract it
and die if the same tools or water dishes are used among your
pets.

If the water snakes dies and you put another reptile in the
cage the water snake lived in, the new pet can also get sick and
die. The only thing to do when you get one of those water
snakes is to *quarantine* it. Put it into an aquarium that is kept
away from all other cages or aquariums. Every time you handle
anything at all connected with the water snake, you must wash
your hands very well with a medicated soap. You must never

use the same dish or anything at all that was in the water snake's aquarium for any other of your reptiles.

The snake should be kept in this quarantine for at least three months. Then, if it is still alive, feeding, and seems contented, you may assume that it is healthy and does not have the amoebic disease. Your precautions can then be lessened. It is still an excellent habit, though, to wash your hands well after handling any reptile before you handle the next one and after you handle the last one. The only thing that will happen to you is that you will have extra clean hands.

Big lizards that feed mostly on meat can get a vitamin deficiency disease. This will kill your pets after a time. Be sure you are feeding them properly. It is not enough to give them just bits of meat. They might eat the meat all right, but they are not getting the proper nourishment from it. Reptiles need *muscle meat*. That means things like beef heart, chicken hearts, or whole small animals like mice.

One thing that will help reptiles who are meat-eaters is vitamin E. This can be given with their food.

The Cayman crocodilians are often the worst sufferers. They *must* have muscle meat in order to live, and they must be kept very warm. Not less than 80 degrees, better 85 degrees. If reptiles are kept too cold, they might eat, but they would have trouble digesting their food. It would remain in their stomachs and finally turn sour. Then the animal would get sick and eventually die.

Sometimes you will find ticks on your reptiles, especially those from pet stores, although you will also sometimes find them on wild reptiles, too. A good way to get rid of the ticks is to dab them with a cotton swab wet with a solution called A-200-Pyrinate. This can be bought in a drugstore. Be careful not to get the solution in the animal's eyes or mouth. A-200-Pyrinate might be good for mites, too, but do not cover the animal with the solution. Just put it on in spots where you know a mite is under the scale.

It is not a good idea to try to pull off ticks. The tick's head might break off and remain under the animal's skin. If this happens, the head is liable to cause an infection that is worse than the tick.

There are several other diseases that attack reptiles, but they are too hard to treat. Generally, if you keep your animals at the proper temperature, feed them the correct food and enough of it, and keep other conditions the way they like them, your reptiles will not get sick. They will live a regular life span, or sometimes even a little longer. They will be contented and not so miserable that they are always trying to escape. Many reptiles become so tame in captivity and are so contented with their food and temperature that they will not go away even if you let them out of the cage.

A snake or a lizard might suffer from a rectal plug. This means that the waste matter in the snake's intestine has hardened at the opening and the animal can no longer move its bowels. A rectal plug, or anal plug, as it is sometimes called, will kill the snake in time if it is not removed.

About the best way to open a rectal plug is to soak the animal for a period of time in tepid water. It should be in the water at least fifteen minutes or longer. Then, with a cotton swab moistened with mineral oil, gently work the plug out of the cloaca. You will be able to spread the opening enough to work the plug out. If the animal has been plugged for some time, it is very possible that when the plug is removed it will have a large bowel movement immediately. For this reason it is well to perform the service on the table on top of a thick pad of old newspaper. You might have to have a helper hold the animal while you work on it. Be very gentle and take care that you do not injure your pet.

After removing the plug, you should watch the animal closely for several days to make sure that the same thing does not happen again. If it has a bowel movement a day or so after feeding, then you can assume that it is cured and that the plug was just a temporary thing. If the animal keeps plugging up every time it feeds, then you might try changing the diet. If you were feeding one kind of food, try another and see if this clears up the trouble.

In taking care of reptiles, a lot of health measures are just plain common sense. Personal hygiene is as important to animals as it is to you. You would not keep your reptile in a dirty cage—wet, sloppy, with the waste matter not cleaned out as soon as it is made—and expect the animal to remain healthy and contented. If it spills the water out of its dish, the animal as well as the cage should be dried off. Cleanliness is the most important thing in keeping animals. Keeping some reptiles clean is a real job. They mess up their cages as fast as you can clean them. The animal is not at fault. Remember, it is not used to living in a small confined space. It is not used to having a dish of water that is easy to upset. It is forced to make adjustments. This is hard for animals, which cannot think or reason as we do. It can hardly be expected to think, "If I crawl over the edge of my water dish, the dish will tip upside down and spill all the water into my cage." You have to do this thinking for it, and fix the dish in such a way that the reptile cannot tip it over, or, if this is not possible, be prepared to clean the cage often.

Do not be unhappy that this is a chore. These are some of the things you must first take into consideration when you try to keep animals. If you want living reptiles for pets, then you must be prepared to do whatever is necessary to keep them healthy, contented, well fed, and alive.

CHAPTER TWENTY

Kinds of Containers
for Reptiles

You have brought your new pet home from the wilds, or from the pet store, and you know how to keep it well and how to cure it. Now you have to have something to keep it in. Fish aquariums make the best cages, because they are easy to clean, you can see into them, and they can be kept either warm or cool, whichever the animals need.

There are many other kinds of cages that can be used for reptiles. You can make them or have them made by a carpenter. Perhaps your father will make some for you, or help you with them. Cages for our native reptiles (except those from the deserts) should be made with a screen on the top and sides, with the back closed and a sheet of glass for the front. That way the cages will be light and airy. You can have the top hinged so it will open for cleaning or to attend to your pet. There should be a good catch on the lid to keep the reptile from forcing it open and escaping.

These kinds of cages can be made of wood and the screen can be hardware cloth with a ¼-inch mesh. This screen is strong and heavy and will not have to be protected against the animal's pushing through it. A good size cage for a medium-sized snake or lizard would be 12 or 14 inches deep, 24 inches long and 16 inches high. That would be high enough to put a small branch inside for the animal to climb on. If you were keeping an anole or chameleon the cage should be higher—24 inches or more—to allow putting in a tall branch. These lizards need to climb and like to be high up in the air.

Cages for iguanas should be even larger. These lizards must have a lot of things to climb on, because if they are unable to climb they do not remain healthy and contented. The smallest cage that is practical for iguanas would be 24 inches deep, 36 inches long and at least 36 inches high. You could, of course, keep them in a smaller cage, but they would not do so well, nor would they live so long. Iguanas grow very large, and the cage should be big enough to allow them to grow without becoming cramped. Also, iguanas are best kept in pairs for company, and the cage will have to hold two of them.

Cages for desert lizards can be low, because the animals do not have to climb. A small pile of rocks in one corner, with an opening under or between them, is all they need to climb on.

Turtles need cages that will hold some water. When turtles are small and young, the plastic dishes sold in pet stores are fine for them. As they grow larger, you will have to move them to larger cages. Many turtles need water in which to eat. Many of them cannot swallow food unless they do so *under water!* Still, even these turtles must have a place on which to climb up out of the water.

In the summer months you can keep your turtles outdoors. The large plastic pools made for babies and little children are fine turtle ponds. An island of stones can be piled in the center of the pool. Fill the pool only halfway. If you put in too much water, the turtles can climb out of the pool by floating on the top and reaching up to catch the edge. Always examine the pool after a rainy day, because it might fill up, if the rain is a hard one, and float the turtles close enough to the top to allow them to escape.

When the water in such pools turns green it must be changed. The green color is caused by *algae* growing in the water. The more sunshine the pool has, the faster the algae will grow. Do not wait until the water is like pea soup, but change it as soon as you notice a faint green color forming.

Outdoor cages are good for many reptiles if they come from places where the climate is the same as yours. You could not put reptiles from hot humid tropical forests outdoors, for instance, but you could keep lizards from Europe and America in outdoor cages during the summer months. They will be better for having a large cage to live in, and for having regular changes of climate during the days and nights.

Outdoor cages must be absolutely tight or the animals will escape. You should never merely place the cage on top of the ground, hoping to keep your pet inside. Within minutes, probably, the animal will have seen a hole that you didn't even know was there to scoot out through.

The very best way to set up an outdoor cage is to put a footing into the ground, on top of which you can fasten the cage. The footing could be located in an out-of-the-way spot in the back yard. It should be not less than 1 foot deep in the ground; and it would be better if it went down 2 feet.

The footing can be made of many materials. The best and the easiest to maintain is concrete. Dig a ditch the size of the cage and 1 to 2 feet deep. The ditch should be about 6 inches wide. You can mix some concrete in an old tub or a wheelbarrow and pour it into the ditch until it is filled to ground level.

If the ground in your yard is uneven, then a form must be made in the ditch to get the top of the footing level. The form can be two boards stood on edge in the ditch and raised or lowered until the top edges are all the same height and all level. An ordinary carpenter's level can be used to set the form boards.

The boards can be held in place by a small stake driven into the ground on the outside of the form and the board nailed to the stake. Your father, older brother, or friend could help you make the form and the ditch. They could also help you mix and pour the concrete.

When the concrete has been poured into the ditch, you can set two steel bolts into each side. Set them about a foot from each end and leave about 3 inches sticking out of the concrete. The head end of the bolt should be put down into the cement. Then, when the footings are hard, the cage can be bolted down tightly to the level concrete and the animals will be unable to dig from under the sides.

A cage for snakes does not have to be covered if the sides are made high enough. The longest snake you will be keeping inside the cage should be measured, and the height of the sides should be one and a half times the length of the snake. This way the snake cannot work its way up in a corner far enough to get its head on top. If a snake can reach the top of a cage with its head, it can hook its chin over the edge and pull its entire body up to escape.

Cages for lizards must be covered, because they can climb right up the screen or the corners. Geckos can walk up the sides even if they are made of glass. In a closed cage, there must be some way for you to feed and water the animals. The top can be made so it can be removed when you want to reach inside. This is easier than trying to make a door that is tight enough to keep the animals from escaping.

CHAPTER TWENTY-ONE

Maintenance of Reptiles
in Cages

In order to keep reptiles, you must have proper cages for them to live in. The last chapter dealt with the *kinds* of cages needed. This chapter will explain what you must have *inside* the cages.

Cages for reptile pets can be divided into several classes: hot, cool, moist, dry, and combinations of all of these. For desert reptiles, cages should be hot and dry. For forest reptiles, cages should be cool and moist. Tropical reptiles are healthiest when their cages are hot and damp. Sometimes it is not possible for you to maintain a cage with the proper conditions for a certain reptile. If that is the case, then it would be best if you did not try to keep that kind of animal. It would only sicken and die.

A cage for desert animals is much different from one for animals that live in water or in humid conditions. It is more difficult to keep a desert cage warm enough, because air heaters are sometimes very expensive to buy, and it would cost too much to set up a cage with a thermostat control for one or two desert animals. One way such a cage can be kept warm enough is to use a short water-pipe heater buried in the sand. These heaters are flat wires that are plugged into an electrical outlet. They come in many different lengths. The short 3- or 4-foot ones are best. Some of them have built-in thermostats, and others are plain. The plain ones are best for heating a cage.

For a desert lizard or other desert animal, you should put in

two or three inches of clean sand or fine aquarium gravel. A
heater wire can be buried in the sand, but not less than an inch
below the surface. Bend the wire in zigzags across the tank, but
be sure that you do not bend it so that it crosses itself at any
spot. If a pipe-heater wire is crossed over itself, it may burn out
at that point. It will get too hot where the two loops touch.
Bring the plug end of the heater wire up one corner of the cage,
so you can plug it into an extension cord for electrical current.

A few small cacti or succulent plants can be bedded in the
sand to the level of the top of the pots. There is no need to put
in a water dish, because practically no desert animals drink out
of a standing supply of water. They drink only dew on the
leaves at night or in the early morning. Make your cage setup so
you can remove part of the lid to water the pets properly. Water
should be sprayed on the plants until drops are left standing.
This should be done each morning and each night.

Soon the animals will learn where their water is, and walk
over to lick up the "dew-" drops. Be careful when you spray the
water so you will not get too much water in the cage. You
should try not to wet the sand. If the plants are all placed in the
same corner of the cage, when you water them the rest of the
cage will remain dry and warm. The animals will move away
from the damp sand around the plants after they have drunk,
and go back to where it is dry.

Lizards native to the forests need cages that are dry and a little cool. They also need a lot of leaves or other forest debris on
the bottom of their cages and a small dead log or branch on
which to climb. Many forest lizards can drink from a water dish.
If you are not sure of the drinking habits of any animal you are
keeping, always put in a small dish of water and watch the pet
very closely for a few days to see if it drinks. You must be sure
that the animal is really drinking, not just smelling the water.

If you see it actually drink from the dish, then you can keep a small dish of water in the cage all the time. Change the water every day. If, after a couple of days, you see that the animal is not drinking from the dish, put a plant with broad leaves (such as a small philodendron) in the cage and spray the leaves well. If the reptile is a dewdrop drinker, it will usually run right over to the plant and begin licking up the drops. If this is what happens, you must water the plant by spraying at least twice every day.

In a forest cage, it doesn't matter if a little water sprays on the dead leaves on the bottom. Leaves in the forest are usually a little damp anyway, and it will not hurt the animals; however, the bottom should not be soaking. You can put some dirt in the bottom of a forest cage if you like, but it should be very clean sterilized soil.

You can buy small bags of sterile potting soil in most supermarkets and nurseries. Then you mix it with an equal amount of sand. The sand should be cleaned by washing it very well in a pan, then spreading it on a flat pan and baking it in the oven until it is dry. Spread the mixture of soil and sand on the bottom of the cage, then cover the soil with the dead leaves. Collect nice clean leaves from under a tree, or from the forest. Examine all the leaves to make sure that there are no spiders, insects, or dirt on them before using them in the cage. A small rock or two and a small log or branch will be welcomed by your pets.

Most reptiles, especially turtles and lizards, require a source of heat under which they can bask as though they were out in the sun. An overhead light bulb at one end of the cage is ideal since it permits the animal to go back and forth into its sunning spot at will.

The most important thing to remember when setting up a

cage for a reptile is to make it as nearly like the natural habitat as possible. Of course the exact conditions cannot be duplicated. You can, however, make it enough like a natural spot that the animal will be contented and stay healthy.

CHAPTER TWENTY-TWO

Reptile Food

Almost all reptiles eat meat—other animals or insects. A few lizards and turtles are *vegetarians*—that is, they eat fruit and vegetables instead of meat. Vegetarian reptiles are the easiest to keep and feed. There is no problem about finding food during the winter months, because lettuce, carrots, and some kinds of fruit are always available. Canned fruit salad, with the juice drained off, is good food for many vegetarian lizards, like the iguanas, which will eat this during the winter.

To keep the meat-eaters that do not hibernate alive through the winter, you must be able to find the proper kinds of food. If they are insect feeders, it is possible to buy crickets and mealworms. There are several companies in the United States that sell crickets by the hundreds or thousands as fishing bait. These companies generally place ads in sporting magazines. Look in the classified ad pages. Mealworms are the larvae of a small beetle. Most pet stores sell mealworms for about a penny each, or a little cheaper by the hundred. Some larger pet stores sell them by the quarter- or half-pound.

Earthworms also make good food for reptiles; they can be collected or bought.

Spiders are a choice bit of food for small lizards. Usually you can always find one or two around the house. Look in dark corners in the cellar, on stairs, in the attic. The only trouble with raising spiders as food for lizards is that you have to feed the spiders, too. This defeats your purpose because spiders are also meat-eating animals.

When you have young reptiles like lizards and anoles, or maybe young geckos, it is hard to find insect food small enough for them to eat. Fruit flies are good for this purpose. They are very easy to raise in "fly farms" and they are a perfect size for tiny reptiles. You can buy cultures of fruit flies from companies that sell supplies to schools. Possibly your science teacher can get you a start of flies.

Sometimes you have baby animals when you cannot get food for them. African animals and those from below the equator have often mated already when the pet stores get them for sale here. Spring in these places is autumn where we are, so in our fall or early winter the tropical pet will surprise you by having its young just when all your food supply is gone because of the cold.

If you have such reptiles for pets, even though you are not sure what sex your pet is, it would be an excellent idea to start some fruit-fly farms in the late summer, just in case. Nothing but a little time and trouble will be lost if your pet does not have any young, but having a few fruit-fly farms producing may mean the difference between keeping the young alive and watching them starve to death if you *don't* have farms ready.

If your reptiles feed on mice or other small mammals, you can buy or raise white mice. Guinea pigs and rabbits can also be kept for larger reptiles. Almost any reptile that has a large enough mouth will eat small mice. There are two stages of young mice that can be used as food for reptiles. The first are "pink mice." Pink mice are the tiny babies that have just been born. These are small enough to feed medium-sized lizards. Larger chameleons will also eat pink mice, as will tokay geckos.

The next stage of mammal food for reptiles is "weaners." These are young mice that have just been weaned by their mothers. They have their fur and their eyes are open. They are good for young caymans and large lizards and for medium-sized snakes. Full-grown mice are used for snakes, caymans, and very large carnivorous lizards.

Keeping white mice is easy enough if you have the space for it, and if you keep them spotlessly clean. If you do not, they smell. No parent will allow a smelly mouse cage around the house. To start a mouse "farm" all you need are two females and one male. They mate and breed regularly, and the females have several young at one time. Naturally, the best time for a mouse farm is in the winter when it is difficult to find food for your pets. If you cannot keep mice yourself, the next best thing is to buy them. There are many wholesale mouse breeders in the country. They make a big business out of raising mice for hospitals, schools, and laboratories. If you are fortunate enough to live near enough to one of these companies, you can usually buy mice rejects from them for just a few cents each. Often they will sell you a whole bunch of pink mice or weaners for practically nothing. If you cannot find a breeder, then try a pet store.

Almost any boy knows how to raise rabbits and guinea pigs. If you have a large snake like a young python or big boa constrictor, small rabbits or guinea pigs make good food. When your cayman gets bigger, it will also eat these things.

At any time you can catch birds for your larger reptiles, such as some of the snakes. It is very easy to trap live sparrows in the summer and juncos in the winter. Just prop a box up with a stick under one edge. Tie a long string to the stick and lead it inside through the window or door. Scatter a handful of wild bird seed, bread crumbs, or dry cereal under the box and sit down for a few minutes. Soon there will be a number of birds pecking away at the bait. Slowly and gently pull the string until the stick falls away from the box. The chances are that you will have more than one bird each time you spring the trap!

CHAPTER TWENTY-THREE

The Best Kinds of Snakes to Keep as Pets

Not every snake will make a good pet. Some of them will not even live in captivity. Some of them will refuse to feed. Others are so easily frightened that they become frantic whenever anyone approaches the cage. I have seen many snakes with sore, bloody noses. They got that way from dashing against the glass trying to escape whenever a person went near them. These kinds of snakes are not good animals to try to keep as pets. Actually, they never become pets, but are merely captive animals. They are miserable, and most of the time do not live very long.

The kinds of snakes you want to keep as pets are those that live well in a cage—the kinds that will let you pick them up and handle them without going mad with fear, the kinds that will curl up contentedly in your lap while you stroke their bellies or backs, and seem to enjoy such treatment, the kinds that will feed out of your hand or at least let you watch them eat.

Many different species of these kinds of snakes are to be found. As we have mentioned in previous chapters, before you select your pet snake, find out what it feeds on, if you can keep it alive through the winter, if you can find food for it without too much trouble or expense and if you can provide proper accommodations for it.

Snakes can be divided roughly into four groups. (1) Those from the Temperate Zones of the world. (2) Those from des-

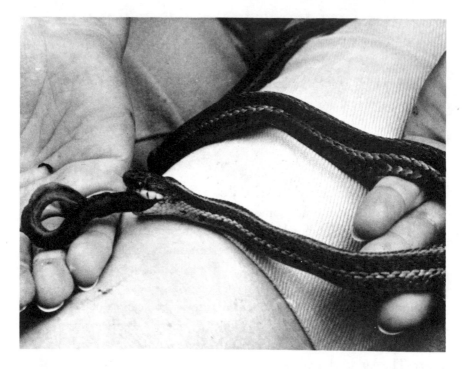

Thamnophis sirtalis. After a few days of kind handling, garter snakes learn they have nothing to be afraid of, and from then on will tame up very quickly, eat out of your hands, and make no attempt to escape when taken from their cages.

erts. (3) Those from the tropics. And (4) a special group called exotic snakes.

Temperate Zone snakes come from the United States, from most of Europe, and a few other places. These snakes can withstand our climate. They generally hibernate during the winter. They do not require special temperatures or conditions of humidity in their cages. And, what is more important, they are readily available in pet stores, they are low priced, and, in many cases, you can catch them yourself.

About the easiest kind of snake to feed is one that eats small rodents and mammals. These are easiest because you can always get food for them in the form of white mice from a pet store. You can also raise the mice yourself if you want to.

Mammal feeders are also the easiest kinds of snakes, other than garter snakes, to find in pet stores. Some snakes that feed on small animals do not make good pets because they never become tame enough. Others live very well in cages and seem to like being handled and played with. They become very tame and do not even try to escape when you let them out of their cages. Of course, any snake will crawl away and escape if you allow it to. Sometimes it is not trying to escape from you but crawls into a hole or a place where you cannot get it back. The result is the same as though it had run from you.

King snakes are about the best mammal eaters you could find to keep as pets. In our country there are several kinds of king snakes. Then there are several kinds of snakes that belong to the king-snake group but are called by other names. The true king snakes belong to the genus *Lampropeltis*. *Lampropeltis* means "shiny skin," and the king snakes have smooth scales and a shiny surface. They are among the most beautiful of all snakes. King snakes are called that because of their ability to kill and eat other snakes. They can kill poisonous snakes such as rattlesnakes and copperheads. They can even let themselves be bitten by rattlesnakes and the venom does not harm them if the bite is not in a critical spot.

The king snake is a constrictor and usually eats small mammals. Because of this, its teeth are very long and it can bite. This very seldom happens, however, since it is difficult to get

King Snake. *Lampropeltis getulus*. One of the most gentle of all snakes, this one will attack, kill and eat a rattler as large as itself!

some king snakes to open their mouths unless they are feeding or drinking. Unless the snake is after food, it does not move very fast. It likes to lie curled up in a corner; sometimes it stays curled up in its water dish, soaking. When you handle your king snake, let it wrap its body around your arm or around your hand. It will hang on tightly, and seems to have a feeling of security if it has a good hold on you. It will remain quiet and calm and you can examine it as long as you like. A good way to hold a king snake is to hold up one hand with your fingers spread wide apart. The snake will wind in and out of your fingers until it is tied in a knot all around your hand. Then it will stay quietly and you can carry it around.

There is no danger in handling a king snake if you do not put it around your neck. It cannot hurt you around your waist, for instance, or around your arm or leg. So you do not have to be afraid to keep a king snake as a pet. They are among the best kinds for this purpose. As I mentioned before, there are several kinds of king snakes in this country. There are also a few species that live in the tropics down as far as Ecuador.

The three main kinds of king snakes are the common king snake, the Eastern king snake, and the Southern king snake. Each has several subspecies, but these are merely local varieties of the same species.

The common king snake is glossy black with large cream blotches all over the back, sides, and belly. The adult length is about four feet but specimens as long as six feet ten inches are on record. The common king snake is found almost everywhere in the United States. Wild specimens may be found under rotting logs, stones, old lumber. They are fond of sunning themselves in the morning and early afternoon. In the hot summer they are out more at night than in the daytime. When first caught, they might strike at you, hiss, and vibrate their tails, but they become tame almost immediately and rarely, if ever, bite.

The Eastern king snake is a beautiful glossy black snake with narrow cream-colored bands running around the body. It can be found in the southern states and the eastern states, west to the Appalachians. The Southern king snake is covered with white or yellow spots all over its body. It is sometimes called the salt-and-pepper snake or speckled king snake. It can be found over the southeastern section of the United States.

King snakes will eat other things besides mice. In the summer, when frogs and salamanders are plentiful, they will devour them. They may eat other snakes, lizards, or small birds when available.

The milk snake is really a king snake. The animal is called a milk snake for a very silly reason. Milk snakes very often go into barns where cows are kept. They look for mice that live among the hay and straw in cow barns. Years ago, if a farmer found a milk snake in his barn he thought it wanted to suck the milk from his cows. The story is not true, but it is how the milk snake got its name.

These beautiful snakes are about three feet long. They are light gray with chestnut-brown or reddish markings on the back. They are found over almost the entire United States. Sometimes they are called house snakes, checkered adders, or spotted adders. They are easy to tame and live well in captivity.

The rat snakes, like the king snakes, are constrictors. They feed on rodents, birds, and sometimes frogs. Rat snakes are also called chicken snakes. This is because they are often found around chicken houses. They might eat a baby chick once in a while, but the real reason they hang around chicken houses is the same reason milk snakes hang around barns—they are looking for rats and mice, both of which live in large numbers in barns and poultry houses.

One type of rat snake is even more beautiful than the milk snake. This is the one called the red rat snake. It is also called the corn snake because it is often seen in cornfields. It is looking for the field mice that build their nests in the rubble in cornfields. Corn snakes are cream, gray, or pale red with dark red, brown, or chestnut markings on the back and belly. They have a beautiful play of color on their belly scales.

The green rat snake comes from Mexico and is grayish green on the back with the scales tipped in black. The belly is white. There are several species of rat snakes, and they are found all over the country. Rat snakes can be found under large pieces of loose bark on dead trees. In the morning or evening they like to go under the bark where it is warm. Rat snakes are very good climbers and spend a lot of time in trees.

Rat snakes, chicken snakes, and pilot black snakes all belong to the group called *Elaphe*. Pilot black snakes are so named because at one time people wrongly thought they led rattlesnakes and copperheads to safety when any of them were in danger of being caught. Black snakes, rattlesnakes, and copperheads all live in the same kinds of places—woodsy and rocky country.

Fox snakes are also members of the *Elaphe* group. They do not climb as much as the other rat snakes and are usually found on the ground in the woods and brushy fields. Any snake of the *Elaphe* group needs a tall cage with a branchy tree or shrub to climb on. They sit coiled up on a high place and sun themselves. In the pilot black snake cage a pile of rocks makes a good sunning area. Be sure to keep the cage in a location where the snake can get out of the sun—or have a cave into which it can go to cool off.

Two more constrictors that make good pets are the famous boa constrictor from Central and South America and the reticulated python from Malaysia, Burma, and Vietnam. These two species belong to the giant snakes of the world. The boa constrictor does not grow much over eleven or twelve feet long, but the reticulated python can become over thirty feet long. Of course, the chance that either of these snakes will reach that size in your cages is slim. They could, though, grow so big that you would have trouble feeding them enough to keep them healthy.

If this happens, you should try to dispose of the snake to someone better able to care for it and get a smaller specimen for yourself. If the snake is a good specimen, healthy and contented with captivity, you might give it as an outright gift donation to

Boa Constrictor. *Constrictor constrictor.* When young, these are among the most colorful of snakes. Chocolate-brown, white and gray markings are vivid.

your local zoo. Or you could sell it to an animal farm that has a display of exotic animals for public view. While both the boa constrictor and the python can climb, it is not necessary to keep a real arboreal habitat for them. A good strong branch will serve well, and the boa constrictor especially will stretch out along it.

South American boa constrictors become quite tame. The Central American ones are a little more timid and sometimes try to bite. When the pythons are first caught they are quite wild and will strike and bite every chance they get. Both the boa constrictor and the python can give you a good bite, since they have big mouths that open very wide. They also have long sharp teeth and can hold on when they catch your finger. However, the bites are not very painful, are generally clean, and do not become infected. Treat them with antiseptic and a Band-Aid.

Both the boa constrictor and the python need large water dishes to curl up in. They like to lie in the water after eating, and may stay there for several days digesting their food.

Sometimes a python will not feed when it is first caged. Weeks may go by before it will take anything to eat. You should put a mouse or small rat in the cage for fifteen or twenty minutes. If the snake does not show interest within that time, you should remove the food. Try again the next day. You may have to keep this up for several weeks, until finally the snake eats the animal.

When your pet starts to feed, there may be danger of overfeeding it. It may take as many mice or rats as you will offer it. If this happens, the chances are that it will become sick and throw them up. It is best to give your snake one little animal a day for two or three days, then one every other day for another two or three days. After that, you can put the snake on a regular feeding schedule. One good-sized rat or a couple of mice once a week should be plenty until the snake reaches six to seven feet. You then might have to increase the food by giving larger animals, such as small rabbits or guinea pigs, or feed it twice the amount of rats or mice.

A python in good health is one of the most beautiful snakes in the world. Its colored skin has all the hues of a rainbow.

These colors keep moving as the snake moves. It looks like a beautiful gemstone. But this color is lost when the snake is sick or dead. Many snakes show a play of color, generally on the belly scales, but none as deep, bright and beautiful as the python. The only other snake I know with such color is a boa that comes from Central America. The colors are so strong and beautiful that the snake is called the rainbow boa. Rainbow boas make good pets, too. They are very tame.

Probably the tamest snake you can find is the indigo snake, which grows to a length of nine feet. It is about the only snake that seems to like to be handled. It will lie for long periods of time while you stroke its belly or its back. Indigo snakes have been known to follow their owners around like a puppy or kitten. They will feed readily and take food out of your hands. They are shiny blue-black everywhere except the throat, which is dark red. There is a play of rainbow color all over their skin. Indigo snakes are the ones used in circuses by snake dancers and snake "charmers" because they are so tame and like to be played with. They are not constrictors and do not squeeze their prey but swallow it alive. They will feed on rats, mice, birds, toads, frogs, and other snakes.

The indigo snake is sometimes called the gopher snake. This is because it hides in gopher tortoise burrows when it is being pursued. It will hide in other holes and burrows, of course, or in among rock piles. It is found in the southeastern United States, and is the largest snake in that part of the country.

Garter snakes are to be found everywhere in the country. They belong to the genus *Thamnophis*. While garter snakes can be kept in captivity, they do not make very good pets because they are generally fearful, and often bite. They have a very bad habit of releasing a foul smell when they are handled. This is caused by the snake emptying its anus or cloaca. Some individual specimens stop doing this after a while. Others never stop. Some garter snakes never become tame enough to handle without biting or trying to escape. Others calm down after a while and seem to accept captivity. It is difficult to say which specimen will do what. I have had a pair of Marcy's garter snakes that seemed perfectly contented in captivity. They had thirteen babies! The young of this species are born alive, instead of hatching from eggs.

Sometimes a garter snake will refuse to eat. If this happens, there is nothing much you can do except to get rid of it. Free it where you found it. You might try to give it to your zoo, except that the zoo will probably not want it either. Zoos are given so many snakes that they have no way of taking care of them all. If the specimen was a rare one or extra large, the zoo might be happy to have it, but for the small common garter snakes there is no room.

Garter snakes need something in their cages to hide under. A small piece of log, a pile of stones, even a flat piece of tree bark is good. They feed on insects, small frogs, worms, lizards, other snakes, and some good feeders will even take strips of raw lean beef. Many species of *Thamnophis* will eat fish, too. The little ribbon snake is a garter snake but does not seem to have the bad habits of smelling up itself or remaining wild. Ribbon snakes will eat fish readily, and they live well in captivity. While some of them may remain wild and fearful, most of them will become tame enough to handle without trouble.

One of the most unusual snakes you can find is the hog-nosed snake. This poor animal is the cause of more stupid and superstitious stories than almost any other living creature. The hog-nosed snake has many local names, each of them pointing to something supposedly frightful about the reptile. It is called the spreading adder, puff adder, blowing adder, hissing viper, flat-headed adder, and others. All the names have either "adder" or "viper" in them. Adders and vipers are some of the deadliest snakes in the world. The hog-nosed snake is not deadly. It is not even poisonous. In fact, it is impossible to make a hog-nosed snake bite you. You can even push your finger into its mouth and still it will not bite. These snakes live in sandy places, and they like to burrow with their up-turned noses. They rarely eat anything but toads, although some have been known to eat frogs.

The hog-nosed snake has a bag of tricks that it uses when it is frightened or attacked by an enemy. This snake can spread a hood like a cobra. It flattens its head and raises it with the hood spread wide, so it looks exactly like a dangerous cobra! While it does this, it hisses very loudly. Usually this is enough for people who do not know about snakes.

If the cobra act does not frighten away the enemy, the hog-nosed snake will coil up with its tail raised in the center of the coil and stretch its neck out in an "S" curve like a rattlesnake. The tail is vibrated very rapidly, but it doesn't make any noise. The snake will strike just like a rattlesnake, but if you watch it closely, you will see that it doesn't even open its mouth!

As a last resort, the snake will go into convulsions, lash its body violently about, and roll its tongue in the dirt. Then it will roll over on its back and go limp. It is now "dead." If you go off a little distance and remain quiet, slowly the snake will roll over onto its belly and start to crawl away. Turn back to it and it will immediately flop onto its back, out will come the tongue, and you have a "dead" snake again.

But in a very short time the hog-nosed snakes can become tame. They are short fat snakes with rough scales and dull brown, gray, or black coloring with mottles showing under the dark ground color. The tail is short and stubby. They do not move very fast, and are easy to catch.

A small brown snake called DeKay's snake is to be found all over the United States. These have even been found in Central Park, in the heart of New York City! The snake does not grow much longer than eight or ten inches, and is a pale brown color with darker brown markings on the back and sides. It feeds on grubs and earthworms. It is a shy feeder, and often, if it is swallowing a worm and you approach its cage, it will disgorge the food and refuse to eat for a long time afterward. This disgorging of food is a defense mechanism. If a snake has just fed, it has a full belly and is sluggish. On being attacked it would be less able to make a fast retreat. So if it disgorges its food it is much less sluggish and can flee rapidly.

Small brown snakes called Sonoras, similar to DeKay's snake, are found in this country also. They do not live in captivity as well as DeKay's snake, but some of them become tame and feed well. Look for these small brown snakes under stones or any other protection such as bark, old boards, or even large leaves. Usually they will coil up when you lift the stone from over them, and you can grab them quickly with your hand. They are easy to keep in small cages and you can keep several together without having trouble between them.

Water snakes can be found almost everywhere in this country. Many naturalists think that they are not very good pets. Usually water snakes do not feed well. They do not get very tame.

Water snakes are not very pretty. They are dull dark brown, with very rough scales, and they have ugly heads. They look as though they should be poisonous, but they are not. They do have a good set of teeth, which can give you a real bite. They feed on fish, frogs, and tadpoles. Their cage should have water deep enough to swim and feed in, and a place for the snake to crawl out of the water.

There are many, many kinds of snakes other than the few I

have mentioned here. Some of them might do well in cages, but many of our common snakes are not good pets. Ring-necked snakes are hard to get to feed. The smooth and the rough green snakes are the same. They are pretty, small, and slender. They like to climb trees and shrubs, but they refuse to feed in cages. Some of the boas will live and feed well in captivity. The rubber boa from the west coast of the United States is very tame and gentle.

The thing to do when you get a new species is to watch it closely for a time. Look it up in one of the snake books to make sure you know what kind it is. Then try to find out what kind of place it likes to live in. You can then make its cage as comfortable as possible for it. Watch when you put food in the cage to see if the snake is interested. If it takes food within a few days of its capture, the chances are that it will feed regularly. If it refuses food for weeks, then the best thing to do is to liberate it and try another kind. It is cruel to keep a snake that will not eat. It will only die.

CHAPTER TWENTY-FOUR

The Best Kinds of Turtles to Keep as Pets

In one way, turtles are easier than snakes to keep as pets. This is because turtles cannot escape so easily. They cannot ooze through small holes. They cannot climb very well. Turtles live a long time, too—some live for more than twenty-five years in the house. You could find a nice turtle, tame it and set up a nice place for it to live in, and then grow up with your pet.

There are turtles that live only in water. Others always live on land. Then there are several kinds that live on land but go into the water, too. Some turtles can eat only under water. They cannot swallow their food in the air. There are several kinds of turtles that make good pets. They become tame easily and quickly.

Turtles sun themselves on rocks overhanging water, into which they can drop when an enemy approaches. You can put your turtle aquarium in or near a window where it will get some sun each day. Be sure, though, that there is a place for the turtles to get into the shade. Sun is good for all reptiles, but if they are trapped in the sun it will kill them. Reptiles are cold-blooded and their blood will heat up if they remain in the sun too long. A temperature will be reached that the animal cannot stand.

Remember that turtles carry the disease salmonella. This does not mean that you should never go near a turtle for the rest of

your life. It does mean though, that you should exercise some
health measures when handling your pet. First, *always* wash
your hands after playing with your turtle or handling it in any
way. *Never* hold the turtle up to your face, kiss it, or allow it to
breathe into your face. It may sound silly for me to tell you not
to kiss a turtle. It isn't very silly, though. Many people love their
pets so much that they regularly hug and kiss them. It is a bad
habit to kiss any animal. There is always the possibility of
catching a disease from it. And, obviously, you should never put
your turtle in any container that is used for food or for cooking.

If you practice these simple precautions, there should be very
little danger of contracting any sickness or disease from your
pets.

There are literally hundreds of different kinds of turtles. I am
not even going to try to list them all here. It is not necessary.
Most of them you will never even get to see outside of a zoo.
Perhaps the best kinds of turtles for you to keep are those that
live in the same kind of climate as you do. This means that most
of the turtles will be those you can see in the streams, ponds,
and rivers where you live.

Ordinary pond turtles make good pets because they will become quite tame, generally feed well, and live a long time in a
cage if properly taken care of. Young specimens should be
taken, rather than the old mossbacks. When pond turtles are
old, moss, algae, and sometimes other water life grow on the
shell. This is particularly true of the snapping turtles. Sometimes their shells are so covered with moss and mud that you
cannot tell they are turtles at all! They lie on the bottom of the
pond and remain very still. Their prey does not know that the
mound of mud and moss is an enemy, either, until suddenly it is
snapped up.

Perhaps the easiest kind of turtle to obtain is a young slider.

They are now sold in such quantities that the dealers are no longer able to find enough wild ones to stock for their customers. For this reason, people have started to breed the common slider turtle. Georgia is the leading state for this industry. Thousands and thousands of young sliders are hatched each year on very large turtle-breeding farms.

The shells are bright green and yellow, and they are really very pretty little animals. The whole turtle becomes grayish when it is old. Male sliders or red-ears have longer claws on their feet than the females. They also have darker shells. Red-ears should be kept in an aquarium or container with a few inches of water and a dry place where they can climb up to sun themselves. The container should be kept in a warm place where it will get some sunshine each day. Be very careful to have a place shaded from the direct sunlight, though, or the animal may become overheated and die. From 75 to 85 degrees is the best temperature range for young turtles of this species. The temperature can drop a bit at night, but should not be allowed to go much below 60 degrees if at all possible.

Young red-ears like to eat in the water. They take food on dry land, but they prefer to feed submerged in the water. They should be fed small bits of *lean* beef, beef heart, small earthworms, mealworms, and small pieces of raw chicken. Do not feed them cooked meat or smoked or pickled meat.

Vegetables should also be given them. A lettuce leaf, small pieces of raw carrot, a freshly shelled pea or two are acceptable. Small pieces of fruit are also good.

Don't forget that the food given young turtles should be chopped into pieces that the little animals can swallow whole with no trouble. Turtles do not chew their food. They tear off chunks from larger pieces and swallow them, but it is much better to chop their food into sizes that they can manage without

Red-eared Terrapin. *Pseudemys scripta.* This is the common little baby turtle sold by the thousands in pet shops, which die by the thousands because of improper food and care.

any trouble. If you plop a large hunk of meat into the turtle cage, it may foul the water before the turtle has eaten enough.

Always change the water as soon as it is no longer clear, clean, and sparkling. This means that you should feed your pets only as much as they will eat, and not so much that a lot of food remains in the water after feeding time. If you feed them one or two bits of meat and watch them eat it, then give them one or two more, you will soon learn about how much your animal will eat at one meal.

Chopped liver is good for turtles and they seem to like it. If your mother cooks fish, the raw entrails, chopped small, are very good for your pets. They contain vitamins needed for the turtles' health which are not found in other foods. A snail, with the shell crushed so the turtle can get at the meat, is also good food. Look for land snails under stones and logs in among the damp leaves of the woods and fields. Pieces of raw fish and small live fish are excellent foods. For live fish, you could use guppies. The minnows sold for fishing bait are too large for the young turtles. They are fine for grown specimens, though. Small tadpoles are eagerly eaten by young turtles.

Some other kinds of turtles found in pet stores, often in the same tank as the red-ears, are young map turtles, young snappers, and a pretty brown turtle with ridges down the center of its back called a sawback.

Sawbacks come from the southern part of the country, along the Mississippi Valley. They need warmer cage temperatures than do the red-ears or the map turtles. The same kinds of foods are good for all the turtles mentioned so far.

There are three main species of painted turtles—the Eastern, the Western, and the Southern. The Southern painted turtle has a bright yellow or white stripe down the middle of its back when it is young. When the animal is older, this stripe becomes red. The Eastern and Western painted turtles are very similar in appearance. The *plastron* (the bottom or belly part of a turtle's shell) of the Eastern painted turtle is orange, and has no markings of any kind on it. In the Western species, the plastron is covered with a fancy pattern. The *carapaces* or top shells of both the Eastern and the Western painted turtles look very much alike. If you have one that you cannot identify, merely turn it over and look at the plastron. If it is marked, your pet is Western. If it is plain, your turtle comes from the eastern part of the United States. The stripe down the back is enough identifica-

Southern Painted Turtle. *Chrysemys picta dorsalis.* The Southern turtle differs from the Eastern painted turtle by having one yellow stripe down the middle of the back.

tion for you to recognize the Southern painted turtle. The front claws of male painted turtles are very much longer than their rear claws. Sometimes the front ones are two or three times longer than the back ones. The males have long tails. Females of the painted turtles have shorter tails, and their claws are all nearly the same length.

Snapping turtles are not too good as pets because they are always nasty and when they get a little old, they try to bite. The very young ones are gentler, and, even if they do try to bite, they cannot hurt you very much. An older snapper can really injure you. Also, snappers grow very large and you would have to have an enormous place to keep them in if you had them for a long time.

Spotted turtles are often seen crossing roads. They are similar to the painted turtles, and they, too, make good pets. They will eat meat, fish, vegetables, and some fruits, and like to feed in the water. They become very tame and are very gentle. The males have longer tails than the females, and brown eyes. The females have orange eyes and a yellow stripe on the lower jaw. The male lacks this stripe.

Spotted turtles must have water enough to swim around in, and a flat rock or log where they can climb out to bask in the sun. When you come near, they quickly slide off the rock into the water, swimming around underneath the rock or log to hide. For this reason they are very difficult to catch in the wild, unless you find one traveling from pond to pond, which they often do, crossing the roads along the way.

Another aquatic or water turtle that lives well in captivity is the musk turtle. When you first catch one, it gives off a very bad odor. But after the turtle has been in captivity awhile and becomes tame, it does not release its smell. However, if a strange person picks it up suddenly, or frightens the animal in any way, it will still smell.

Mud turtles also give off a bad odor. The yellow mud turtle is a smooth, trim, and pretty animal, and becomes tame after a short time in a cage. Male musk turtles and male mud turtles both have thicker, heavier tails than the females. They also have a hard tip on the tail that the females do not have. Males have two heavy rough scales on each hind foot. Females do not. Both these species are water turtles and need water deep enough to swim around in, and big enough in area to afford them a good pool. It would be difficult to keep them in an outdoor pool because they can climb. Of course, if you could cover their pool with an escapeproof screen of some kind, you could easily keep them outdoors. Float a piece of wood in their water or have a flat rock sticking out so they can climb up out of the water if they like.

The musk and mud turtles eat meat, fish, and some water plants. If you go to a tropical fish store, you can get bunches of anacharis, cabomba, and other water plants that are used in fish aquariums. These are very good for turtles, too, and you can plant them in gravel in the bottom of the water in your turtle tank. The animals will enjoy nibbling on them when they are hungry.

Often turtles eat meat and insects when they are very young. These form their main diet at that time. Slowly, however, they will eat more and more leafy vegetables, fruits and berries, until, when they are fully grown, they are almost entirely vegetarian.

Land turtles may be a bit easier to keep than water or semi-aquatic ones. The prettiest of the land turtles, we think, is the wood turtle. While we class this turtle as a land turtle, it is really a semi-aquatic species. However, it lives so well on land and lives so long in the house, that you really do not have to give it a semi-aquatic home for it to be contented and healthy. This one has a dark brown shell that is beautifully marked in a regular pattern of designs. The plastron has dark patches of color around the edges. The center is plain. Male wood turtles have much stronger and more curved front claws than the females. The plastron of a male wood turtle is slightly hollow. The plastron of a female is slightly rounded out.

Wood turtles make wonderful pets. They live a long time and

Wood Turtle. *Clemmys insculpta.* The carapace of wood turtles is very beautifully sculptured with shell-like markings.

become very tame. They eat almost anything that you eat—raw fruits, vegetables, lean beef, fish, chicken. They should also have some muscle meat like chicken or beef heart. Liver is good for them, too. Once a week or so you could put a drop of cod-liver oil on the bits of meat you feed to your wood turtle. In fact, this would be excellent for any of your turtle pets.

Another land turtle is the box turtle. There are several species of box turtles in this country. The common box turtle is found in the eastern part of the United States. Blanding's turtle is found in the northeastern part of the country. The three-toed box turtle comes from the southeastern part of the United States and around the Gulf of Mexico. The ornate box turtle is the one found in the central and western part of the country. There are a few other species of box turtles, but some of them are just subspecies.

Most box turtles like the same kind of habitat. A woods aquarium should be set up for them. They like dead leaves, a small log, and a few rocks. The leaves can be kept slightly damp but not wet. You can have some dirt on the bottom of the tank, and a dish of water that is large enough and deep enough for your pet to get into. Some box turtles like to eat with their heads under water.

Male box turtles generally have lower carapaces than the females. There is a fairly deep hollow at the rear of the plastron of the males. The eyes of the males are brightly colored pink or red. The eyes of the females are darker and sometimes are gray or brown or very dark red.

If you keep your box turtles outdoors, you must give them a place in which they can dig down into the dirt when they hibernate during the winter. If possible, they should have not less than eighteen inches of dirt to dig into. If there is less than this, after they have dug down for the winter, you can pile hay on top of their burrow to help keep them from freezing.

CHAPTER TWENTY-FIVE

The Best Kinds of Lizards to Keep as Pets

There are so many different kinds of lizards in the world that I could write a book or two on them alone. Many lizards make good pets, yet some cannot be kept in captivity. They will not live. Some of them grow so big that it would be very difficult to keep them in a cage in the house. Of all the reptiles, I believe the most brilliant and beautifully colored ones are found among the lizards. They have metallic colors: blue, green, gold, red—all the colors of the rainbow. There are several that make good pets, and that you can obtain easily, either by catching them yourself or buying them in pet stores.

The most common lizard found in pet stores is the little green anole, which is often called a chameleon.

The only way an anole can drink is by licking drops of dew off the leaves of plants. In their natural habitat, the animals drink in the early morning or the late evening, when the dew forms on the grasses and plants. In captivity the only way they can get their water is by having a plant growing in their cage and having water sprinkled on the leaves of the plant two or three times each day. It is an easy matter to put a small potted philodendron in the cage for your anole, and to sprinkle it in the morning and evening.

Anoles eat small mealworms, flies, fruit flies, spiders, small grasshoppers, and many kinds of insects. Their cage should be

American "chameleon." *Anolis carolinensis.* These little lizards will get to be tame if you handle them often and feed them properly. You can wear them on your shirt after they get to know you.

kept warm. The ideal temperature is between 80 and 85 degrees. The temperature can drop a little at night but remember that the nights where these animals come from are quite warm. The atmosphere should be kept humid in their cage. The easiest way to do this is to cover the bottom of the cage with coarse aquarium gravel that has been washed until the water runs clear. Then, when you put the gravel in the cage, wet it with a cup of water. As the gravel dries out, you can add a little water. You do not want to have the water standing in the bottom of the cage, just damp gravel.

In most parts of this country, swifts are very common. These are called by a lot of different names in different areas. Fence lizards, fence swifts, rail lizards, blue-bellied swifts are a few of the names given to these interesting animals. They have rough scales and the bellies of the males have two dark blue patches on the sides. As their name implies, they are swift. It is almost impossible to get close enough to catch them. As soon as they see you they jump away.

About the easiest way to catch them is with a long slender pole and a noose made of heavy sewing thread. Remember that a fence lizard will bite when it is first caught, so do not be so surprised that you let it go when it nips your finger. The bite is nothing. It rarely even breaks the skin. Actually it is a little pinch rather than a real bite. After a fence lizard has been kept for a while, it will become tame enough for you to handle and play with. Remember its name, though. It is a swift! At any time, unless you have a secure hold on it, it can dart away so fast that it is gone before you know it. It can easily run up a wall, up a tree or anything at all.

Blue-bellied swifts eat all kinds of insects. They love moths and butterflies, and will eat mealworms, grasshoppers, crickets, different kinds of beetles, and many other insects. They can drink water out of a water dish, lapping it with their tongues. Some dirt and leaves should be on the bottom of the cage, with a rock or two to hide under, and a log to sit on in the sun. They love to stretch out on a fence rail and sun themselves. The temperature should be warm in the daytime. About 80 is fine; although they will be comfortable at 75 degrees, it should not be much less than that except at night.

In the western and southwestern parts of this country there is a very good-looking reptile called the alligator lizard. This lizard is reddish brown, and its skin is like the skin of an alligator. There are black and white markings down the back and sides. Its diet consists of mealworms and almost all other insects, and it will also eat small lizards of other species. The cage for the alligator lizard should have some sand and leaves in the bottom, and a log or a couple of rocks to climb up on. The cage should be very warm with a lot of sun, but there must be some shady place where the lizard can go to cool off if he gets too hot. The alligator lizard drinks out of a water dish.

Also from the South and West in the desert country come the little fat roly-poly lizards that are incorrectly called "horned toads." These animals are not toads but true lizards. They must be kept hot in order to live and remain healthy. They do well at temperatures between 80 and 90 degrees. They are "dewdrop drinkers," which means that you should have a plant or a few leaves to sprinkle water on for them to drink. They will some-times lap at a water dish, but they must have sprinkled water to do really well.

Their favorite food is ants, and they will eat hundreds of ants at a meal. In the summer, you can take them outside in a porta-ble cage without a bottom, and put them over an anthill. If it is warm enough, your pet will sit at the opening of the anthill gobbling up the ants as fast as they come out of the ground. You must be certain, though, that the cage is secure and tight all around the bottom, or the pet will crawl out and escape. They can get out of a very narrow space, because their bodies are so flat.

When horned lizards are frightened, they react in a very odd way. They squirt a few drops of blood out of the corners of their eyes. Nothing much is known about this defense action, but we think that the blood stings the eyes of its enemies.

The cages for these animals should have not less than three inches of sand in the bottom, a rock or two to climb on, and some kind of plant to sprinkle with water, as well as a small water dish. Besides ants, horned lizards will eat mealworms, spiders, moths, crickets, and other insects.

From the desert, also, come the collared lizards. These are beautifully colored in bright green, bright blue, with a black and white collar around the neck. They do not live too well in captivity. One reason is that the cage is usually not kept warm enough. It must be hot! The best temperature is not less than 80 degrees and up to 90 or even 95 degrees. Since collared lizards are fast runners, they should have a long cage in which they can run when they want to. When a collared lizard gets up speed, he runs on his hind feet with his body upright. Collared lizards, like most desert animals, drink dewdrops from plants and rocks in the early morning and at night. They eat all kinds of insects and, if you are not careful, your fingers as well. They are particularly fond of grasshoppers, katydids, locusts, and crickets.

A very interesting lizard, native to this country, is the "glass snake." It is really a legless lizard. It has eyelids and can close them, and has ears—two things that a snake does not have. The fact that it is quite large—"glass snakes" reach a length of almost four feet—and has no legs makes some people think it is a snake. Usually "glass snakes" are not good pets, because they frighten so easily that they cannot be handled at all.

The "glass snakes" eat all kinds of insects, but seem to like spiders best of all. They also drink water out of a dish. They are burrowing animals, and should have three or four inches of clean, slightly damp earth in their cages. They do not climb, so a branch is not necessary, but a couple of rocks for them to bask on are appreciated.

Green lacertas are sometimes offered for sale in pet stores, and these are among the gentlest and most beautiful of the lizards. They are easily identified as to sex. The males are solid yellow-green, and the females, although they are the same color, have two whitish stripes bordered with black patches running down the back. These beautiful lizards come from Europe and can adapt to our climate quite well, although they should never be allowed to get very cold. They eat mealworms, moths, grasshoppers, crickets, and many other kinds of insects and they drink water out of a dish.

The proper cage for lacertas should have clean dirt mixed with equal amounts of clean sand or aquarium gravel in the bottom—about three inches deep. Pieces of moss, a slab of bark, and a small log can be set on top of the soil. A few rocks should be piled to make a small hill with crevices between large enough for the lizards to crawl into and hide. The soil should be kept just slightly moist, but not wet. Dead leaves from the woods can be put on top of the dirt not covered by the moss, bark, log, and rocks. The pets will come out and bask in the sun on top of the log or rocks, going under the bark or rocks at night.

They are very calm animals, and not at all hysterical as some of the lizards are. The best temperature for lacertas is about 75 to 85 degrees, and must not drop to less than 50 degrees at night.

Probably the easiest of all lizards to keep as pets are the beautiful common iguanas from Central and South America. These are easy to keep because they are strictly vegetarian. This means

Common Iguana. *Iguana iguana.* These handsome animals live very well in captivity, and, indeed, make one of the very best reptile pets.

that they eat fruits, vegetables, and melons, all of which are available throughout the winter. Iguanas must be kept warm. They come from very humid, hot countries, where the daytime temperature often goes well above 100 degrees. From 80 to 90 degrees is fine for your pets. It can drop as low as 55 or 60 at night, provided you can warm them up in the morning. If it is cold in your house, then you should keep an electric light bulb in a reflector on top of the cage to supply them with warmth.

Iguanas drink from a water dish, but they love assorted plants in their cage. They nibble on a leaf or two during the day. They should be fed chopped vegetables such as lettuce, grated carrots, raw peas or raw string beans, and chopped bits of almost any fruit. They love pears, apples, peaches, cherries, bananas, and many more. Chopped raw spinach leaves are eaten readily. In the winter months when fresh fruit may be hard to find, canned fruit cocktail is acceptable. Drain it well before giving it to your pets, and chop the pieces smaller than they are in the can.

Until the iguanas are a year old, you should put a few drops of cod-liver oil on their lettuce leaves every other day, or at least twice a week. A few small mealworms should also be dropped in with their vegetable food. They will stop eating mealworms after a time, but they seem to need some when they are young. Iguanas do not chew their food, but swallow it whole. This is why you should chop everything fine for them. If you put a few different kinds of plants in small pots in their cage, you will find them nibbling on one or more. As soon as you see which ones they prefer to eat, you can make sure that one of this kind of plant is always in the cage.

Iguanas have very long tails—as long as the head and body together, sometimes even longer. They need a large cage to live in. Also, they must have something in the cage to climb up on, such as branches. Unless they can climb, they will not remain healthy, and will soon die.

The real aristocrat of the lizard family is the true Old World chameleon. There are many species of this animal. Chameleons have all kinds of unusual head shapes. Some of them have a shield that runs from the back of the head over the neck. Others have heads that are squared off with a hollow on the top like a basin. Still others have one horn on the top of the head, or two horns, or three, and one even has four horns!

African chameleons are not very often available in pet stores, but sometimes the larger stores carry them. Nothing is quite like these strange, strange creatures. They move so slowly that you want to reach in and give them a boost with your finger.

Their feet are like pairs of tongs. Of course, their feet are perfect for their way of life. Chameleons are completely *arboreal*. This means that they live only in trees and shrubs, and practically never live on the ground. They cannot walk too well on the ground, and have a very funny waddle when they try. It is a different story in the trees, however. There their tong feet grasp around slender twigs and branches, giving them a very secure hold.

Their tails are prehensile. They can grasp with their tails just as well as some monkeys. Often you will see one walk out to the very tip of a branch, then let go with both front feet and extend its body away out in the air. Behind it, it hangs on with its hind feet and a curl of its tail. Slowly it extends itself out—until you think it is going to fall down, but the tail just straightens out more and more to allow it to stretch. Suddenly POP! its tongue shoots out for a distance equal to the entire length of the body and snaps up a fly or other insect. The tongue moves so fast that you can barely see it.

The eyes of these marvelous animals are mounted in little turrets like the guns of fighter planes. Each eye can move independently of the other. The animal can look forward with the right eye and rearward with the left eye at the same time, or up with one eye and down with the other.

One great difficulty in keeping African chameleons is the fact that they must be kept hot—not less than 80 degrees and 90 degrees is better. At night the temperature can drop to 60 degrees or so. During the winter, feeding them is a big problem, since they feed only on living insects and do not like mealworms very much. Once in a while a specimen will eat mealworms, but not usually.

Chameleons are dewdrop drinkers. They *must* have lots of water, and the only way they can get it is by licking drops off plant leaves. Keep a wide-leafed plant in the cage and sprinkle the leaves with water until they drip, at least twice every day. Four times would be better and six times best.

PART IV

Birds as Pets

INTRODUCTION

Throughout the world, the keeping of animal pets has reached proportions so great that it would be impossible to estimate the number of persons involved. In the United States alone, the pet business takes in many hundreds of millions of dollars each year. In 1971 alone, the amount of money spent on veterinarian and health service for pets in the United States ran nearly one half billion dollars. This does not include the initial cost of the animal or bird, nor the cages, equipment, food, and other necessities that go with the keeping of a pet.

At least since the time of the Egyptian Pharaohs, men have kept animals in captivity, either for sport and fighting, or as pets. Birds have always been popular, especially in China and the other oriental countries. In the early days, Canaries were unknown, since they originally came from the Canary Islands and the Azores. They were not discovered until around the 1300s by Portuguese explorers.

Most of the birds kept in captivity were Parrots or parrotlike species, and it was early discovered that these birds were capable of mimicking human speech. Training them, however, was done differently than it is today. The birds were hit over the head with an iron rod to make them speak! How many succumbed to fractured skulls before they could learn a word or two is not known, but certainly those captive creatures must have led miserable existences for the most part.

Birds were generally available only to royal families or to the very wealthy, since the only specimens finding their way to civilized shores were brought in by sailors returning from a lengthy voyage to the exotic places where the birds lived. A systemized method of breeding was unknown in the beginning.

Later, much interbreeding and crossbreeding of birds, were done in foreign countries. Now we have cage birds that in no way resemble the original stock. Fancy feathers, colors, body shape, and song have been bred into the various species.

Until recently, most birds sold in this country were imported from other lands. The raising of birds in captivity has reached the point where most of the specimens sold in pet stores are bred rather than caught in the wild. I am speaking mainly of the small birds like Canaries and Budgerigars, although the latter are still wild-caught in great numbers.

Birds—some birds—live a long time if they are cared for properly. Fifteen years is not at all unusual for a canary, for example. But they must be cared for. They cannot be neglected, so before you undertake to keep a pet bird, you should be made aware of the fact that keeping a bird does not mean buying it, popping it into a cage, and then paying some attention to it *if* you happen to think about it. Birds require daily care, and unless you are prepared to give them this, it would be better if you did not get one, since it would only lead a short and miserable life.

Birds are not really alarming carriers of disease, but they *are* responsible for two. *Psittacosis,* or "parrot fever," has been known for some time. A few years ago an epidemic was forecast in this country. Importation quarantine and subsequent health measures enforced by the government soon checked the advance of the disease to the point where it is no longer a threat to man to keep the hook-bills of the parrot family.

Now, however, comes along another ailment called *Reniket,* or Exotic Newcastle Disease. This is a virus which, being carried by wild birds, attacks domestic fowl, chickens, ducks, and the like, and is almost invariably fatal.

In order to protect our fowl farming, a law has been passed forbidding the importation of birds into the United States from all other countries. As a consequence, only birds bred in the United States are now available to persons wishing to buy them. For this reason, considerable attention will be paid to breeding in this book, since some readers may wish to try their hand at this very interesting and profitable hobby. Good luck.

CHAPTER TWENTY-SIX

A Little About Birds

Birds come in two kinds—*Altricial* and *Precocial*. Precocial comes from the same stem as the word precocious, meaning developed earlier than usual. And that is just what precocial birds are—developed. They are hatched almost completely feathered out and within minutes, or at most an hour or so, are able to run about and feed themselves, and they are not dependent upon their mothers for anything other than possibly warmth at night.

Altricial birds are hatched naked and helpless, with their eyes closed and their mouths open yelling for food. They are completely dependent upon their mothers for everything. The mother has to feed them. She has to keep them clean. Even when they finally feather out to the point where they can begin to fly, the mother must teach them to do this!

You were an altricial baby. When humans are born, they are naked and helpless. While their eyes may be open, they cannot see anything out of them. They must be fed, clothed, cleaned, and pampered. Deer, elephants, and most other animals are more precocial, since, wobbly at first, they learn within a matter of hours to stand alone, then run about following their mothers. They nurse for a time but eat other food as well.

Birds are, we believe, descended from the reptiles. This is not to say that birds replaced the reptiles, but they were an offshoot of reptile development. Certain characteristics indicate this.

Birds, however, are unique in one thing—they have feathers, something no other living creature has.

Birds are believed to have started their development from reptile stock somewhere around 150 million years ago. Mammals had already evolved, so this makes birds the youngest group of animals.

There are about 8,600 species of birds now living, and scientists think there may be a hundred or more species yet to be discovered. Birds live in every climate and under every condition. From the frozen wasteland of the antarctic to the searing desert, birds, well adapted to their environment, are to be found. The foods birds eat are as varied as the birds themselves. Birds are fish eaters, vegetarians, carrion feeders, reptile eaters, insect eaters. Some eat only fruits, others only seeds. And there are some who combine several different things in their diets.

Birds are divided into 27 different orders. These are further divided into 155 families, each family containing from one to thousands of species. While several orders will be discussed in this book, we are mainly interested in just two—*Psittaciformes* and *Passeriformes*. To the former order belong the hook-billed birds like Parrots, Budgerigars, Parakeets, Lovebirds, Macaws, and several others. To the passeriformes belong the perching birds such as Canaries, Finches, Larks, Thrushes, and many, many other species. This huge order contains 55 families and over 5,000 species. Actually, Canaries are a kind of Finch, but more of this classification in the proper chapters.

The passerine or perching birds are the most highly evolved of all birds and are the most recent development in the bird world. Passerines first appeared about 50 or 60 million years ago. Other orders go back 120 million years or even farther. Perhaps the most intelligent of the passerines are the Jays and Crows, including the Starlings. However, some of the Finches

A Sulphur-crested Cockatoo. They are usually very tame and affectionate and can learn to talk.

are also very intelligent. One Finch—Darwin's Finch of the Galápagos Islands—even uses a tool in order to capture its prey, succulent grubs in holes in trees. This Finch holds a long, sharp thorn in its bill, using it to probe for the grubs, then, when one is discovered, pierces it and hauls it out of its hole on the end of the thorn.

Some of the passerines are marvelous architects as well, building most complicated nests as a deterrent to predation. The Weaverbird is one of these and the nests are hung on the outer ends of branches. Whole colonies of birds build their nests in the same tree.

The construction of the body of a bird is rather wonderful. Everything is designed for lightness and for strength. The feathers are particularly interesting, having great structural strength as well as being practically weightless. The stiff quill is rigid for support at the base, tapering to a flexible tip at the outer end. From the quill, alternate barbs extend from each side. These barbs, in turn, are equipped with a series of hooks on their outer sides and filaments along the inner sides.

When the feather is preened into sleek smoothness, all the hooks are caught over the filaments, making a web, or flight surface, with which the bird can push against the air. Feathers can become disheveled either by getting caught in branches, in fighting with another bird, or by being caught by man. The bird is usually able to preen the feather back to its normal sleekness with its bill, using oil from a gland near the tail. This oil is also important in making the outer feathers waterproof in order to shed rain when the bird is caught without adequate shelter.

The contour feathers are the ones that make the outer shape of the bird, form the wings, and support it in flight. Under these are downy feathers called *Filoplumes*. Filoplumes are hairlike, and you may have seen them many times if you cook freshly killed chickens in your family. The "hairs" that must be singed from the chicken, prior to cooking, are filoplumes.

Many birds also have actual down feathers on their bodies. The down feathers are for insulation. Perhaps you have observed birds in cold weather, sitting on a branch, huddled to-gether, their feathers all puffed up until the bird resembles a ball. This is because the down feathers are held erect to supply thicker insulation in order to combat the cold. It is like putting on an overcoat, since, by the erection of the down, the bird places a much thicker layer of feathers between its body and the elements.

Because feathers are subject to damage, they must be re-placed. Once a year the bird is able to change its coat of feathers completely by the process known as molting. Some birds un-dergo an additional partial molt, but all birds molt completely once a year. As a rule they do not lose all their feathers at the same time. This would tend to eliminate the bird, since it would be able neither to fly nor to forage for food, to say nothing of the inability to escape its predators.

In most birds the molt is a symmetrical affair. A flight feather from one wing falls off, and its opposite number on the other wing follows at the same time. This leaves the bird with a hole in its flight feathers, but still able too fly and maneuver sufficiently well to survive. When these feathers have been renewed by replacement growth, another pair falls off. The growth of replacement feathers is rather rapid, and in a compar-atively short time the molting process is completed, six weeks being the average.

Sometimes an artificial molt may attack birds, especially those kept in cages in the house. Too warm a location is not healthy for them. Birds can tolerate more coolness than you may think—it is drafts that quickly kill them. Even Canaries have been known to be bred and raised in outdoor temperatures through the winters, but they were protected completely from drafts and windy gusts.

The bones of a bird are another marvel of engineering. Since the creature must maneuver in the air, sometimes attaining great forward speed, its bone structure must be both light and strong. The skeleton of a small bird is practically weightless. The bones are hollow and the walls are thin. The backbone is fused for rigid strength instead of being flexible as your backbone is. The rib cage is fused together as two broad plates, and there is a keel on the breastbone to provide anchorage for the relatively enormous flight muscles. These may equal 25 per cent of the total weight of the bird, or even more in some species.

Compared to the birds, man is very nearly blind. Some birds, especially the birds of prey, have vision eight times keener than man's. Because the eyes of birds are set at the sides of their heads instead of on an equal plane in front—Owls being an exception—they have far better vision than does man. Birds have no trouble seeing behind them as well as to the sides and straight ahead. As a matter of fact, their monocular side vision usually overlaps both to the front and to the rear into binocular vision such as we have. At the worst, there is only a narrow band of blindness to the rear for most birds.

A Woodcock, with its eyes set higher on the head, and farther back than most birds, has binocular vision both to the front and to the rear. In this way it can watch for predators and attacks from behind while it is probing for worms with its long bill buried in the ground.

An Owl's eyes are very nearly immobile in its head, not revolving as are the eyeballs of a man. But it has the ability to turn its head in a complete half circle, to look straight to the rear or any angle in between. When an Owl sights in on its prey, it performs a curious sideways bobbing motion, to fix the range of the victim for the pounce.

The bills, or beaks, of birds are nearly as varied as the birds themselves. They are ideally suited to the needs of that particular species. Raptors—Hawks, Owls, Eagles, etc.—have hooked bills designed for tearing chunks from a carcass and for ripping off the hides of their animal prey. The large, strong, hooked bills of scavengers such as Vultures and Condors are just what are needed for ripping up carrion and rotting meat. The short, sharp bills of small perching birds cannot be bettered as seed-cracking devices.

Perhaps the most marvelous parts of perching birds are the feet. True, this part of the animal is not very pretty to look at. The legs and feet of most birds are covered with scales, pointing to their reptilian ancestry. They have long curving claws which, in the case of birds kept in cages, must be periodically clipped. The wonderful part of a perching bird's foot is the musculature.

Perching birds perch on twigs and branches. They perform most of their life processes in this position, including sleep. Normally an animal relaxes when it sleeps, but if you ever tried to perch on a branch smaller than your feet, then tried to fall asleep, you would shortly find yourself flat on the ground beneath the tree. Not so perching birds. Their leg muscles are connected with those of the toes in such a manner that when the bird alights on a branch and squats slightly, bending its legs, the muscles pull the toes into a fist, clamping the branch tightly. As the bird relaxes, it squats lower and lower, placing more and more tightening effect on its toe muscles until not even a hard wind could blow it off the branch. In this way it is able to sleep safely and soundly, with no fear of falling off its perch.

Many of the small birds will breed in cages, and much work has been done by man to develop new strains, new colors, and improve the songs of such birds as Canaries and Finches. Several kinds of Canaries we see often in the pet stores are completely domestic breeds developed from the wild stock and unknown in nature. The wild Canaries only slightly resemble the birds we know. They are darker, mottled, greenish, and brownish. Their song, while sweet and clear, in no way is as beautiful as the song of a bred Roller or Chopper Canary.

Some of the other Finches will also breed in cages, and these are very popular cage pets. Budgerigars, Cockatiels, Parakeets, and Parrots can be bred—some easily, some with difficulty. Mynah birds have been known to breed in captivity, but only very rarely and not with much success. All Mynah birds in the country are imported, and now, with the new law that forbids bird importation in effect, it is doubtful if any more will be available. A fortune is waiting for the person who discovers how to breed them. One of the difficulties of breeding Mynahs is telling the sexes apart. Both the males and females look alike, and there is no sure and infallible way to distinguish them.

Some of the cage birds live for a long time. Canaries have been known to live for twenty-four years and longer. Parrots are the patriarchs of the cage birds, living for fifty years and sometimes much longer. This is a bird that you can get when you are very young, and grow up with. Peacocks can live over one hundred years.

CHAPTER TWENTY-SEVEN

How to Care for Birds

Naturally, each species of bird requires some special kind of care and treatment, but all birds need much the same method of care for their health and welfare. Common sense is probably the most important ingredient for the successful keeping of bird pets. Unfortunately, this is not an item you can purchase in the pet shop where you go to buy your bird. You will have to work out commonsense methods for yourself, with the help of books on the subject. We will try to tell you here some of the ways to make the chore of birdkeeping less troublesome.

Because keeping a bird *is* trouble. It is a responsibility that you must be prepared to meet fully even before the pet arrives in your house. You must be made aware of the fact that a bird cannot be neglected, even for a day, without suffering some ill effects which, if the neglect continues for any length of time, will end with the poor creature on the bottom of the cage, feet in the air.

Food is the most important single item in the life of every living thing on this earth, from man to plants. And birds are no exception. Rather, they require more attention to their diet than do many other kinds of animals—dogs, cats, reptiles, and so on.

Also, a dog, cat, or reptile can be made to go without proper food and even water for long periods of time, while a bird cannot survive such treatment. When a person says his friend "eats like a bird," intending to convey the message that the friend is a very light eater, he could not be further from the truth.

Birds eat constantly, throughout their waking hours, and a supply of clean, fresh food must be in front of them at all times. Also, not having a digestive system like man, most birds require some kind of assistance in order to grind up their food. This assistance takes the form of fine gravel, or sand, which is clean and sharp. The birds eat some of this material which aids in grinding up the seeds and other foods they eat.

The gravel which is kept at all times on the bottoms of the cages is not the only gravel which should be supplied to the birds. During the course of the day, this gravel will be contaminated by the bird's own droppings, and the creature may be seen picking in among the grains. It is far better, from the point of view of health and cleanliness, to provide additional grit in a small cup hung from the bars of the cage.

In such a cup may be kept a mixture of two parts clean gravel, four parts crushed oystershell, and one part bird charcoal. When the cup becomes soiled from droppings, it may be emptied and refilled with fresh mixture. Using this mixture the bird is assured of sharp gravel to fill his crop in order to help digest food, oystershell to keep him supplied with calcium, and charcoal to keep the crop from souring.

Clean water is also essential, and this should be placed in cups so designed to protect the water from droppings when the bird sits on a perch above the cup. Finches and Canaries will use a cup attached to the outside of the cage, with a hole leading to the reservoir. The same style cup can be used for seed as well as for water.

Budgerigars do not use this kind of cup to advantage, because these little members of the Parrot family dislike putting their heads through a hole. However, once you have gotten the Budgerigar accustomed to feeding from an outside cup, they seem to have no fear of the opening and will use it as readily as other species of birds. This is especially true of the newer style cups which are square instead of round and have a large square opening in place of the small round opening of the old-style cups.

If the cage you use does not have accommodations for the seed and water cups on the outside, then you should use "hooded" cups inside the cage, placing them in a position protected from the droppings from a perch overhead.

It is useless to try to give a bird anything in a cup placed on the floor of its cage. Within minutes after placing the cup inside, the bird will have overturned it, spilling the contents all over the floor.

The water used for drinking should preferably be boiled for fifteen minutes or so, then put into a clean container to cool to room temperature. If you have only one or two birds, a quart of boiled water will last you up to two weeks, so it is not a great chore to keep a supply on hand.

Water used for bathing purposes need not be boiled, necessarily, but, since there is the possibility of the bird drinking some of its bath water, it is a good idea to use the same treatment that you do for drinking water. It, too, should néver be given the bird to bathe in until it is at room temperature. Birdbaths which are fastened to the outsides of cages are available, and these are the best kinds to use.

Attention should be paid to the kind of perches in the cage. Plain wooden perches are fine, as are the telescoping plastic ones, ridged for stability. You should never use perches made with a sanded surface. The idea that they afford more traction for the bird's foot is wrong. The bird does not need such traction because of the clamping action of its toes. Then too, the sanded surface abrades the feet of the birds to the point, at times, of

An indoor bird room. The baths fit over the doors of the cages.

even making them bleed. This not only injures the bird but leaves it wide open for infections which could very easily kill it in a very short while.

The same is true of the bottom of the cage. Sandpaper sheets are sold for placing on the bottom, and these have the same danger as a sanded perch. The very best thing to use on the bottom of cages is newspaper. This is also the easiest to maintain. A pad of several sheets of newspaper is torn to fit snugly into the tray.

A *small* handful of clean gravel is sprinkled on the paper. Each day, you merely pull out the tray, remove the top sheet of paper and the gravel, shake out any seed and gravel from around the edges of the remaining sheets, replace the handful of gravel with clean material, and return the tray to the cage.

This operation can be done in less time than it took you to read the instructions. And your pet is set for the entire day. The cleaning is best done in the morning, but it could be done in the evening, too, I suppose. The only thing about evening cleanup is that the birds go to sleep as soon as the sun goes down, and you may disturb them.

For birds like Finches, Canaries, and related birds, toys and gadgets in the cage are only a bothersome clutter, both for you and for the bird. A swing suspended from the top of the cage is all that is necessary, and sometimes a bird will not even use this. The more free room for jumping from perch to perch, with a cage big enough to permit a flutter or short flight, the better your bird will get along. They should have some exercise. And, if you intend to breed them, they *must* have room enough to exercise.

Birds of the hooked-bill group—Parrots, Budgerigars, and others—like a toy or two. The only two I would recommend are a mirror for them to admire themselves in—and, indeed, a Budgerigar can spend hours every day preening himself in front of his mirror—and a small bell, hung from the side or the top of the cage. Possibly, for these inquisitive little pets, a ladder if they are in a large cage and the ladder does not take up too much jumping or flying room. They seem to enjoy hopping up and down the rungs.

Budgerigars should have larger cages than Canaries or Finches, since not only do they jump and fly, they climb adroitly. It is an odd sight to see a parrotlike bird—almost all the family do it—walking along the bars of its cage upside down. Tall cages are fine for Budgies, while wide cages are better for Canaries. Cages which are large in all dimensions are necessary for the larger birds like Cockatiels, Cockatoos, Macaws, and the big Parrots. Also, it is a good idea to make certain there is a positive latching device on cage doors used for the parrot-family birds, since you will be amazed to see that in a very short time they have mastered the method of opening their door, and you will find them flying about the house.

There are several ways of protecting your birds in their cages. Remember that a bird in a cage is captive, and it cannot go anywhere except in the relatively small area of the inside of the bars. So use your common sense. Sunlight is an important factor in keeping birds in cages. Direct sunlight can quickly kill a bird if it has no way of getting out of the glare.

Birds can help themselves keep warm a little by fluffing up their feathers to afford more insulation, but they have no way of cooling themselves off when subjected to too much heat. Hence, a bird kept in direct sunlight can suffer sunstroke or heat prostration and, if not removed immediately from the light, will die. Even if it is taken to a shady place, the experience cannot but be harmful and debilitating for the poor creature.

The same thing is true of wind. Birds will get pneumonia from a draft and in a very short time you will have a dead bird on your hands. This is the reason people cover bird cages at night. This is not necessary if you take precaution to see that they are maintained in a draft-free location. Avoid sudden changes. For example, don't open a door in cold weather when the cage is situated where the blast of incoming air will blow right on it. Your birds will not last very long under these conditions.

Most small birds are hardier than you may suppose and can

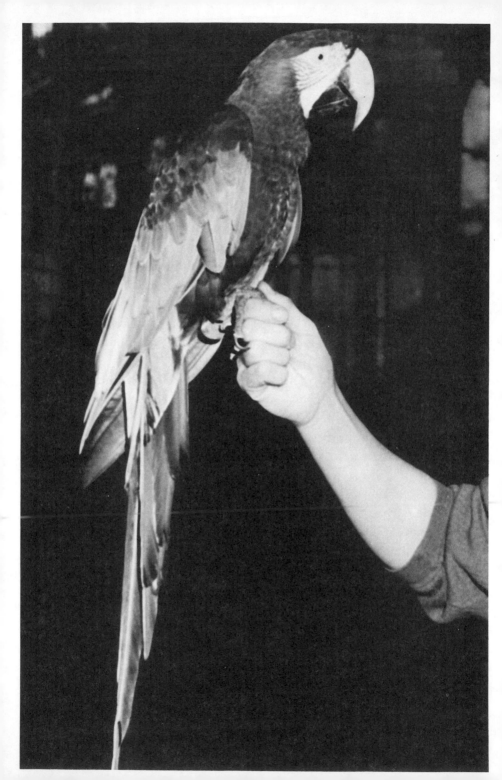

be bred in outdoor cages right through the winter in locations not subjected to prolonged subzero weather. One very large bird farm keeps thousands of birds—Canaries, Finches, Budgerigars, and other exotic specimens—in very large walk-in cages, covered with sheet plastic, throughout the entire year. It freezes many nights in winter but warms up a bit during the day, at least above freezing.

Birds purchased from such a dealer can be kept outdoors, but the average bird purchased from a pet store would be dead by morning if it were subjected to these conditions. You cannot take a bird, bred and kept indoors for its entire life, and expect it to survive when placed under "wild" bird conditions. True, the birds bred outdoors are far hardier than those bred indoors, but unless you are interested only in breeding for sale, your pet should be protected from the elements.

In warm climates, a very large outdoor cage is a wonderful break for the birds in summer. They can be turned out there to fly and exercise their wings to their heart's content.

Birds must be kept clean, and they are very willing to perform this service for themselves if they are provided with the proper facilities. A daily bath is very beneficial for Canaries, Budgies, and Finches. Most birds will use a birdbath fastened to the outside of their cage and filled with cool water. Some will not, but will bathe in a shallow dish placed in their cage.

If your bird will not use the bath, sprinkle some water on it and the chances are it will then go into the bath. Sometimes they do not recognize what the bath is for, and they are reluctant to enter what may seem to be a trap.

There may be a mess for you when the bird shakes itself dry,

A Scarlet Macaw, sometimes called a Red and Yellow Macaw, is nearly three feet long.

but this is merely one of the things to cope with when you keep a bird. If you are unwilling to do the things necessary for the welfare of your captive, then it is better not to have one.

Messes made by bathing birds can be dealt with, perhaps, by placing the cage with the dish for bathing in the bathtub, closing the shower doors or curtains, and leaving it there until the bird has finished splashing and shaking. Then the cage may be returned to its regular location after drying the bars and changing the paper in the bottom. Morning is the best time to let your birds bathe, since morning is the best time to clean the cage, change the food and water, replace the paper in the bottom, and perform any other chores of maintenance needed. Give the bath water first, then the cleanup you do will perform all servicing at the same time.

Different kinds of birds require different kinds of cages. For Canaries, the cage should be not less than 15″ in one dimension, and the higher it is, the better, since this will give the birds room for short flights. Finches are smaller than Canaries and require cages with bars spaced closer together—not more than ⅜″ spacing, or the little Finches will easily slip through. Some Finches, notably Zebra Finches, are smaller than a Wren. They are really tiny, and a standard Canary cage is entirely unsuitable for them.

Budgies will live in Canary cages, but they should have as large a cage as you can get, and no more than one pair kept in one large cage—that is, one male and one female. Two males should not be kept in the same cage unless you want feathers flying about the room, finally resulting in a dead bird. They fight without provocation. Cages for Budgerigars should have horizontal bars, at least on two sides, because Budgies use their bills for climbing, and the horizontal bars act as a ladder, making it easy to get around in the cage. Vertical bars would only

An indoor flight cage. Note the slant of the perch racks to eliminate droppings falling on the birds below.

let the birds slip and slide to the bottom, and there is the good possibility of their toes catching in the wires and being injured.

For Cockatiels a very large cage is needed. One of the large Parrot cages is fine, and the birds should be kept separately unless you are breeding them. The same kind of large cage is good for a Parrot or a Mynah bird.

Attention should be given to the positioning of the perches. First of all, they should never be placed so the vent of the bird overhangs either the food or the water dishes. Birds, as explained earlier, eat almost constantly. They also make droppings almost constantly, and these should be kept out of their food and water dishes. Next, depending on the kind of bird you are getting, the perches must be placed far enough from the sides of the cages to permit room for the tail feathers to hang free. A perch placed close to the bars of the cage will result in broken and ragged tail feathers, and your bird will always look ruffled and unkempt.

Cages which are to be hung from a bracket, or in a floor stand, in one of the lived-in rooms of the house should have a seed guard of some kind attached to them. These are in the shape of plastic strips wrapped around the cage, or as plastic aprons slipped into guard holders made on the cage itself. The seed and water cups are kept below the top edge of the seed guards, and thus most of the seed scattered by the bird will fall within the cage rather than being shot all over the floor of the room, making a mess that will soon dampen the ardor of a bird lover. Such seed guards will also help keep down the water splashed about when the bird bathes in a dish.

Often a Canary can be tamed enough so that it will sit on your finger, or perch on your head or shoulder, riding about the room as you move. Budgerigars, too, are easily finger trained as well as trained to talk. These birds can be let out of their cages for a time each day, or several times a week, and the freedom and extended flight room is very beneficial to them. It is not a good policy, however, to release birds which are not very tame, since the hysteria generated when attempting to return them to their cage is worse for them than the extra freedom is beneficial. Some birds, when tamed enough to be released, will fly about for a time, then, of their own accord, return to their cage for the night. If you have such a pet, thank your lucky stars, and enjoy it.

The claws of perching birds should be clipped about twice a

year. They grow long and curved, and sometimes will grow so much as to prohibit the bird from grasping the perch. Regular nail clippers can be used for this service, but you must be careful to avoid injuring the creature.

Each claw in a bird's foot has a vein running part way down it. Most of the time this vein is clearly visible, and the claw is clipped just above the vein. If the vein is severed, it hurts the bird and the foot bleeds—sometimes for a long time. A bird may actually bleed to death through the careless cutting of its claws, although this is not something you need constantly fear. Just make sure you clip off the outer ends of the claws, and you— and the bird—will be all right.

When clipping, the bird should be held completely enclosed in the hand with its wings in a natural folded position, close to the body. The leg is held between two fingers, close to the foot, and care is needed to make sure the bird does not jerk its foot at the instant you clip, or you may clip off a toe! On the other hand, a bird's leg—that of a small cage bird, at least—is a very fragile object, and a rough or hard grip on it can easily break it.

If you are hesitant about the job of clipping, or think you cannot do it properly, then the best thing to do is to take the bird to a veterinarian, or to a pet dealer who knows what to do, or to a friend who knows how to clip them. A very easy way to make sure you are clipping the nail at the proper point is to wear a set of magnifier lenses while doing the job. The kind with lenses of 7″ focal length are the easiest to manage, since with this power you can work at a comfortable distance and still have plenty of room to hold the bird and operate the clipper.

The great majority of birds kept as pets are seedeaters. But some of them are insectivorous, and some of them eat both insects and seeds. Seeds of many kinds are available from companies specializing in pet foods

On the following page is a table of nutritional values, with percentages of protein, fat, and carbohydrates. All hemp seeds available from seed companies have been treated so they will not germinate, to eliminate the possibility of a person buying it as bird food but raising their own marijuana as a side business. The percentages are useful only as a guide as to which seeds are higher in protein or in fat or in carbohydrates. The table does not represent a laboratory analysis. The difference between the combined percentages and 100 per cent represents moisture content.

It is important that the seeds fed to cage birds be fresh. A seed that will not germinate, for example, has little nutritional value. The exception is hemp, or marijuana, of course, which would be capable of germination if it had not been "killed" artificially.

Some seeds should not be given in large quantities, especially the oily seeds which for a captive bird in a small cage would be too fattening. Niger is a particular favorite of almost every bird, and a mixture of several seeds, predominately niger, is given in small cups as a treat to Canaries, Finches, and many other birds. One such small cup a day is plenty. More would be too much. Some breeders only give a treat cup of this mixture to their Canaries once a week.

Seed	Protein	Carb.	Fat
Anise	18	55	12
Buckwheat	10	75	2
Canary	14	70	4
Caraway	22	53	17
Corn	9	75	4
Fennel	16	55	12
Flax	25	22	37
Gold of Pleasure	22	40	30
Hemp	22	40	30

Seed	Protein	Carb.	Fat
Millet	13	75	3
Milo	12	72	4
Niger	20	30	43
Oats	12	74	5
Peanuts	28	23	36
Poppy	21	22	50
Rape	20	28	45
Rice	8	78	2
Sesame	21	30	47
Spray Millet	15	70	6
Sunflower	15	49	28
Wheat	12	76	2

There are many other seeds used in the feeding of captive birds, but the ones described here are the most common. If you buy the excellent mixes available from seed companies, you need not bother getting individual types of seeds and mixing them yourself. It is better to get seeds from a regular supplier in bulk than to purchase packaged food, and if you have a large number of birds, it is far cheaper to buy in quantity.

CHAPTER TWENTY-EIGHT

Breeding Finches and Canaries

The breeding season for cage birds, especially Finches and Canaries, extends from about the middle of March to the end of June. Budgerigars and others of the psittacines will breed all the year around if kept indoors in cages, but only during the regular breeding season if kept in outdoor aviaries. Cockatiels will breed indoors whenever you give them a nesting box.

Probably the most important single part of breeding birds is bringing them into breeding condition. This is not just to see that they have seed and water, but they must be given special foods in special quantities, and at certain times, before they are ready to lay and raise a family. The birds must be in breeding condition before they are mated and the hens permitted to make their nests. There are nearly as many recipes for nestling food as there are breeders. Below is one that has proven itself for us. The base of the recipe is English Nestling Food, obtainable from the Hershey Seed Company, 41 North Moore Street, New York, New York 10013. They will ship via mail if desired. The recipe follows:

English Nestling Food . . . 6 tablespoonfuls
Royal Lunch Crackers . . . 2 tablespoonfuls
2 hard-boiled eggs, mashed through a sieve
1½ tablespoonfuls strained carrots

All ingredients are thoroughly mixed together with a fork, then placed in a covered container and kept in the refrigerator. DO NOT USE THIS FOOD AFTER THE SECOND DAY! The reason for this precaution is because the minute you open a hard-boiled egg it begins to spoil, and while you may eat such an egg two or three days later, a Canary cannot eat it without the danger of becoming sick. Chicks can be killed by spoiled food.

The Royal Lunch Crackers used in the recipe are a Nabisco product and can be purchased in almost any grocery store or supermarket. The crackers are rolled into crumbs with a rolling pin before using them in the bird-food recipe. The strained carrots are those which are sold everywhere as human baby food. Strained sweet potatoes may also be used, but the carrots seem to be the best.

If you are breeding only a hen or two, you might cut the recipe to suit your needs. Conversely, if you are breeding a large number of birds, the recipe may be doubled, or increased as many times as necessary, to provide you with a two-day supply. Keep the food mixture refrigerated at all times, removing it to use it, then returning it to the cold immediately. Discard any leftovers at the end of the second day, and make up your new batch the next morning when you are ready to feed the birds.

Beginning about the first of January, the food should be given to each bird, male and female, in a treat cup, once a week. This is continued for the entire month of January. At the end of the month, increase the amount to two treat cups each week for each bird. After the middle of February, the food is given daily from then on until the hen lays her first egg. At this time the conditioning food is stopped until about two days before the eggs hatch, when the food is again offered in a treat cup.

There are three ways commonly used in breeding birds. One

is in an outdoor aviary, another in an indoor aviary, and the third in individual cages.

Outdoor-aviary breeding is practiced when quantity is desired, with little or no regard to blood lines or type of stock. In this method, as many breeding birds as the aviary will accommodate are placed together, nesting boxes or nest baskets hung around the walls, a supply of nesting material placed where the birds can easily locate it, and the birds left to their own devices. It is obvious that with the birds interbreeding, no check can be kept of their parentage. The point is to let the birds breed as freely as they will, and gather the harvest of young ones at the end of the season.

The season is short in the outdoor aviary, one or, at most, two nests being the norm, since the birds wait until warm weather to begin to mate and make their nests; and the spring is well advanced before the first nest is fledged and the hen is ready for her second nest.

Indoor-aviary breeding is almost identical with breeding in an outdoor aviary, with the difference that the birds can be brought into breeding condition much sooner, since the temperature indoors is much warmer than it is outside. Thus the indoor breeder can obtain an extra nest each season, and, if he is breeding many females, this can result in a considerable increase in the number of young obtained in any year.

The serious breeder, however, is reluctant to breed in a community system like this but does his mating and rearing in individual cages, with accurate records kept of all hens and males, as well as the progeny obtained from them.

In this method of breeding birds, exact records may be kept of all adults, blood lines, type, color, or whatever you desire. The young may be family-banded so that their ancestry is known at all times; thus line breeding is possible without getting your stock mixed up. Faults may be bred out of stock, desirable points bred into them, colors fixed or developed; for any kind of breeding, including breeding for song, can be performed in the individual cage.

In this method, also, any hen (or male) which shows undesirable characteristics may be removed in order not to propagate those faults. Often you will find a hen which, while laying full nests of fertile eggs, fails to rear her young properly. Either she does not feed them sufficiently for vigorous growth, or perhaps she does not cover the chicks well enough, permitting them to chill. Such a hen should not be used for breeding. You will only waste time, lose the chicks, and become exasperated with the whole thing. Better to sell her or give her away and use another hen.

Sometimes the male is at fault. Males will sometimes breed very well, and the hen will have healthy chicks. She may feed them well and cover them well, but the male will interfere. Either he will keep chasing her off the nest, or perhaps throw the chicks out of the nest himself. It is often the case that a male will actually pick the chicks to death.

In cage breeding you can watch out for all of these things, where in aviary breeding you will miss most of them, since you cannot possibly watch individual pairs in the aviary the way you can in a breeding cage.

Double breeding cages are by far the best to use, since in these both the hen and the male can be placed at the same time, being kept apart by the screen or solid partition supplied with the cage when you buy it. The hen is placed on one side and the male on the other. The wire partition is the best to use, since this enables both birds to see each other and so become acquainted.

It is not at all uncommon for a pair of birds, on being placed into a breeding cage without a partition, to fight viciously, resulting in the death of one or the other, or at the best, injury and nervous damage to the point where neither bird is of any use for that breeding season.

When the partition is used, food and water cups are, naturally, placed on both sides of the partition for each bird. Then you watch them for several days to see how they get along. If both birds are in fine breeding condition, the male will perhaps begin to feed the female through the bars of the partition. If this is observed, you may without concern withdraw the partition to put the two birds together. It is best to remove the barrier at night, so the birds will find each other at dawn, more or less naturally.

As soon as the partition is withdrawn, the nest should be placed in the cage. Probably the easiest and the best type of nest, especially for Canaries, is the basket or strainer type. These look like nothing more than a large tea strainer without a handle, but with two clips on one side. The strainer is hung over the bars in one end of the cage. Such strainer-type nest baskets are usually supplied with each breeding cage, and, with the double cages, two nests are supplied.

The strainer nest baskets must be lined before the bird can use them. Linings are also sold ready-cut to size and shape, and these liners may be used more than once, by turning them over after the first use and placing them back in the strainer. Since they cost only a few cents each, it is very economical to use the manufactured liners rather than to try to make your own.

The nest liners serve as a soft bed for the chicks, as a support for the hair lining which the bird will make, and, most importantly, to keep the air from chilling the bottoms of the eggs while they are being incubated and the bottoms of the chicks after hatching.

The first day or two after removing the partition, the birds should be observed frequently, to make sure they are really compatible. Particularly important is the mating procedure. Make certain that the hen accepts the attentions of her mate without too much objection. If persistent avoidance of the male's attention takes place, the birds should be separated and the hen tried with another male, and the male given another hen. Of course, they should once again be placed in partitioned cages to do this.

Usually, however, after a pair of birds are introduced through a cage partition, there is no trouble with the mating, and you may continue with the breeding schedule.

Five or six days after removing the partition, the hen should begin picking at the paper or even at the feathers of the male. She is showing a desire to make a nest and is looking for nesting material. At this time you should place a supply of nesting hair in the cage, confined in a small hopper of some kind. Such hoppers are sold at bird suppliers for a few cents, and they last for many years. Goat hair is commonly used for making the nest, and this material is sold in pet stores in small boxes containing a fraction of an ounce per box. One box will supply enough hair for about three nests. Goat hair is also sold by the pound for breeders who are mating a large number of birds.

The hen should begin to line her nest within a day or two after being given the hair. Sometimes—usually, I find—either the hen, the male, or both birds, will pick the hair out of the hopper and scatter it all over the bottom of the cage. I put it back in the hopper once or twice, but if the birds persist in scattering it, leave it alone after that, and let them use it as they will from the cage bottom. If they soil the hair too much, then it is best to remove it and give them a new supply. This is not too great a nuisance, however, since most hens take the hair from the hopper and line the nests with it without too much waiting around.

You will find some hens lining their nests really neatly, tucking the hair in tightly, and making a snug, even lining all around. Others simply pile the hair inside the nest loosely, and when they lay their eggs, get them all tangled up in the loose hair. With such a hen, it is a good practice to wait until she has laid her first egg, then, remove the nest from the cage and the egg from the nest, rub the hair down with your fingers until it is tight against the felt lining, or even work it down with an electric light bulb as a form. The nest is then replaced in the cage.

As the hen lays, each egg is carefully removed from the nest and a clay nest egg, obtainable from pet stores, is substituted. A Canary clutch consists of from three to five eggs, and they lay one egg each day, usually in the morning between 6:00 and 9:00 A.M. A small covered container is used to hold the eggs while the hen is laying, and the lid of the container is labeled accurately with the number of the hen, the date she began to lay, and the cage number if you use that system. The container should be partly filled with birdseed as a bed for the eggs.

Canary eggs are unbelievably fragile, and if you pick them up by your fingertips, I can almost guarantee you will squash them. Rather, use a spoon, bent into a scoop, or, if you *do* use your fingers, roll the egg partly up the side of the nest, then let it roll down your fingers into your hand without putting any gripping pressure on the egg itself. Tip it gently out of your fingers into the birdseed in the container, but do not let it *fall* into the seed, or the side of the shell hitting the seed will crack or cave in.

The eggs are removed daily as they are laid, and the nest eggs substituted for them until the fourth egg has been laid. Sometimes a hen will lay only three eggs. You will know she is not going to lay any more if one day elapses without an egg being laid. In other words, she will lay an egg a day for three days, and the fourth morning no egg will appear. When this happens —which is by no means unusual—you may assume that she has completed her clutch.

When the fourth egg appears, or, as just mentioned, the fourth morning with only three eggs, the clay nest eggs are taken from the nest and the genuine eggs returned to the hen. She will begin to set them, and all her eggs will hatch on the same day, or, at the most in two days for the entire clutch. It is best to give the hen back her own eggs in the morning.

Let us interrupt again to tell you about the candling of eggs. Candling is nothing more than looking inside an egg to see if it is fertile and developing into a chick. It is the easiest thing in the world to do, but remember the fragility of the tiny eggs, and handle them accordingly. Actually, all you need for candling is a flashlight, turned on and placed on a table, so you can hold the egg in front of the ray to look through the shell. It is much more accurate and easy if you use some method of blanking out the light around the egg, to concentrate the light through the egg itself.

A candler can be made with squares of cardboard and masking tape. Five squares are cut, and four of them taped together to make a box. The fifth is then taped to the other four, to close one end of the box. Into this square a small hole is cut with a sharp knife or heavy shears. The hole must be smaller than an egg so it will not fall through. The size of the box is unimportant. It can be anywhere from 5 to 6 inches square, and deep enough to accommodate whatever light you intend using. One of the small high-intensity lamps is perfect for a candler, but a flashlight will also serve. In use, the light is turned on and the box placed over it, positioned so the hole is directly above the light beam. Now an egg placed over the hole will appear almost transparent to the eye, and you can very readily observe the yolk and the white inside.

If the inside of the egg shows any darkening or any color other than the tiny yolk floating in a clear fluid, you may assume that the egg is fertile. If, on the seventh day after the hen has set her eggs, the yolk is still clearly defined, the egg is infertile and should be discarded.

On the morning of the fourteenth day you should gently nudge the hen off her nest to see if the eggs did hatch. Sometimes they do not hatch until the evening of the fourteenth day, and often will carry over, or at least one or two eggs will carry over to the next morning. In any event, when the chicks hatch, the red label is fastened over the green one, and the date the *last* chick hatched is placed on this space.

A Canary hen can lay eggs for a considerable length of time without debilitating herself. She may also set eggs with no ill effects. It is the rearing and feeding of the chicks that wears her down, which is the reason for limiting the number of nests you take from a hen each season.

Since the laying and the setting of the eggs does not wear her out, you candle the eggs to determine fertility. If the eggs are fertile, you return them to the nest and the hen continues to set them. It is at this time you fasten the green label with the hatching date—fourteen days—written on it. If the eggs are infertile, you remove them and the nest. Then you either remove the male, leaving the hen alone in her breeding cage, or place the hen in a flight cage for about one week. The hen is then put back into the breeding cage, the male placed beyond the partition for a day or two, then the partition removed, the nest placed in the cage, and the cycle begun all over again.

If a hen deposits two nests of infertile eggs, the chances are she and the male are not compatible. In this case she should be introduced to a different male. Likewise, the male can be given a new hen in another cage.

After the chicks are hatched, the hen is kept supplied with the nestling food at all times until dusk, when the food remaining in the cup is removed from the cage. A regular feeding schedule should be established for hens with chicks, and, while it is a bit of trouble, and you will lose a little sleep over it, still, in the best interest of the growing birds you must follow it.

The first feeding should be as close to dawn as possible. You may have to set the alarm clock in order to get up then but the feeding takes only a couple of minutes, then you can go back to bed.

The feeding schedule is as follows: First feeding at dawn. The food cup is partly filled and placed inside the cage, then

A busy mother Canary feeding four hungry chicks.

leave the birds alone while you go back to bed. The next feeding is around nine o'clock in the morning. The food cup should
be empty or nearly empty by then. At this second feeding, I
sprinkle three or four drops of wheat-germ oil into each food
cup right on top of the nestling food. This seems quite
beneficial to the birds, and you may do the same if you wish.

Wheat-germ oil is obtainable from the Hershey Seed Company, or from health-food stores. Never leave food in the cup
during subsequent feedings. Empty out the stale food and put
in fresh. Remember that baby birds need no great amount of
food, so do not heap the cup full. Only partly fill it. One or two
feedings should tell you the right amount to give them. Around
one or two o'clock the birds should have their third feeding, and
the last feeding about four in the afternoon. This food is left in
the cage until dusk, when the cup is removed from the cage; the
paper on the bottom of the cage is also removed, and fresh
gravel is sprinkled on the fresh paper.

The removal of the paper is most important, and the reason is
that, during the day, in feeding her chicks the hen will scatter
particles of food all around the bottom of the cage. This food
will spoil, especially during the hot days, and if the paper is not
removed at early dawn, before you get to the first feeding, she
will pick up this food and feed the chicks with it, usually killing
them in the process with food poisoning. We lost several nests
of babies because of this problem before we discovered what was
wrong. Since the method of paper changing was put into operation, the infant-mortality rate dropped to zero. It is well worth
the trouble, since the entire operation of changing paper and
gravel takes not more than a minute.

About sixteen to eighteen days after the chicks are hatched,
the hen will be ready to make a second nest. At this time, both
the hen and the male should be partitioned off in the end of the

cage opposite the one containing the old nest and the babies. The parent birds will continue to feed their chicks through the bars of the partition.

If the chicks are left with the adult birds at the time of the second nesting, there is a better than good chance that the hen will pull the feathers out of the chicks to line her new nest. Partitioning them off eliminates this possibility, and the hen will make her new nest in the usual manner, provided you supply her with fresh nesting hair and another nest.

At the time of partitioning off, a small dish of nestling food should be placed on the floor of the cage on the chicks' side, in addition to the regular supply given the hen. The baby birds will soon learn to eat this by themselves. When you see them picking at the nestling food, you can sprinkle a small quantity of regular seed on the floor of their cage, or even better, a shallow jar lid containing seed may be placed on the floor where the young birds may find it easily. After a few days the seeds may be put into a treat cup, mixed with the nestling food.

When the chicks are from twenty-one to twenty-three days old, they should be picking seed for themselves and can then be removed from the breeding cage to a small cage of their own. They should be closely watched for several days, to make sure they are feeding properly. If a chick peeps constantly in a plaintive tone, it is crying for food and is unable to fend for itself. A young chick will literally stand ankle deep in food and yet starve to death, simply because it does not know enough to feed itself. If the chick does peep without letup after removal to its own cage, it must be replaced with the hen for another day or two, for further instruction in feeding. Then it can again be transferred to its hardening cage.

After the chicks have been in their own small cage for a week, they are transferred to a large flight cage. They may be left in this cage for the remainder of the year, or they may be taken from the flight cage to individual cages after they have been in the flight cage for about a month.

While in their own cage and while in the flight cage, the nestling food, mixed with seed, is fed to them. Seed cups are also kept supplied, along with the shallow lid of seed on the floor. When finally you see them eating seed several times during the day, you may start cutting down on the amount of nestling food and increase the amount of seed in proportion until they are weaned entirely to the seed. This should take from three weeks to a month. When the birds are about six to seven weeks old, they should be given greens daily the same as the adults, and from then on their diet is the same as that of the adult birds.

Close observation of the young birds in the flight cage should tell you which of them are males. From one month to five weeks old, the young chicks make attempts to sing if they are males. They go through all the motions, mouth open, tongue moving, and throat vibrating, but no sound is heard. They cannot yet produce notes but can only exercise their singing apparatus. When a bird is observed going through these motions, it is almost certain that it is a male. They can then be color-banded, or some other method of identification can be used, to help you identify them when the time comes to segregate males from females.

About August the birds go into their first molt, and it is then almost impossible to sex them. During this time, a good molting food, also obtainable from Hershey Company, should be given them daily in addition to their regular diet of seed.

About the only important difference between breeding Canaries and breeding other types of Finches is that the Finches prefer a closed nesting box to the open-basket-type nest used for Canaries. It is just as important to bring your Finches into breeding condition and to supply them with the proper diet.

When breeding the gorgeous Lady Gould Finches, you should use a somewhat different approach. Among the big problems with this species is that they do not incubate very well in cages, and they do not take very good care of their young. For this reason, Lady Goulds are usually fostered out to other species of Finches—mainly Society Finches. These interesting birds are probably the easiest of all birds to breed. They mate readily, either in individual cages or in community in an aviary. They will accept eggs from other hens and hatch them. They will feed their young with no trouble and will also feed other hens' young if community bred.

When attempting to breed Lady Gould Finches, you should condition at least one or two pairs of Society Finches simultaneously with the Goulds. When the Gould hen lays her eggs, they are removed from the nest and placed under a Society hen. This bird will hatch them and rear the young as if they were her own. However, there is one hazard that must be understood and taken into consideration when using Society Finches as foster parents for Gouldian chicks. Society Finches mature a few days earlier than do the young Gouldians, and, if not watched carefully, the female will desert the fledglings before they are able to feed for themselves, in order to start her second nest.

This trouble may be overcome by removing the female when she shows the first signs of wanting to nest again. Leave the *male* with the young, and he will continue to feed them as long as necessary.

The Lady Gould Finch is probably the most colorful of all the Finches. Certainly it is striking in its vivid, gaudy coat. The head and cheeks are deep red to maroon, the throat black. The nape and collar are pale aquamarine and the back green. The chest is purple to violet and the abdomen deep yellow, fading to white at the far rear end. The tail is black, blue, and gray. Altogether the color scheme is little short of unbelievable, yet on the bird everything blends in to make this creature a prize among the cage birds.

There are three recognized varieties of Lady Gould Finches, two of them occurring in the wild. These are the red-faced and the black-faced. The third, the yellow-faced, is found only in captivity and appears to be a cultivated sport. The species is indigenous to Australia.

The diet of Gouldian Finches should be kept simple instead of giving them a pampering selection. A standard Finch mixture of seeds, with a little extra-small yellow millet, is excellent. In addition, spray millet should be offered, and a supply of this kept before the birds at all times. Canary treat can be offered in a small treat cup, as a daily addition, and greens can be fed to them daily as well. A cuttlebone must be fastened inside the cage, and a small cup of grit kept filled. The grit can be the mixture of crushed oystershell, charcoal, and gravel used for almost all cage birds.

In the summer, heads of seeding grasses are welcomed and beneficial to the birds. Dandelion greens, cabbage, almost any table green should be offered daily; and fruit such as sweet red apple, pear, a cherry or grape, or a section of sweet orange makes a good biweekly supplement. Too much rich food causes liver disorders, and it is very possible that improper diet is one of the governing causes of their often sudden death.

Society Finches are not nearly as colorful as the Gouldians, but they are very interesting birds in their own right and, besides, are the ideal foster parents for the more temperamental species; so no bird fancier interested in rearing Finches should be without two or three pair. The price of Society Finches is nearly as low as that of Zebra Finches; therefore, the purchase of a couple of pair should not drain your resources very much.

Society Finches come in many different degrees of color. I say degrees because some are all white with dark markings. Some are pure white. Others have from a very little amount of black or brown mottling to, at times, so much as to appear all black or all brown, with a few white flecks in the feathers.

While they do not sing, as do Canaries and Siskins, they do have a cheerful chirp. Society Finches are unknown in the wild, and their ancestry is also unknown. They have been bred through so many stages of hybridization throughout the centuries, by the Chinese, that it is no longer certain what the parent stock was. Strictly speaking, Societies are not true Finches, but rather belong to that group called Mannikins. True, Mannikins are Finches, but that name has been attached to include some of the Finches as well as some of the Waxbills as a separate classification.

These little birds prefer the wicker-basket-type nests or wooden nest boxes, such as are used for the Gouldians, to the open Canary nests.

They will nest as readily in a small cage as in an aviary. They are brought into breeding condition by a substantial diet of nutritious foods just as are Canaries. The incubation period is the same as for Canaries—thirteen days—and they will nest any time of the year.

Everything said about Society Finches can be said about Zebra Finches. They are considered the easiest of all the Finches to breed, although I think both species are about equal in this respect. However, Zebra Finches are just a little unpredictable as foster parents, so it is best to breed them for their own species rather than as fosters for Gouldians.

Zebra Finches are more nervous than most other Finches, and they are considerably smaller than the other popular species. They are very fond of spray millet, and when this is offered to them, it has been my experience that they will eat the entire spray before going back to their regular seed cup.

Basket nests are preferred to box nests, but they will accept a box if nothing more is available to them. The box should be partly filled with dry grass or other nesting filler before the Finches use it. They will hollow out the cavity and line it with nesting hair, grass, shredded burlap, or any other material available. Four- to six-inch squares of burlap, hung on the side of the cage with a safety pin, will be carefully pulled apart and the strands used to line the nest.

The eggs are tiny, white, and very fragile. Both birds incubate them, and both male and female will sleep together in the nest. The incubation time for the eggs is about twelve days. No special diet need be offered; their regular diet of Finch mixture seeds is sufficient for their continued well-being.

Zebra Finches mutate frequently, and at least two different strains have become fixed as definite varieties. White Zebras are very pretty, solid dazzling white birds, with deep orange legs and bill. The males have redder beaks than do the females. Gray Zebras are another fixed strain that is very popular. There are several other strains, but these are variations in marking or coloring, and they are rather rare. Some work is being done in England to standardize the different color strains of the Zebra Finch and to arrive at a standard classification for the different mutant species.

The next most popular species of Finch is the Ribbon Finch, also known by the unfortunate name of Cutthroat Finch, taken from the fact that the bird carries a narrow band of vivid red across its throat.

While Ribbon Finches are fairly easy to breed, they do not approach the ease of either the Zebra or the Society Finches in this respect. They require a larger cage for breeding than do the other two species just mentioned. One of the standard flight cages, about 21″ deep, 26″ high, and 30″ wide, is obtainable from any of the cage manufacturers and will serve for quarters for two to three pairs of Ribbons. Basket nests should be pro-

A male Ribbon Finch. Note the band of dark red color across the throat.

The female Ribbon Finch does not have the red band.

vided, and the birds should be permitted to pair up and select
the nest to their liking. You should place one more nest than
you have pairs of birds in the cage, to eliminate any source of ri-
valry and fighting over their nesting site.

The diet for Ribbon Finches is the same as that used for
Societies and most other Finches. No special conditioning foods
need be provided, but a cuttlebone and a supply of crushed oystershell, mixed with gravel and charcoal, must be in the cage at
all times.

Many other species of Finches, Mannikins and Waxbills are
known to breeders in this country. The more beautiful, both as
to color and shape, are the Australian species. Several African
species are also bred. With the present embargo on imported
birds, these colorful and interesting birds are becoming more
and more scarce and will continue to do so until the breeders in
this country who already had a supply in stock have managed to
breed enough to put them back in the market.

CHAPTER TWENTY-NINE

Breeding the Psittacines

The diet for Lovebirds, Budgies, and Cockatiels is Budgie mix, sunflower seeds, greens offered daily, fruit a couple of times each week, and a cuttlebone kept always in the cage, as well as grit and crushed eggshell, or crushed oystershell. A small amount of avian charcoal mixed with the shell and grit is beneficial and will help sweeten the crop.

While it is easy enough to breed the parrotlike birds in captivity, certain things must be done in order to achieve success. One of the most important conditions in successfully raising chicks is sufficient humidity during laying and nesting periods. The eggs of the psittacines harden if the shells dry out, and if this happens the weak chicks are unable to peck open the shells from within.

Many methods have been resorted to in an attempt to prevent this during the hot, dry months. Some of them work; others fail. Yet every method will work for some breeder at some time or other; so a method should not be discarded just because you had no success with it the first or second time you tried it.

Dampened wood shavings are used with good results by some breeders and sworn at by others. It has been my experience that, in the case of Budgerigars, at least, the birds spend more time throwing out every single shaving than they do laying eggs or setting them.

A piece of blotting paper cut to fit under the nest block, and kept moistened by a strip laid as a wick, is also favored by certain breeders. Of course, if you can afford to keep a humidifier in the breeding room, it would be the simple answer to the humidity problem. However, unless you are breeding top-quality birds which can command a high price, it would take a great number of chicks to pay for this piece of equipment.

One or two pails of water placed in the bird room where the birds cannot get to them will help a great deal to keep the air moist. The water should be replenished as it evaporates.

Budgerigars used to sell for three or four dollars in pet stores, with breeders running up as high as fifteen dollars or a bit more. I am afraid those days are gone forever because now young birds, which are nothing really more than cull stock, bring anywhere from eight to twelve dollars each, and a good breeder bird will bring whatever the owner can ask for it. It is not at all uncommon to pay a couple of hundred dollars for a good pair of birds, and there are records of exceptionally fine breeders selling for as high as one thousand dollars!

A box is used for the nesting site, and the standard Budgerigar box measures about 6" by 10" high. It is made out of ¼" plywood, with a ½" lumber top and bottom. The front and back are nailed to the top and the bottom, and the sides, made of ⅛" masonite, slide in grooves cut into the plywood front and back, which project out from the top and bottom about ¾" to permit the sides to be installed. A ½"-diameter hole is drilled through each side, and two through the back, about 2½" down from the top of the box. These provide ventilation. The hole for the birds to use, going in and out of the nest, is about 2" in diameter, centered 3" down from the top of the box, and a ½"-diameter perch is fastened about one inch below the opening to the nest. The easiest way to fasten the perch is to drill a ½" hole and push a piece of dowel through to project an inch or two inside the nest box, and 3″ outside.

The nesting block is placed in the bottom of the box. This is a square of one-inch pine cut to fit snugly inside when the sides are in place. The block is scooped out to make a shallow depression in the center. This may be done with a gouge or on a lathe if you are making your own boxes, but Budgie nest boxes are so cheap that it hardly pays to make them yourself. The depression in the bottom block resembles the rounded-out hole in a tree. More importantly, though, it serves to keep the eggs rolled all together in the center of the block, to be more easily covered by the hen when she sets them.

Some breeders say to put shavings inside the nest box. Others advocate sawdust. Still others offer dry grasses to their nesting Budgies. Usually Budgies will toss out everything you put inside their box, laying their eggs on the bare wooden bottom and raising the chicks there as well.

Breeding condition in Budgies is fairly easy to tell. First of all, you must have mature birds to mate and lay fertile eggs. Young Budgies have barred feathers covering the head and forehead. When a Budgie is adult, these barrings recede to leave the forehead and top of the head solid in color. Surrounding the nostrils is a bare patch of skin called the cere. In adult male Budgies this cere is blue, and in adult females, brown or gray. When the bird is in breeding condition, the female cere is a deep, rich brown and that of the male is a deep, bright blue.

The sexes should be kept in separate flight cages until mating time. When the males strut about the cage and rattle their beaks against the bars, or the feeding cups, and when the females keep calling the males, it is time to put a pair together.

If the nesting box is hung on the outside of the cage, a single breeding cage is plenty large enough to take the pair of birds.

The pair should be watched closely the first few days after putting them together. If they fight, of course, they should be separated and paired with other birds. If they show no sign of mating after several days, they could be separated and the hen given to another cock, and vice versa. Best results seem to be accomplished when either the hen or the cock is older than the other. For example, it is better to mate a one-year-old hen with a two-year-old cock than to try mating two one-year-olds.

Budgies apparently resent interference while breeding. Interference by the breeder, I mean. Constantly looking into the nest box is apt to cause the hen to abandon her eggs. It is better to leave the birds alone as much as possible, watching to see other signs of laying. A large pile of droppings is almost a sure sign that she has begun to lay.

Budgies lay an egg every other day until the clutch is completed with from four to seven eggs. They begin to sit on the eggs after the second or third is laid. When the chicks hatch out, there is, of course, the same lapse of a day between hatchings, which means, that with a clutch of six eggs, the first chick will be twelve days old when the last chick comes out of the shell. As soon as you find that the hen has laid the first egg, stop looking into the nesting box because every time you open the box to look, the hen throws a fit and thrashes around inside in a mad scramble to get out of the hole. Usually in doing so, she stamps all over the eggs, puncturing them with her toes. It is better to note the date you saw the first egg in the nest, then in about two weeks you may start listening outside the box. When the chicks hatch, you will hear them peeping as they are being fed by the parents. This is when you start watching the nest. At least every two days look inside—a quick peep, to make sure that none of the chicks have died. They must be removed immediately or they will spoil, and possibly the decomposed matter will kill the other birds.

This ugly little Budgie chick has hatched four days before the next egg. He will have all his feathers by the time the last egg has hatched.

When all the chicks have hatched, again stop looking into the nest for five or six days. At that time, you take the chicks out to band them, returning them immediately, and leaving them alone for another two weeks, when you may begin to handle them.

Most writers will say that the chicks should be closely examined each day after hatching, and if signs appear that they are not being fed well enough, they should be taken from their parents and given to a foster hen to rear. This is fine, provided you have an unlimited number of Budgerigars, all in breeding condition and all ready to have chicks. If a pair of birds has no chicks of their own, there is no use giving another hen's chicks to them to rear, since they will not accept them. If a hen has chicks of her own, she has enough to do to rear them without adding to her burden by dumping another nest on her.

Many of the same breeders advocate using poor quality, or at least, lesser quality birds than your "good" breeders as the foster parents, throwing out their eggs as they are laid, replacing them with the eggs from the better quality birds.

This does not seem like a practical practice to me at all. It takes exactly as much time, as much trouble, and as much expense to rear and feed a bad bird as it does to rear and feed a good bird. Why then, waste all that time, trouble, and expense keeping stock you have no use for in the off chance that a pair will be in the same condition at the same time as a pair of your regular fine-breeding stock?

It is far more practical to try to foster out your chicks among other pairs of good stock, I should think, or, if this is not possible, then let the birds do whatever they are going to do anyway, and be glad of what chicks you end up with. A pair which persistently refuses to feed or care for their chicks should be culled out of your bird room. You should certainly not try to keep them as breeding stock.

A much better way to rear Budgies, in my opinion, is to let them nest as they will, and keep yourself from disturbing them as much as possible after the chicks hatch. About seven or eight days after hatching you can remove them from the nest to band them if you wish, and, at the same time you can clean up the nesting block, which by this time should be pretty dirty. Then return the chicks, close the box, and leave them alone. The hen will provide whatever care the chicks require.

Chicks will die for no apparent reason. Perhaps the hen did not cover them well enough, and one got chilled. If this happens, the food given to the tiny creature will not digest properly, and the bird will die of malnutrition even with a full stomach. Or a chill will give it a cold which ends up with the same result. The other chicks in the nest, having been kept warm by their mother, do not suffer the same calamity.

After the chicks have hatched, you can change the nest block for a clean one, and now you will be able to put in a small handful of cedar chips. These will absorb the liquid droppings of the baby birds and help keep the nesting box clean. The shavings can be renewed every couple of days. The chicks leave the nest anytime after they are twenty-eight days old. At this time they should be cracking seeds for themselves, but you should watch them closely to make sure they are being fed by the parent birds if they are not already self-feeding. As soon as you are certain that they are feeding themselves and are cracking seeds with no difficulty, they can be transferred to a flight cage for hardening up. There they will exercise their wing muscles and come into full plumage.

Budgie chicks should be banded as soon as the foot is large enough to retain the band. Foot size varies with the amount of food the chick receives, and with the breed. Some of the very large imported Budgies may be banded when they are three or four days old. Others—most all others—could not hold the band in place until they are at least one week of age. You will have to use some judgment of your own as to when exactly to band the youngsters.

Budgies' toes are short, fat, and stubby, as are their lower leg bones. Sometimes you will have difficulty slipping the back toe through the band because the toe is so short. When this is the case, push the band as far up over the knee joint as possible, taking great care not to wedge the band too tightly on the knuckle, or to skin the joint. Now a sharpened pencil point may be inserted under the rear toe and with gentle pressure, pull it up through the band. The toe will bend like rubber, so you need not fear breaking it if you are careful.

A popular group of psittacines are the African Lovebirds, of which there are many species. We will discuss the three most popular, and the easiest of the group to breed.

Lovebirds look like diminutive Parrots. They have the same general shape of body and beak and many of the same habits and characteristics of behavior. They will also learn to talk and can be tamed to the finger, but both instances require more time and patience with Lovebirds than with Budgerigars and Cockatiels. Lovebirds are usually hardy and live for a long time, and they are very colorful. Unfortunately, some of them are also very aggressive toward other birds, and for this reason must be kept to themselves. It is extremely difficult to sex Lovebirds, and even if you have two birds that make a nest and lay eggs, it is no insurance that you have a sexual pair, since two females will go through all the motions of mating and produce eggs in abundance—infertile, of course. Only if an egg hatches are you certain you have a real pair of breeding birds.

While Lovebirds will nest in a standard Budgie box, a good supply of nesting material must be provided, since they build elaborate nests within the box when the time comes. Strips of green bark, grasses, hay, feathers, squares of burlap, which the birds will strip into strands, are all accepted. Raffia, cut into 4″ to 6″ lengths is excellent nesting material, and this may be found in hobby stores throughout the country. Do not use just one type of material. They may not like it and will then fail to produce a good nest. If several kinds of material are made available, they will usually build the nest out of one of the stiffer varieties and then line it with a softer kind.

The best way to breed Lovebirds is in an outside aviary. If this is covered with heavy plastic sheeting on the top and three sides, they can be kept in such a cage the year round. In very cold weather, plastic should be hung over the fourth side as well. Use clear or white plastic rather than the black. Many of the Lovebirds are community breeders, but they will also breed as pairs in cages. They like a fairly large nesting box, or, even better, an old hollow log in which they can make their nest. Outdoor cages can be occupied right through the winter if the birds are placed in them in the spring and permitted to become acclimated as the seasons change. Protection must be provided from drafts and some sort of shelter given them during the winter, especially on freezing nights.

PEACH-FACE LOVEBIRDS are perhaps the most common species we discuss in this book and the most readily obtainable. They are also one of the largest of the group. They are pugnacious among themselves as well as with other birds and must be given room to dodge each other, so do not keep more than one pair in a fairly large cage. In an aviary, where there is plenty of flying room and where thickets of brush are provided as shelters and refuges, several pair may be kept together.

An odd habit these birds have is of tucking nesting material in among their tail feathers, then flying to the nesting box with them. The eggs hatch in about twenty days, and number up to eight in a clutch.

BLACK-MASKED LOVEBIRDS are second only to the Peach-faced species in popularity, and some breeders like the Black-masked

A pair of Black-masked Lovebirds.

ones better because of the more striking appearance of the birds. The neck, shoulders, and chest are bright yellow, and the remainder of the bird, bright green. The beak is a shiny bright red. The entire head is black and the eyes are surrounded with a stark-white ring. This contrast gives the bird the appearance of owlishly watching you all the time, and at the same time being slightly comical.

Black Masks breed easily in a Budgerigar box, although they do better in a hollow log. They, like most of the Lovebirds, build a rather elaborate nest out of twigs and grasses, filling the box to the point where they themselves have difficulty in entering.

Black-masked Lovebirds also differ from the Peach-faced species in that the former are very affectionate birds, both with themselves and with other species. They will mate and rear their young in large outdoor cages occupied by Cockatiels or different birds about the same size as themselves. The only time these creatures show any fierceness is during their mating time, and, if they are left alone by other birds, even at this trying season they go about their own business quietly.

There is a mutation of the Black-masked, called Blue-masked Lovebird. This one has a blue and white body, with the black mask and the white eye rings. The beak is whitish instead of bright red. They are not nearly as striking as the normal variety.

CHAPTER THIRTY

Training Your Birds

Some birds will become tamer than others, and most of the psittacines will actually become very affectionate and tame toward human beings to the point where they seem to prefer the company of their owners rather than that of other birds of their own species. It is fairly easy to tame a Budgerigar, Cockatiel, and some of the Parrots; and besides taming them, you can, with patience and perseverance, teach them to talk!

Finger-trained birds—those that will sit on your finger, or ride on your shoulder, whenever you wish—are much more expensive than ordinary birds of the same kind. If you are raising birds to sell, it might pay to put the extra time and effort into making them tame so you can get higher prices for them.

Some birds tame up if you hand-raise them. Crows, for example, when obtained as fledglings and hand-fed to maturity, will become so tame as to be almost a pest. You won't be able to move without the bird being underfoot. They make excellent watchdogs, raising a rumpus whenever anyone approaches the house. On the other hand, they make so much noise as to nearly drive you up the wall when you want peace and quiet. Crows can be taught to talk. Pay no attention to the old tale that to teach a Crow to talk you must split its tongue. This is not only not true, it is an unnecessary cruelty to the bird. A Crow can manage to talk perfectly well with a whole tongue.

Mynah birds are also able to talk. Teaching these birds and Crows requires much time and patience, but the result is a bird that finds it difficult to keep its mouth shut.

The secret of taming a bird is to get it when it is just out of the nest, feeding itself, before it has had time to pick up fear of

Clip the outer ends of the flight primaries of one wing only, to stop a bird from flying all the time, when you want to tame it.

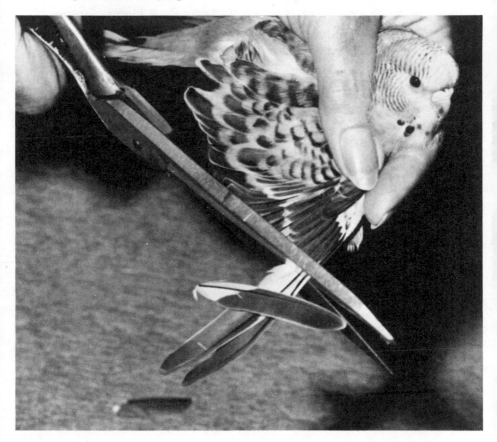

humans from the adult birds. The parents of a bird you want to tame may be wild and completely unmanageable, but that will not stop the young bird from becoming perfectly tame and docile with a very little bit of attention.

To finger train a Budgie or a Cockatiel is simplicity itself, and the method is used for other birds as well. Other birds just take more time than do the little Budgerigars or the colorful Cockatiels.

As soon as the young are feeding themselves, the chicks you wish to finger train are put into individual cages. Now you have to make up your mind as to whether you are going to clip the wing feathers or not. This seems to be a matter of preference among breeders and trainers. Some say that clipping the wings makes the bird so insecure that one has difficulty in managing it during training. Others say that it makes the bird more easy to manage, since it soon learns it cannot fly and pays attention to the training as a consequence.

I would say that a lot depends on the bird itself. If it persistently tries to fly away while you are training it to sit on your finger, then, certainly, wing clipping is the answer. If the bird is naturally docile and tractable, then the clipping is unnecessary.

Just in case you do want to clip, however, the feathers that are cut away are the flight feathers of one wing only. These are the stiff primaries on the front of the wing, and the other ends are cut off—not the entire feather. Each quill is hollow for a part of the length, but at the base it is filled with blood vessels. If you cut past this point, the bird will bleed profusely and suffer pain. It is as painless as clipping your fingernails, to cut off the outer half of the feathers, however. Use a heavy shear because the quills are tough. If the bird is afraid, to restrain it you should wrap it in a towel, with one wing exposed, while you cut. This way it is more difficult for the bird to bite you, which it may try to do while being subjected to the indignity of clipping.

If you are yourself afraid of being bitten by a bird, then certainly you must either overcome this fear or let someone else train the bird because you will only be asking for trouble. Bear in mind that when climbing around a tree in the wild, or its cage in captivity, a psittacine bird uses its beak as a third hand or foot. It reaches out, takes hold of the new support with its beak, then pulls its body up to the position where it can take a new purchase with its feet. The bird is not trying to bite you, but the beak is hard and sharp, and the nip you get depends upon the weight of the bird. If he is heavy, he must grab hard to pull himself up. A light bird needs a lesser grip.

When you offer your finger to the bird, he grabs it with his beak, then yanks his feet up afterward. If you jerk your finger back as he attempts to take it in his beak, this frustrates the creature. No animal will tolerate teasing for very long, including you. After you have yanked your finger away enough times to arouse your pet, he will finally snap at it with a vengeance, and then you will really feel what it is like to be bitten by a hook-bill!

If it reaches for you, let it take hold. The grip will not hurt, or, at any rate, not hurt very much, and, as soon as he has a good grip with his feet, he will let go with his beak.

When you have clipped your bird, put it back into its separate cage for a couple of hours. Then the finger training can begin. Put your hand inside the cage with one finger extended in front of the bird. If he does not step up on the finger, nudge him just at the tops of his thighs, and, as you push gently backward, he will step up on the finger to keep his balance. Remove your hand slowly from the cage, with the bird on your finger.

You should keep up a steady conversation with the bird as

you handle it, using simple words and a soft, even tone of voice. Since the hearing range of birds is more toward the high end, pitch your voice as high as you comfortably can when talking to it, or the sounds will be inaudible. It is for this reason that girls usually make better trainers than men. Their voices are pitched higher.

It is best to sit on the floor when first training a bird. That way it will not fall so far if it flies from your finger. Remember that it is a very young and very little creature, and until it has become used to using its wings, it can fall just like a human baby.

The lessons should occupy not less than one full hour, and it will be a good idea to place a clock where you can see it from the position on the floor. The reason for this is that ninety-nine people out of one hundred cannot accurately estimate elapsed time, and, after working with the bird for what seems like half the day, you will be shocked and surprised to find that only fifteen or twenty minutes have passed.

Work with the little bird until it sits on your finger facing you. Then use the other hand to extend a finger in front of him, and push against his body until he steps up on the second finger. Keep up your running talk as you work. Keep repeating the transfer from finger to finger. Some trainers advocate the use of a key word every time you make the bird step onto a finger, such as "Step," "Hop," "Up," or any simple word, to condition the bird to what he is supposed to do. The use of key words is fine except that there is the good possibility that the bird will not step onto anyone's finger after it is trained unless the same word is used each time. This means that the key word must accompany the bird throughout its entire life, passing from owner to owner. Without it, the bird may not respond to handling.

The first day should be enough to finger train a Budgerigar or a Cockatiel. Perhaps two or three days are needed for larger Parrots. The next step in training is to put the bird on your shoulder, spending an hour at this training, the same as with the finger. You simply keep repeating the process of placing it in position, talking to it all the time. Soon it will perch by itself, with no attempt to fly away, and then you may get up and slowly walk around the room, with him riding your shoulder. As soon as the training is over, the bird should be handled by as many other people as possible, using the same motions and words, so it will lose fear of all people, not just of its trainer.

In training a Parrot, you should use a short perch of wood instead of your finger. One reason for this is that the Parrot's beak is stronger and larger than the beaks of small birds like Budgerigars and therefore capable of giving you a more severe pinch. It may even draw a bit of blood, especially if the bird is startled while you are trying to train it.

Anyhow, the perch eliminates this danger, and you will note that the Parrot takes a secure grip on the perch, then tries to move it before he steps on it. Birds like a secure perch and hesitate to step onto anything that may fall away from beneath them, so hold the perch securely in your hand while training your bird.

Food, especially one of the favorite foods of that particular bird, is always a big help in training. Offer a bit from your fingers as you work with the creature, when you want him to step forward to the perch, step on your finger, or your shoulder. If you see he is getting nervous, the food will help to calm him down considerably. Always offer the food from your fingers. I won't give you my opinion of people who feed their birds food from their own mouths. Let it be enough to say that if they are bitten on the lip or tongue, it is just what they are asking for. This is to say nothing of the mutual passage of diseases or germs if they happen to be present.

All the finger and shoulder training should be completed be-

fore you attempt to teach a bird to talk. They must first have
overcome all their fear of humans and be docile and manageable. Talking takes a long time—as long as a year or even more
in some cases.

The bird should be confined in a cage that is covered to ex-
clude all outside influence. It must be kept in a room away from
other birds, and where it cannot hear other birds' noises. A
white cloth over the top and three sides of the cage should be
enough. The front is left open for the regular maintenance
chores, and to let you observe the bird.

Begin by repeating a simple word, or, at most, two simple
words, such as "Hello, there," or, "Pretty bird," or anything else
that you like. The words should be repeated many, many times,
and every time you approach the cage. When you change the
food and water keep repeating the words. Do not say anything
to the bird except the words you are trying to teach it to memo-
rize. Weeks, and sometimes even months, may pass without the
bird saying anything except a squawk or two. Sooner or later,
however, you will hear the little fellow softly repeating his new
vocabulary. Continue to repeat the words to him until he says
them clearly and frequently. Each time he talks, you might give
him a bit of choice food as a reward. Perhaps a piece of whatever fruit he most likes.

One thing you must be made aware of, if this is your first attempt at teaching a bird to talk, is that the bird's voice does not
sound like the voice of a human being. First of all, the bird's
vocal apparatus is differently put together than yours, and next,
the bird is quite considerably smaller than even a human baby.
The voice of a Budgerigar, for example, is very tiny and thin,
and it takes some practice for you to distinguish the words at
first. Soon, however, you will clearly understand the creature
when it talks.

The next important thing in training birds is to continue its vocabulary as soon as it has learned the first word. There seems to be a wide ability in Parrots and parrotlike birds to learn, once the ice is broken, and you can teach the bird whole sentences, questions and answers, poems, whatever strikes your fancy. Remember that the bird has absolutely no reasoning power, nor is it able to make up sentences of its own. It is a mimic, pure and simple, and will faithfully mimic what it has been taught, or what it has heard, but no more.

Perhaps the easiest way to start training is to obtain a training record, of which there are many on the market. Most of them are good, but you should avoid those which are not repetitive. These records have a simple phrase which is repeated over and over. Such a device placed on an automatic phonograph can run for as long as you can stand it. It is even better if you can go outside while the bird is having the phrase dinned into its memory. As soon as the bird has picked up that particular phrase, the record playing is stopped, and you then begin to talk to the bird, using the identical words from the record, and trying to use the same inflection of voice.

When the bird responds to your voice as it did to the record, then the second side of the record is put on and the process repeated. After the bird responds to the second lesson, you can either go on with advanced-training records, or go on by yourself. If you have the time and patience, it is better for you to take over the training after the bird has come to know what is expected of it. If you haven't, then by all means continue with recordings until you have exhausted the supply of them, and then you will have to improvise from that point. Records should be played to the bird for about an hour in the morning and for the same period of time in the evening before dusk.

Training without records should also be given in two sessions, as much to rest yourself as to rest the bird. One half hour in the morning and the same in the evening should be enough for both of you. During the training time, no one else should be around, of course, and if other people are in the house, you and the bird should go someplace where their voices cannot be heard. As you talk to the bird, you should hold him on your finger, facing you, and close to your face so he can watch your mouth to know that the sounds produced are voice sounds.

Since the first training you gave it was finger training, this should present no problem at all. And remember, as it learns more words, the learning progresses more and more rapidly. There seems to be no limit to the number of words and phrases a psittacine bird can learn.

CHAPTER THIRTY-ONE

Diseases of Birds

Birds become ill just the same as human beings, and, while something may be done to help some conditions, it is far better to try to prevent illnesses than to try to cure them. As with all animals, in order to cure a disease you must first be sure just what the disease is, and this means you have to learn the symptoms and perform an accurate diagnosis. In some cases, taking a suffering bird to a veterinarian who is familiar with bird diseases will yield a diagnosis and treatment schedule, but usually the treatment is up to you alone.

If symptoms of illness are caught at an early stage, effecting a cure is far simpler than if you wait until the bird is far gone in its ailment. Your birds should be observed often. Healthy birds should have bright eyes, a perky, alert manner, be frisky, hop about their cages, and sing often if they are singers. A sick bird has dull or droopy eyes, ruffled feathers, or a puffed-up appearance, acts listless, sometimes with its head tucked under a wing, or sitting with its eyes closed most of the day.

As soon as any of these symptoms are noticed, you should take some first-aid measures. The most important of these is warmth. A bird's body temperature is high—102 degrees and higher—and, unless it is kept warm, it will lose interest in feeding. If this happens, the bird will fail rapidly, since the metabolic rate of birds is extremely high.

A healthy bird assimilates its food in a short time, which maintains its high body temperature automatically. A sick bird, however, eats less, and, as a consequence, lowers its metabolic rate to the point where external heat must be supplied in order to keep it alive. This may be in the form of a heating pad placed under the cage, a light bulb suspended inside the cage, or by any other practical means that may occur to you.

The bird should be isolated from your other birds by placing it in a "hospital" cage in another room, out of drafts and excessive activity. A section of old sheet, or an old towel, may be draped around three sides and the top of the cage to hold in any warmth provided. If you suspend a light bulb inside the cage, use one not over 25 watts in size, and take care that the bulb does not rest against any fabric cover used. There would be danger of the fabric igniting from the heat of the lamp. By far the safest and easiest to use is an electric heating pad. Taking the cloth cover off the pad will help, since the rubber base cover will be easier to keep clean. If the bird being treated is one of the psittacines, take care to place the heating pad in a position which makes it impossible for the bird to reach it with its beak and chew a hole through, shorting the pad, and possibly electrocuting the bird in the process.

Hospital cages are available, equipped with built-in heaters, thermostatically controlled. If you have valuable birds, it would pay to purchase such a cage, since the cost of the equipment would more than be covered by the value of one of the birds.

Only a few things are needed to prevent most disease onslaughts. Cleanliness is of prime importance in the cages and room. All seeds should be kept in covered containers so that feathers, droppings, and other airborne particles will not fall into them. The bottoms of the cages and especially the perches should be kept clean. Water should be drawn fresh each time it is put in the cups, and the seed and water cups themselves washed as often as necessary to keep them clean.

Newspapers, cut or torn to fit the bottom trays of the cages, should be kept in the trays in stacks of about ten or twelve sheets. Sprinkle a handful of clean bird gravel on the paper, then, when cleanup time arrives, which should be not less than every other day, the top two sheets of paper are discarded, the gravel shaken out of the tray, a new handful sprinkled in place, and the tray returned to the cage.

Two or three drops of wheat-germ oil (vitamin A) in the seed cup daily will be very beneficial to the bird's health. Cod-liver oil will do the same thing, but the trouble with this is that it goes rancid very quickly, and the rancid oil may do more harm than good. Peanut butter is an excellent food for birds, and most birds relish it. A small dab on the inside edge of the seed cup will soon be cleaned up, or, if it is too much work for you to wash the seed cup daily, then the peanut butter may be supplied in a treat cup.

As far as medicines are concerned, there are a few that you can give to your creatures. Probably the most valuable of all is the soluble chlortetracycline—also called aureomycin. This is sold by pet dealers without a prescription and is must useful in the treatment of many bird ailments. As a regular treatment, when obtaining new stock, it is a good practice to give the new arrivals this antibiotic as a preventative, in the proportion of two teaspoonfuls of powder to a pint of water. The solution is given in lieu of the regular drinking water for one week, after which the birds may be placed on their regular clear water for drinking.

New birds should be put in isolation cages for at least four weeks after bringing them home, before putting them into your bird room. During this time the preventative dosage of chlortet-

racycline can be given, and the birds watched for any symptoms of disease or illness.

Bacterial diseases are particularly dangerous in the bird room,
since they are for the most part airborne and can spread through
an entire flock of birds in rapid time. The treatment of such disorders is sketchy at best, and the bird, even if recovered, is never
the same as before. There is also the chance that the sufferer
will be a carrier of the disease even though it has recovered, or
rather, did not die from the disease itself.

Some bird ailments and the treatments for them are described
here, but the reader should bear in mind that the suggested
treatment is by no means a sure thing. Rather, it is the best one
can do, and you can only hope that it works. It might work for
one bird and not for another. This is not to say that the treatment is always at fault. The diagnosis may be wrong.

COLDS. The symptoms of cold in a bird are very similar to those
in a human being—runny nose, bleary eyes, listlessness, and
sneezing. The bird sits with its feathers fluffed up and head
drooping. About the only thing to do is to put it in a hospital
cage and raise the temperature to around 85 degrees, covering
three sides of the cage and the top. Administer chlortetracycline
solution in place of drinking water, and continue this treatment
for at least two weeks. Two teaspoonfuls to a pint of water for
the antibiotic solution.

PNEUMONIA. While a cold is a virus disease and pneumonia is
a bacterial infection, the latter is often the result of the bird
catching a common cold and becoming so weakened that it
catches the more dangerous pneumonia. The treatment is the
same as for colds, but you might increase the strength of the antibiotic by 50 per cent, that is to say, three teaspoonfuls to a
pint of water, and continue the treatment for three weeks.

RICKETS. The main cause of rickets is the lack of calcium in the diet. This can be brought about either by the chick being given a calcium-poor diet, or perhaps by chilling when very young. The chilling itself would not cause rickets, but it would slow the metabolism of the bird to the point where it could not assimilate its food properly, thus resulting in a lack of calcium. Not much can be done to cure this malady, since, by the time it is discovered, the bones have already lost their rigidity and the bird is more or less helpless. Sprawling flat in the nest is one telltale sign of rickets. The kindest thing to do is to put the bird out of its misery.

PLUGGED OIL GLAND. On the upper side of the base of the tail, birds have an oil gland. This is used in preening their feathers. The bird picks up oil from the gland with its bill, then rubs it through the feathers as it smooths and combs them out. Once in a while this gland becomes plugged for one reason or another, and the oil backs up until the gland becomes distended and swollen. The cure is to remove the plug with a toothpick, then gently apply pressure on the swelling until the oil oozes out.

ASTHMA. This is usually the aftereffect of a cold, and the treatment is long and tedious. The bird has difficulty in breathing. It wheezes and heaves with every inhalation. The cure often takes six months or longer and consists of keeping the bird warm—85 degrees at least—in a covered cage, and using an electric vaporizer with a bird inhalant daily.

SOUR CROP. Usually caused by a mold. Keeping a supply of bird charcoal mixed with oystershell and grit in the cage at all times will do much to sweeten the crop and prevent this ailment. To cure it, one teaspoonful of baking soda in a quart of water, given in place of the regular drinking water, will end the trouble in a few days.

DIARRHEA AND CONSTIPATION. While these two ailments may

seem directly opposite, the treatment is the same for both. A simple laxative. Either one teaspoonful of epsom salts in a quart of water, or two or three tablespoonfuls of molasses in a quart of water, is given in place of the regular drinking water for two or three days. Repeat in five or six days if the birds are not cured.

EGG BINDING. If your bird is kept under clean conditions, with proper and sufficient diet, there should be no instance of egg binding. Once in a while, however, this malady will affect a laying hen and, unless prompt measures are taken, may result in her death. If you have a laying hen, she should lay one egg each day until her entire clutch of from three to six eggs is laid if she is a Canary or a Finch. A psittacine bird should lay an egg every other day, from three to eight eggs making the clutch. If she misses a day before the clutch is completed, hold her in your hand and examine her vent. If she is egg bound, you will see the bulge of the egg at the vent.

Keeping the bird warm at all times, put a few drops of warm mineral oil, or olive oil, inside the vent with an eyedropper. Try to apply the oil all around the lower part of the egg. The bird should pass the egg soon after the application of the oil. If she fails to do so, or continues to strain obviously in her attempt, a gentle pressure above the egg should help her expel it. After the bound egg has been passed, the hen will continue to lay her clutch as though nothing had happened, and she may not ever suffer egg binding again.

SCALY FACE AND SCALY LEG. Scaly leg is more common to Canaries and scaly face to the parrotlike birds, but both may contract both troubles at times. Scaly disease is caused by a tiny mite which infects the bird, causing inflammation on the legs and the bare parts of the face and causing the scales to stand erect. The legs and face have a rough appearance and often the scales peel off in patches. Bacitracin or neosporin ointment rubbed into the affected areas will help soften the rough scales and kill the mites. The treatment should be continued for three or four days, then again in a week. The preparation sold commercially under the name Scalex is made expressly for the treatment of this ailment and should be of use in eliminating the trouble. Use according to the directions on the bottle. Severe cases of scaly face on Budgies can be painted two times a week with tincture of gentian violet. Your druggist can make up this solution for you. Apply it with a Q-tip.

BROKEN BONES. Sometimes a bird will break a wing or a leg. Sometimes you yourself will break a bird's wing or leg. If the

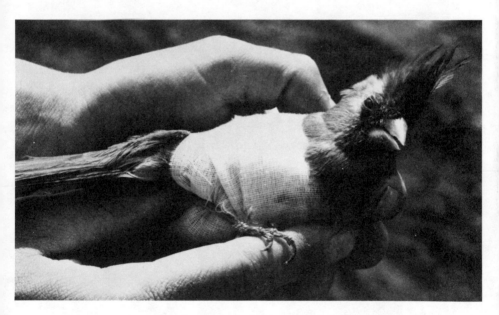

A broken wing may be bound close to the body until it heals, as with this female Cardinal, hit by a car.

break is a simple one, as in the case of a wing, nothing need be done except to place the bird in a cage from which all perches except one very close to the floor have been removed. Food and water dishes should be open and placed where the bird can have easy access to them. The break will heal by itself in about ten days. For a simple break on the leg, a splint can be fashioned out of a stiff feather, matchstick, or short piece of wire, taped snugly but not so tightly as to block the flow of circulation to the leg. The taping must be secured well because the bird will probably pick unceasingly at it. Compound fractures where the bone penetrates the skin are much more difficult to treat and should be left to a veterinarian.

PART V

Wild Mammals as Pets

INTRODUCTION

This section is not intended as a guide to encourage persons to catch, trap, or otherwise obtain small wild mammals and hold them in captivity as pets. Rather the intention is to discourage this practice as much as possible.

However, there are times when an animal is in need of help to enable it to survive, and this book is designed to tell you just what to do to keep the little creature in good health and a measure of contentment. Most small wild animals are under some kind of protection by most states, and you need a permit to keep one.

The deaths of thousands of small animals each year is a tragedy. This is largely due to the fact that people just do not know how to care for these animals, or what they need in order to survive. The animal "fortunate" enough to fall into the hands of a well-meaning person who thereupon sets about to raise it, is but very little more fortunate than those left to die unattended. This is because, while having the very best intentions, the person simply does not know what to do.

We will not tell you *how* to capture wild animals and cage them, but to tell you what to do and how to do it *if* you get an animal that needs help. This is, in fact, a kind of field book of life histories of small animals. It deals with a large number of wild animals, divided by families. It tells you what they eat, what they must have in the way of treatment, how to handle them, how to house them, and a short thumbnail sketch of their behaviors.

One thing we want to stress right at the beginning is the necessity of knowing the laws of your state governing the possession of these kinds of animals. Information about the detailed regulations that exist in every state may be had for the price of a postage stamp, by writing to the conservation department of your state. The information is free, and you should certainly take advantage of the opportunity of studying your animal laws if you intend to keep any of them.

One thing we should like to bring to your attention is the attitude of many persons toward some animals. Certain animals are called "bloodthirsty," "ferocious," "mean," "killers," and other derogatory names. As a general rule, these appellations are untrue. With very few exceptions—I can only think of two—animals kill for food or for the protection of their young. Sometimes they kill in defense of their mates, or their territory, but usually these last two conflicts end in the retreat of one or the other contestant, rather than in death. Unlike human beings, animals do not kill for "sport."

To the animal's prey, it may very well be ferocious and bloodthirsty, but only to the prey. To another animal, or to a human being, the creature is not. That animals try to bite, or fight to regain their freedom when caught is not bloodthirstiness, it is pure fright. A weasel, for example, is thought and said to be one of the most bloody of killers, slinking through the forest murdering as it goes. It probably is—to a mouse—but as an animal, it is docile, very interesting, and easily tamed.

CHAPTER THIRTY-TWO

What Is a Mammal?

What *is* a mammal? Well, an animal, in order to be a mammal, must have several things. It must be warm-blooded, it must suckle its young with milk, and it must have hair. Maybe it will not have a lot of hair, but somewhere on its body, you will find a hair or two on every mammal. There are a few hairs even on scaly animals like armadillos.

Mammals are found in every part of the world, from the polar icecaps to the hottest parts of Africa. They are found in the air and in the sea. They occur underground and in caves. There is practically no habitat in which a mammal or two cannot be found. They live in the deserts and on the highest mountains.

Mammals come in all shapes and sizes. From the tiny shrew, which weighs one tenth of an ounce, to the giant blue whale weighing 125 tons and more! It would take more than *forty million* shrews to equal one blue whale!

The food that mammals eat is almost as diversified as their size and shape. There are mammals that eat nothing but insects. Others eat only other animals. Some feed on plant life exclusively, while still others eat almost anything they can swallow. Some mammals eat meat that is rotting—carrion—while the larger carnivores eat meat that they kill fresh for each meal, tearing their dinner from the still warm carcasses of their prey.

There are about five thousand different kinds of mammals living today. There have been more, but many species have become extinct, through earth changes and upheavals, and through the murderous attentions of mankind. Many more species are on the way to extinction right now, and some of them will, in fact, disappear from the face of the earth during your lifetime. This is a terrible thing to think about, because once an animal is extinct, that means there will never be another one for all time! This is why conservation is such an important thing. We all should do whatever we can to help animals survive in a world we are making impossible for them to live in.

Each year thousands of "lost" baby animals are picked up and taken home, under the impression that an act of kindness is being performed. Actually, it is an act of cruelty, since the baby animal may not be lost at all. The fact that adult animals are not visible means nothing. They may be near, in hiding, and, sometimes, ready to attempt to lure you away from the immediate vicinity of their young, but, if the baby animal is scooped up and carried away, the adult animals can do very little about it.

Thus starts a period of misery for the young animal, usually ending in death after a time of lingering malnutrition or other horror. Not the least important item in keeping a young animal, especially if it is really a young one, is the matter of temperature. They must be kept hot, and this means twenty-four hours a day, not just warmed up once in a while. Next comes the matter of food.

Suppose you find a vole, for example. Voles are those silken-soft little meadow mice with short tails and dark fur. Before you think about running home with it to keep it as a pet—consider the fact that voles must eat their own weight in food every day in order to survive. This means that the better part of your day will be spent in hunting food for your little pet, which very quickly becomes your little pest. Then what are you going to do with it?

If you dump it outdoors, the chance of its surviving overnight are slim indeed. Animals are very territorial-conscious. They establish their own territories and defend them against all comers —their own kind or other species. When you put an animal outside in another animal's territory, there is the chance that it will be discovered and killed by the owner of that particular territory. If you have kept the animal in captivity for a period of several days or weeks before letting it go, even though you took it back to the exact place from which you got it originally, it is more than likely that a new animal has moved into the vacated territory and your "pet" will then become an interloper and be driven off or mauled or killed.

The point is, baby animals seen in the wild are usually not lost at all. They are either out being taught by their parent animals what to eat, how to climb, hunt, swim, run, or whatever. As soon as a human being approaches, the adults fade away. Presumably the baby does, too, but often they are so young that the danger is not apparent to them, and they remain right out where you can see them. More often than not, the training they are getting is given to them long before they are weaned. Since some animals are difficult to feed and care for before they are weaned, it often amounts to murdering them to take them at that time.

Baby seals, for example, are almost impossible to nurse when they are still in the suckling stage. The mother seal does not have projecting teats like most mammals, and the young animals do not know what a nipple is for. The best way to suckle a baby seal is to soak up the milk formula in a clean sponge, and the little animal will, in turn, suck the sponge dry. Having read this, you now know about a baby seal, but suppose you found a "lost" one on a beach *before* you read this? You'd have a very difficult time of it, and the animal a worse time, if it survived!

You may think voles eat a lot. Their own weight, daily? A

shrew eats over three times its own weight daily, and this food
has to be living creatures—other animals, insects, frogs, etc.
What do you think of the task of feeding a shrew? It will literally starve to death within one day, if food is not constantly supplied it. And this feeding must continue throughout the night as
well as the daytime. Shrews for pets, anyone?

So we come down to asking, if baby animals in the woods are
not lost and should not be taken, where would we find an animal for a pet? There are several ways you can be certain that
the animal needs care and could be kept as a pet. One is the discovery of an adult animal killed on a highway with young
nearby. If you examine the dead animal and determine that it
was the female, then the young animals are orphans and almost
surely will die or be killed if nothing is done to help them.

Sometimes the baby animals will stay by their mother after
she has been killed, not leaving her, nor yet able to find food.
These are the pathetic cases, and the little animals survive only
until some predator chances along. Raccoon families often go for
walks along the highways, and the three or four babies playfully
skip around, with their peculiar and distinctive waddle. If they
venture out on the roadway, the mother will go after them, and
that is the time she can be struck by a passing car.

Baby animals are orphaned in other ways too. A predator can
catch the mother and kill her, leaving her young alone and
defenseless. Usually there are some signs of the struggle and kill
near the spot where you find the babies. Bits of fur, a few bones,
a partly eaten carcass, blood on the disturbed plant growth—all
signs of a predator having taken its prey.

You may actually witness the abandonment of a small animal
by the adult. This is usually the case if the young animal is injured or sick, and, if it is injured or sick, the chances of your
being able to keep it alive are pretty slim anyway. If the injuries

are internal, there is very little hope for its recovery, and the most humane thing to do would be to put it quickly out of its misery.

But if the injury is external—say a broken leg—you stand a pretty good chance of saving the animal. The leg can be set and splinted, and will, in all likelihood, heal. The animal may limp and be unable to catch prey for food, but if you keep it, it can live its life span without too much distress.

Young, or even fully grown animals can be purchased from pet stores. There are stores specializing in captive wild animals. If your state requires a permit in order to keep a wild animal as a pet, then you should inquire of the department as to the availability of such animals. Often the conservation officers have a number of animals either confiscated or found, or brought in to them by other persons. These are kept for a time in "game farms" and the department might be very pleased to give away one or two to a properly licensed person who knows how to care for it.

However you obtain your animal, you should not think of getting it until you have read up all you can on that particular species of animal—so you know what its requirements are going to be—and until all arrangements have been made to keep it properly. You need the right kind of cage, large enough, easily cleaned, food and water provisions (what the animal eats and how much it eats), whether or not its food is going to be easy for you to obtain, not just now, but in the winter. For instance, will you be able to carry it through without it becoming such a big chore that you tire of the task?

The next thing you want to take into consideration when selecting a wild animal as a pet is what it is going to turn into. When babies, most animals are darling, cuddly little things that are a lot of fun to have and play with. But—little baby animals

Two young raccoons raiding a pear tree.

may grow up into great big animals, and when they are large, they are quite different from when they are small. For example, when a raccoon is a baby, there isn't a cuter animal possible, nor one more friendly. Right out of the wild, they will cuddle up to you, nibble on a finger or an ear, and like nothing better than to be rolled about, tickled, and played with. This is the baby stage.

They grow a little and become a teen-ager. They are still the most friendly of animals. They still want to play almost all of the time, and they still playfully nibble a finger or an ear, but their nibbling draws blood. Their teeth are as sharp as needles and very nearly as long. They're not so much fun to play with, at this time, they hurt. But wait. They are still growing, and after a time they become adult. Now your itsy-bitsy cuddly baby is nearly three feet long and weighs twenty-five pounds or more. When it nibbles at your ear, it is more apt than not to rip it off your head. When it playfully chews your finger, it gashes it to the bone.

Yet it is still a tamed animal and is not attacking you. It is merely doing what it was trained to do, and what comes naturally for it—playing with you. Only you're not another raccoon and cannot defend yourself.

The point of all this explanation is simple and should be self-evident—you can tame a wild animal, but you cannot tame its reflexes. I think that sentence is the most important lesson a person can learn when dealing with wild animals. In order successfully to handle animals of any kind, you must become familiar with its behavior. You must know how it acts in times of stress. The animal may be perfectly tame (and I have never found an animal of any species, which, if taken young enough and treated with enough care and tenderness, cannot be tamed), but you must take into consideration that sometime or other, through no fault of your treatment at all, the reflexes of that animal might take over and this can result in drastic consequences.

And the danger increases with the adult size and behavior of the animal being kept. A mountain lion cub is roly-poly and playful. An adult mountain lion, as tame as a kitten from having been raised in a household, can still, at a sharp moment of fright, disembowel you with one blow of its paw, and this is the normal reflex of a mountain lion. Oh, it will come over to you and purr, and lick the blood gushing from your fatal wound, and wonder why you don't get up and play some more, but you will not be any less dead.

Now we come to the other big item in the keeping of a wild animal. When it does get to a size that is unmanageable for you, or when, after growing up, its disposition changes and it becomes vicious and ornery, what are you going to do with it? How are you going to get rid of it? Who will take it?

You cannot, after raising an animal from a baby, just take it out to the woods and turn it loose. It will not survive. It would be the height of cruelty to do this to an animal just to afford you the pleasure of having it while it was young and cute. It will not have been taught to hunt for prey, it will not know how to protect itself from the elements or from predators. It will be used to human beings and walk up to the first one it sees, more than likely getting itself shot on sight. It is defenseless and vulnerable.

Give it to the zoo? Zoos do not want these kinds of animals. They usually have their quota of small animals and are not geared to take in all the unwanted charges of the public. They have no funds to feed and house them, and, usually, the new animal will not be tolerated by the ones already in the cages. It smells like people.

Give it to someone else? If you cannot manage it, why do you suppose someone else can? Unless, of course, he is a field biologist who just happens to want a specimen of that kind of animal.

Sometimes universities want animals and will take a specimen, but usually they want it for biological studies, inoculation and/or dissection. The result is death for the animal. If that is what you want, give it to a university lab.

One small ray of hope is in the privately owned "game farms" that are located in most states. These small zoos are run for the profit of the owner, and anything they can get for free is usually welcomed. There is the possibility that they may have so many of a common animal that they do not want any more, but that is not very often the case.

Some of these game farms are very well run and operated for the greatest comfort and welfare of the animals. Such a farm is the Space Farm in Beemerville, N.J., near Sussex. This is a very good zoo, run by a father and son. Besides the zoo, there is an enormous mink ranch, where sixteen thousand mink are raised for fur each year. The zoo is open to the public. The mink ranch is not. Some may call game farms wildlife refuges. Do not confuse this with the state-owned wildlife refuges, which are designed as resting, nesting, and breeding places for wildlife. The animals are not on display in these areas. The conservation department of your state will be able to tell you the locations of persons who are licensed to keep animals on exhibition and of any game farms in the state.

CHAPTER THIRTY-THREE

How to Handle Mammals

In helping young animals to survive, the three most important conditions are: temperature, housing, and food.

Young animals are usually one of a litter, except, of course, in the case of those creatures who only have one or two young at a time. The members of the litter remain in close contact with each other, and their body warmth is distributed among them all, keeping each one warm and cozy. At intervals the litter shifts, so that those animals on the outside of the group are shifted into the center where they can be warmed, and the center ones move to the outside and cool off a bit.

Most baby animals cannot survive for long even though they feed well and are cared for properly, unless this heat distribution is constantly maintained. About the best way to keep a baby warm is by the use of an electric heating pad. These usually come with a switch that can be set for two or three different degrees of heat. The pad can be wrapped in an old towel and laid in the bottom of a carton large enough to accommodate it. The animal, lying on top of the towel will be bathed in the rising heat. At first, keep the setting of the pad at the lowest heat. If the animal's body becomes warm to the touch and feels loose and relaxed, this degree is high enough. If, after the lapse of three or four hours the animal still feels cool or cold, turn the switch to the next higher setting.

It is useless to cover most young animals with a blanket or towel since they will only squirm out of it quickly and generally end up all tangled in the material. It would help preserve the heating pad if the fabric cover with which it is supplied is removed before using it for animals. The pad itself is made of rubber, or neoprene, which can easily be washed off or wiped clean. Young animals, especially those not weaned or ailing for one reason or another, are not housebroken and they pass urine every few minutes. The removal of the fabric cover keeps the pad cleaner and makes for less upkeep of the nesting box.

If the animal being cared for is *very* young, regardless of the species, it will not be necessary to cover the box. Not until they have their eyes open and are well on the way to being weaned, need you provide some method of keeping them confined to their heating box. When this time arrives and the animal becomes active and wants to explore, you can provide an intermediate cage to house it.

Cages for animals differ according to the type of animal you wish to keep in them. Animals like squirrels, flying squirrels, and other tree-climbing species, need vertical cages with something sturdy to climb on. Their lives are spent high off the ground for the most part. Naturally, they like to come down to earth once in a while. Squirrels run around on the ground looking for nuts and for places to bury them, but they are essentially high-living creatures and require height in their cages.

Animals like chipmunks can climb, but they are essentially ground-living animals and need low cages with a lot of horizontal room and hiding places, such as piles of rocks into which they can scamper when they are frightened or think they are in danger. As a rule, very active animals need more room in their cages than sedentary ones. Thus chipmunks want a much larger cage than a hamster, for example. Weasels need a lot of room, too, as do raccoons, but opossums can be kept in a smaller cage, equipped with something to climb on, because they are not as active and inquisitive as raccoons. Skunks can be housed in smaller cages than raccoons for the same reason—they are not quick and active animals.

Considerable thought should be given to the making of cages for small mammals. You should know what kind of animal you are going to keep, then the cage should be designed for its greatest comfort and for your greatest convenience.

An animal cage should have several things, regardless of the type of animal it is intended to house. First, you should be able to clean it easily. Next, you should have easy access to the inside while the animal is in it. By this I mean that you cannot keep an animal in a cage if you have to herd it into a corner every time you open the cage to keep the animal from jumping out. And, no matter how tame you have made your animal, it will always want to jump out every time its house is opened.

Third, the cage should be set up inside so that you have little trouble catching the animal if you need to. If you are making a pet of a wild animal, it should be handled frequently. If you are keeping it merely for survival, raising it until it will be able to fend for itself, then it should not be handled at all. As a matter of fact, the less it sees of people, the better off it will be since no taming is desired or the animal will lose some of its fear of human beings, possibly resulting in its death after it is released.

When rearing an animal that you intend to release, you should not go near the cage while it is active. If it is a nocturnal animal, then all feeding and care of the cage should be done when it is inactive—that is to say, during the day. Toward evening, but still while it is early enough for the animal to be sleeping, you can quietly put its food and water in the cage. If the animal is diurnal (active during the day), then late at night would be the best time for feeding and watering. In this way, you have the minimum personal contact with the creature.

Although it may seem silly, or even cruel, the more you teach the animal to be afraid of you, the better it is for its eventual survival upon release. So make some noise when feeding it. Frighten it a little, not by physical treatment, do not hit or poke it, just make no attempt to soothe it or cajole it into tolerating you. Plunk its food down with a bang, if you wish, bang the cage shut and walk away. When the poor creature stops shaking it will feed, and with this treatment it will only wish it were far, far, away from the two-legged monster who holds it captive. This response will carry over when it is released. Whenever it hears, sees, or smells a human being, it will make itself scarce in a hurry, and that is exactly the response it *must* have in order to survive.

Particular attention should be given to the bottoms of your cages. The most practical bottom is concrete, but this makes the cage a permanent fixture in your yard, so you should pick a spot for it that will not be in the way of your normal living. The actual making of a concrete bottom for a cage is not at all difficult. Concrete can be mixed by hand in small quantities, purchased in large paper bags as a ready-mixed preparation needing only the addition of water, or mixed in a portable concrete mixer if you have one, or have a friend who can loan you one. In most cities and rural areas there are machine rental places where you can rent a small concrete mixer for a very small amount by the day. One day would be all you would need it for.

If you mix your own concrete, you should use a 1-2-3 combination. This means one part of portland cement, two parts of builder's sand, and three parts of cracked rock or gravel. You can use whatever measure is easiest for you, one shovelful, one pailful, or one boxful. Add enough water while mixing to make the concrete a fairly loose material so it will pour readily and be easy to level out when in the form.

You must use wooden forms to pour concrete into, and these can be made of four short lengths of 2×4 nailed together to form a box large enough to accommodate the cage you are making. The cage should be built first, because it will be needed for a pattern for the hold-down bolts.

When the form has been filled with concrete, it should be leveled off either by puddling the concrete with a rake or by screeding. This means dragging a board across the top of the concrete to level it, letting the edge of the board rest on the sides of the form, and sawing it back and forth as you move it across the surface.

After the concrete has been leveled off, wait just a few minutes for the surface water to soak in, then carefully place the cage in position on the wet concrete. Press the cage just enough to make a mark all around on the surface of the soft concrete, then carefully lift the cage off and place it aside. Now you can see where to put the hold-down bolts. These can be ¼″ carriage bolts, long enough to imbed about two inches in the concrete and leave enough sticking out to go through the bottom rails of the cage, leaving room for a washer and nut. Carefully puddle two bolts into the concrete on each side of the cage, making sure that they are straight and solidly set.

Allow the concrete to set at least overnight before installing the cage. Wait for three or four days before removing the 2×4 form lumber. Set the cage down over the bolts, the bottom rails of the cage having been drilled to take the bolts, of course, and tighten the cage to the base with a washer and nut on each bolt.

This method of making cages is some trouble while in the making, but they are so trouble-free afterward, and so easy to clean and keep up that it is well worth the effort, time, and ex-

The completed cage makes a permanent home for the animals. This one will house a family of flying squirrels.

pense. Cement is cheap, and the forms can be used over and over to make as many bottoms as you want.

With a concrete bottom, gnawing animals find it impossible to chew holes in the cages and escape, provided, of course, that the wire screening covers the entire inside of the cage members. The cage can be cleaned with a small flat shovel like an old-fashioned coal scoop; it can be hosed down in the summer to keep the animals cool if need be; and there is no danger of the bottoms rotting out in one season. The cage can be painted before fastening it to the base, and is easily removed for repainting each year.

Cages themselves can be made out of 1″×2″ lumber and either ½″ mesh hardware cloth or 1″×2″ mesh "hog wire." For animals like raccoons, or opossums, skunks, and species of larger animals, the hog wire is fine. The thing to look for in selecting the screening is the size of the animal's head. If they can get their head through the opening in the wire, then they can get their body through, so, obviously, the 1″×2″ mesh wire would not be suitable for animals like weasels, chipmunks, ferrets, and similar species.

The cages should be made as large as you can possibly accommodate. The more room you give the animal, the more contented it remains. Frames are made of the wood, and the corners reinforced with triangular gussets of plywood. Use ½″ exterior plywood, and cut it into squares about 10″×10″ or 12″×12″. Each square is then cut diagonally from corner to corner to make the gussets. The side frames can be fastened together with wood fasteners at the corners, then the gusset placed in position and fastened with several roofing nails. These are galvanized and have large heads, and hold securely. The side for the entrance should have a second frame built into it to accommodate a door. The door is also made of 1″×2″ lumber and screened to its edges to keep the animals from chewing the wood away.

Horizontal cages are made a bit differently, since they are low and long, and you are not able to walk into them. The top should be divided, and one half of it hinged to permit access to the inside. If the cage is very long, then both halves of the top are hinged so they can be opened individually to permit access to both ends of the interior.

Depending upon where you live, the fastenings of the doors can be simple hooks and eyes, or a hasp with a padlock. In populated areas where there is the likelihood of vandalism, you should use a hasp and padlock. This will discourage people from opening the cages and releasing the animals. It is unfortunate, but this happens quite frequently.

It is an excellent idea to make a "holding" cage. This is a cage of medium size, and is used to hold animals when they are first brought home, especially if you already have an animal in the regular cage. They are useful because the stranger must be acclimated for a while before feeding, handling, or putting in its regular cage. In the holding cage the newcomer can be de-fleaed, cleaned up, and otherwise cared for. You can watch it for several days to make sure it is not sick or diseased. After it has been quarantined for a time, you can transfer it to a permanent housing.

Boxes for transporting animals are made in many styles and sizes by Alco Carrying Cases in New York City. These carrying cases are ideal for transporting animals and for shipping them. Some cases have screened fronts, and make fine temporary cages. Others have transparent tops to permit a view of the animal within. They are equipped with latches and handles. An easy way to ship an animal in one of the cases is to attach a shipping tag to the handle and simply send it parcel post. Some states may have restrictions against the importing of non-native animals, and you should inquire from the conservation department before having an animal shipped to you. The larger sized carriers with larger animals in them can be sent by express. The usual way is to mail the empty carrier to the person having the animal, and they return it with the animal inside.

In carrying cases, and in cages with solid bottoms, litter should be placed to absorb the waste products of the animal. While wood shavings are useful, the best kind of litter is one that absorbs readily, is easily cleaned out, and that kills odors to a certain extent. Such a material is called Cat-Comfort, which is made by the Georgia-Tennessee Mining and Chemical Company of Atlanta, Georgia. This granular, claylike material is very absorbent, easy to use, and clean to handle. An inch of this in the bottom of the cage keeps the animal clean, dry, and comfortable. Cat-Comfort is sold in most pet stores or pet departments and is reasonable in price.

Reliance Sales in Hempstead, New York, makes animal cages in several styles and sizes. These are excellent for containing small animals and also for use as holding cages. Most of them are equipped with a cleanout tray which is easily filled with Cat-Comfort, and which can be cleaned without any danger of the animal escaping.

Another possibility for holding animals temporarily is with the use of the larger sizes of live animal traps. Several companies make traps that are designed to catch the animal without hurting it. Mustang Manufacturing Company of Houston, Texas, manufactures a complete line of such traps, from quite small ones to very large ones. The very large traps will make excellent holding cages for temporary use for larger animals, and the smaller sizes do nicely for little creatures.

One thing to remember when setting live traps to catch animals, is (especially when going after large animals such as raccoons or skunks), that the trap must be fastened securely so the animal within cannot tip the whole contrivance over and escape.

It should be weighted down with a concrete block, or, if this is not convenient when setting the trap in the woods, possibly laying an old log across the top will suffice. Or tying the trap to a tree may work.

These Mustang traps are very useful for trapping the young of animals that you know have been orphaned. For instance, if a fox has been killed, either accidently or by design, and you know she had a den with young kits inside, a Mustang trap set at the opening of the den will almost surely net at least one of the young. Subsequent settings will most likely gather in the entire litter, if you bait it with goodies that the young foxes cannot resist.

Feeding young animals that have not yet been weaned is probably the most taxing part of keeping them alive. In the first place, baby animals nurse with considerable frequency, and often nurse through the night as well as in the daytime. This is especially true, of course, of nocturnal animals, whose normal nursing time is at night and which may be very difficult to get to feed during the day.

Then there is the matter of what to feed these charges. Plain cow's milk, contrary to most persons' thinking, is not very good for the young of wild animals. First of all, it is not rich enough. Secondly, for some reason or other, baby wild animals seem to languish on a diet of cow's milk unless it is made into a formula of some kind. The addition of honey, a little cream, some salt, or some corn syrup makes the milk more palatable and more nutritious, but how much to mix with the milk is a problem.

I have found that the prepared baby formula Similac, made by Ross Laboratories and sold in drug stores, grocery stores, and supermarkets all over the country, is nearly a universal food for the young unweaned wild animals. Similac is made in concentrated form to which you add water, in plain formula ready to

An armadillo will become a lifelong friend if you feed it lots of honey from a spoon.

use, and also a ready-to-use kind with added iron. This last variety, with the addition of infant vitamins, has worked very well, so far, with a very wide assortment of wild species.

Weaning these animals presents yet another problem. What do you wean them on? The very best thing, of course, is their natural food, but often the natural food of an animal is hard to come by. When you do obtain such an animal, the best thing to do is to get it into the hands of someone who is competent in rearing it. However, this is often impossible, and then what are you to do? You have the choice of two avenues—either kill the little fellow to "put it out of its misery," or you can try to get food that will fill the nutritional needs of the animal. This business of putting an animal out of its misery has always given me some bad times. To begin with, who is the judge of just how much misery the animal is enduring? Most of the time, it isn't miserable at all, but just plain hungry! This, it is understood, if the animal has not been injured in any way.

So, as one of the very important items of information in this book, I am listing, within the life history of each animal mentioned, as many of the natural foods of each species as I can dis-

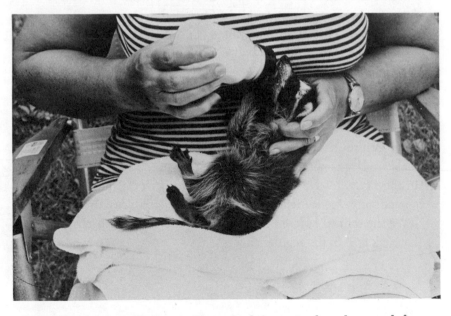

A baby bottle will do nicely to feed an animal such as a baby raccoon.

cover. These, then, would be the foods you should try to get into your pet when weaning it, and which you should feed it after it is weaned. And one thing you should keep always at the front of your mind is that you are feeding a *wild animal*. You are not feeding yourself, and while some of the foods, in the condition which is acceptable to that animal, might, in your estimation, gag a maggot, don't let that worry you. The animal will relish it and it will taste good to him. As a matter of fact, even maggots are excellent food for many species of wild creatures, including human beings!

One other thing that is important to the comfort of young animals is the matter of fleas. Most animals taken from the wild have fleas, and some of them are literally crawling with the parasites. It is comparatively easy to de-flea the little creatures, if a few simple precautions are taken. One of the ninety-day flea collars can be used, not on the animal, since usually the young animal is too small to wear a collar around its neck. The collar is wrapped in a strip of metal screening, or small-meshed hardware cloth to discourage the animal from chewing it. Form the screening into a circle, with the collar inside, then lay it in the nesting or sleeping box so the baby animal will have to sleep inside the ring. Within a short time the fleas will all be gone. If the animals are large enough, the collars may be put around their necks in the normal way. It would be better to perform the de-fleaing operation in your holding cage, so that any fleas that might leave the animal before being killed by the collar, will not transfer back to it in the regular cage.

CHAPTER THIRTY-FOUR

Marsupials as Pets

ORDER: Marsupialia.

FAMILY: Didelphiidae.

SCIENTIFIC NAME: *Didelphis marsupialis.*

POPULAR NAME: Opossum.

RANGE: From New England south to Mexico. West to Iowa. Introduced to California.

GESTATION PERIOD: Twelve to thirteen days.

BIRTH MONTH: June–July. Sometimes two litters annually.

NUMBER OF YOUNG: Up to twenty. Only thirteen will survive.

NURSING PERIOD: Eight weeks.

LIFE SPAN: Eight years.

PHOTO PERIOD: Mostly nocturnal.

This is the only species of marsupial in the United States.

Opossums are very primitive animals. Most of the marsupials are found in Australia, Madagascar, and Tasmania, but the opossum is a true marsupial and, in recent years, has made its way far north in this country, even though it is, strictly speaking, a tropical, or at least a warm climate animal.

The fact that it is a marsupial, and that its diet is varied, probably accounts for its success in invading the colder regions of its range. In common with most primitive creatures, the opossum is a dull-witted animal, usually slow in its movements, although it can move quite rapidly if the occasion warrants.

These animals can climb very well, because they have an opposed digit on the hind feet, and a prehensile (grasping) tail. A female can climb with her brood of young hanging on to her tail by their own tails. It is not an uncommon sight to see a female opossum walking along, her tail held stiffly horizontal over her back, and a row of small upside-down babies hanging neatly along the length of it.

Very young opossums are difficult to feed. Their mouths are not adapted for taking food from a large nipple, or even from an eyedropper. When baby opossums are born, they are smaller than a honeybee, and are not fully developed. They crawl into their mother's pouch and fasten themselves to one of her thirteen teats. Since an opossum can have as many as twenty young at a litter, those that are late in reaching the teats automatically die. The young animal remains attached to the teat and suckles without letting go.

The growth during the first week is absolutely amazing. They can reach a size of five inches from that of a bee within this time. The young animals nurse for two months. At the end of the first month, they may come partially out of the pouch for short periods, but do not actually leave it until they are about eight weeks old. They may come clear out of the pouch at about five or six weeks, but scamper back inside to feed and sleep. At two months the young opossum is able to shift for itself.

Once in a while a female opossum will be hit by a car and killed or maimed, but not squashed. In her pouch may be a brood of youngsters. These can be removed from the pouch all right, but it will be very difficult to rear them if they are not very close to being weaned. The best substitute for their mother's milk is Similac with iron. The first morning feeding should have children's vitamins added and an egg beaten into the formula.

The young animals should be fed four times daily, which is the barest minimum for this species of baby. Six or even eight daily feedings would be even better.

Usually a baby animal wiggles and squirms around while it is in the box and when you pick it up, but the instant you start to feed it, all wiggling stops and the creature settles down to the very serious business of filling up its little tummy. Not so opossums. They wiggle, and they wiggle, and they squirm until it is

The litter gathered around the festive board was taken from the pouch of the mother which was killed by a car.

almost impossible to get an eyedropper into their mouths. Then when you do get it in, they chew the dropper instead of sucking on it. This results in the milk spilling out the sides of their mouths, since they cannot chew the dropper and swallow at the same time.

When they are this young, though, they really are truly charming. Their fur is not unkempt as it is when they are adult, and they haven't yet begun to smell. Two very bad things about opossums are that they have a musky smell about them when they are big, and they have an unfortunate expression on their faces. Opossums *look* vicious and mean. Their lips are shaped in a perpetual snarl, and, being the primitive animal that they are, they have a full complement of teeth which look as though they could tear your arm off. Fifty teeth, as a matter of fact. Their fur is coarse and straggly, and their ears and tail naked.

Weaning opossums is quite a deal. Their food is varied, and they eat almost anything. Mice and insects are their staple diet in the wild. They go absolutely batty over raw eggs, and probably, being good climbers, birds' eggs form a large part of their diet. Opossums are a real pest to poultry raisers too, because they not only eat eggs and are not loath to take all they can find, but they like chicken, and think nothing of polishing off a fat hen each night. About the easiest way to wean them is with insects. Catching grasshoppers and crickets is not hard, and these can be offered to the babies who can chew them with their tiny baby teeth, since they are soft-bodied insects. Fruit, especially soft pulpy fruit, is readily taken. Bananas are difficult, since they are dry when ripe and stick in the small animal's throat. When they are adult, bananas are relished, as is any meat, preferably raw, and raw or cooked vegetables, any kind of fruit, milk, or eggs. You should have no difficulty feeding an opossum after it has been taken past the rough time of weaning.

It is almost useless to take an adult possum and try to tame it. They are much too dull-witted to tame up and become pets. Even when you get them very young they remain completely aloof as they reach maturity.

CHAPTER THIRTY-FIVE

Insect-eaters as Pets

In this country, this group includes moles and shrews. We will list only a very few, because of the great difficulty in keeping them. It would require many hours each day to supply food to most of these creatures, and some of them would have to be fed right through the night as well.

ORDER: Insectivora.
FAMILY: Talpidae.
SCIENTIFIC NAME: *Scalopus aquaticus*.
POPULAR NAME: Common mole.
RANGE: Over the entire United States.
GESTATION PERIOD: About six weeks.
BIRTH MONTH: April.
NUMBER OF YOUNG: Four or five.
NURSING PERIOD: Three to four weeks.
LIFE SPAN: Probably about two to four years.
PHOTO PERIOD: Both nocturnal and diurnal.

Moles are often dug up in lawns or found in fields. Moles are very interesting animals, very soft and quite slow of movement, although they can scamper if necessary. Their eyes are so small and so hidden by their fur that to all intents they are blind. In this species, they are apparently missing.

To keep moles contented, you should have at least six or eight inches of dirt in the bottom of their cage for them to tunnel in and around. They will live without the dirt, but not feel very secure.

They are fed beetle grubs, earthworms, insect larvae of all kinds, mature insects, and some vegetable matter. Earthworms and beetle larvae (grubs) are their main diet, and these must be supplied to them in fairly large quantities. The average mole will eat over one half its own weight each day. In feeding insectivorous animals, you have recourse to persons selling fishing bait as a food source when you are unable to find enough food yourself. These places have worms and sometimes insect larvae —mostly aquatic—for sale as bait, and you can buy enough to feed your animal, usually at very reasonable prices.

It would be useless to try to keep unweaned baby moles alive, if you found any. They nurse for about one month.

Mole fur is soft and silky, very short, and it grows straight up out of the body. The fur does not impede the progress of the animals when they are crawling through their tunnels. If the fur lay pointing toward the rear of the animal, or toward the front of it, there would be the likelihood of its catching against the sides of the burrows, making it difficult for the animal to move in that direction.

One thing it is important to know about moles is their feeding habits. The animal feeds voraciously at any time of day or night. This feeding is interrupted by periods of sleep—lasting from five to six hours. When the animal awakens, every bit of food has been digested and utilized by the body, and, unless food in large quantities is made immediately available, the creature will literally starve to death while you watch it. The same is true of shrews, only they require even more food at shorter intervals.

The metabolic rate of insectivorous animals is incredible, and it is this one detail that makes both moles and shrews very poor risks as pets. You would simply be on the run twenty-four hours a day to keep the tiny creature filled up enough to keep it from dying of starvation in the palm of your hand!

ORDER: Insectivora.

FAMILY: Talpidae.

SCIENTIFIC NAME: *Parascalops breweri.*

POPULAR NAME: Hairy-tailed mole.

RANGE: Northeastern United States to Ohio.

GESTATION PERIOD: Four weeks.

BIRTH MONTH: April to May.

NUMBER OF YOUNG: Four or five.

NURSING PERIOD: Three weeks.

LIFE SPAN: Five years.

PHOTO PERIOD: Nocturnal and diurnal.

This is a much rarer animal than the common mole and it is a little smaller. The habits are very like those of the common mole, but this animal requires more food, consuming its own weight each day. Earthworms and grubs form the major part of the diet.

The fur of the hairy-tailed mole is a little coarser than ordinary mole's fur. Moles are considered pests, not because they are actually pests themselves, but because they make such extensive burrows, which, after completion, are used by mice that do damage to the root structures of economically important plants.

CHAPTER THIRTY-SIX

Meat-eaters as Pets

We come now to the large order of animals that eat meat. This group, and the gnawing animals, comprise the two largest groups of mammals discussed. Many carnivores are really omnivores, since, not only are they meat-eaters, they eat vegetable foods as well. This makes it far easier to feed the animal, especially in winter, because even if wild animal foods are not available, there is always a kind of meat we eat that will serve for your pet. Also, white mice and rats are available throughout the entire year from pet stores, or wholesale from breeding companies, which breed these small animals by the tens of thousands for use in laboratories. The companies sell their exhausted breeders for a few cents each, and it costs practically nothing to keep an animal on this diet.

ORDER: Carnivora.
FAMILY: Procyonidae.
SCIENTIFIC NAME: *Procyon lotor.*
POPULAR NAME: Raccoon.
RANGE: Everywhere but the far western part of the country.
GESTATION PERIOD: Sixty-three days.
BIRTH MONTH: April to May.
NUMBER OF YOUNG: Two to six.
NURSING PERIOD: Two months.

LIFE SPAN: Twelve to fifteen years.

PHOTO PERIOD: Nocturnal.

Raccoons seem to be born tame. Any young raccoon can be picked up and handled for a few minutes, and from that point on, it will follow you around like a puppy. For two years, at least, the animal will remain tame and very friendly. After two years they become unpredictable and may even turn belligerent. Since they have an excellent set of needle-sharp teeth, this belligerency may become painful, if not to say dangerous. An adult raccoon's bite is nothing to pass over lightly. A fully grown raccoon can kill a large dog if it is cornered.

Raccoons are one of the most curious of animals. They get their noses into everything. Every nook and cranny must be thoroughly investigated, and, if easy access is denied them, they merely set about taking things apart until they can get into whatever it is they are examining. A half grown coon can climb right up a tiled bathroom wall, hang on with three hands while it uses the fourth to open the medicine cabinet and sweep off the top shelf to make a "den" for the night.

Raccoons are omnivorous and will eat anything. The story about the animal washing its food before eating it is not exactly the case. In nature, much of a raccoon's food are water creatures. Fish, which it is adept at catching, crayfish, clams, and mussels. The animals does not search for this food with its eyes, but stands near the edge of the water puddling around with its forepaws, instantly grasping anything that moves as soon as it makes contact. In captivity, the animal may carry its food over to its water dish and drop it in, then scrabble around in the dish until it again finds it. In doing so it is only satisfying its feeding instinct, not washing the food.

Infant unweaned raccoons may be fed Similac, either plain or fortified with iron and with an egg beaten up in it. The formula should be warmed and strained before pouring into a nursing bottle. The stringy parts of the egg white may otherwise clog the nipple. A raccoon will take readily to a baby bottle. They can be weaned on almost anything. Start with large insects like grasshoppers or large crickets, soft fruits, soft vegetables, meat in small pieces, and fish.

Vitamins should be given unweaned animals, mixed in with the Similac. One dose a day is sufficient, and liquid children's vitamins are the best to use.

Once a raccoon has been raised for a time it can be turned loose outside, if you live in a convenient location, and the animal will stay around the house like a dog or cat. A doghouse-type structure can be provided for it, and, at first, it should be confined within the house in any practical manner, being fed right outside the opening. In a day or two the confining barrier may be removed and your pet raccoon is part of your family. The disadvantage of keeping the animal in this kind of freedom is that it will range at night. The ranging itself is not bad. But the animal, being friendly, will walk up to any human being it may come across, and many of these human beings have the unhappy philosophy that anything that moves should be shot. The other danger is that the raccoon may be killed on the road by a passing car. They are at best a slow-moving animal unless they are fleeing or chasing; then they can really get along. Countless thousands are road-killed each year because they simply do not get out of the way in time.

Almost every state in which raccoons live protect them in one way or another, and you will have to have a permit to keep one as a pet. Investigate this law before you procure your animal, and you may be saved a lot of grief.

ORDER: Carnivora.

FAMILY: Procyonidae.

SCIENTIFIC NAME: *Nasua narica.*

POPULAR NAME: Coati, coatimundi.

RANGE: Extreme southwestern part of the United States, also Mexico and Central America.

GESTATION PERIOD: Ten weeks.

BIRTH MONTH: July.

NUMBER OF YOUNG: Four to six.

NURSING PERIOD: About eight weeks.

LIFE SPAN: Up to fifteen years.

PHOTO PERIOD: Mostly diurnal, but is sometimes abroad at night.

Coatimundis are closely related to the raccoons, and have much the same habits. They also eat the same foods as raccoons, and dig with their rubbery snouts for roots and tubers. They also eat scorpions and tarantulas.

While they can be tamed when young, coatis often turn vicious when they mature, and for this reason they should be carefully watched as they obtain their full growth. Usually the females are more belligerent than the males. Aside from the superficial outer markings, these animals do not resemble raccoons very much because they have long bodies, a very long tail, which is more often than not held stiffly erect, more like a cat than a raccoon. The face has the same kind of black mask as the coon, however, and the coatimundi is an even better climber than the raccoon.

Young animals thrive on Similac and are easy to feed. Their mouths are extremely wide, and with their flexible snout curled up they can almost swallow the entire feeding bottle, so keep a good hold on it at feeding time!

The mother will attack viciously if the babies are taken away

A little pug-nosed coatimundi makes a good pet only while it is young. They are apt to become mean when adult.

from her, even to play with, and it is not a good idea to keep the adult with the babies in captivity, unless you allow her to perform all the maternal duties.

ORDER: Carnivora.
FAMILY: Mustelidae.
SCIENTIFIC NAME: *Mustela erminea.*
POPULAR NAME: Bonaparte weasel.

RANGE: This species, or closely related species are found over most of the country.

GESTATION PERIOD: As long as eight to ten months.

BIRTH MONTH: April to May.

NUMBER OF YOUNG: Four to eight.

NURSING PERIOD: Six weeks.

LIFE SPAN: About ten years.

PHOTO PERIOD: Usually nocturnal, but may be abroad during the day.

There are several species of weasel, all looking very much alike. The differences among them are slight. Several of them become pure white in the winter, with only the black end of the tail colored. Then they are called ermines. Their fur is useful for women's apparel, although its use has fallen off considerably the last few decades.

Weasels are very important animals economically, aside from their fur value, because they feed abundantly on mice and other small rodents. Millions of mice, rats, and other harmful rodents are killed annually by weasels, and in captivity, mice must be the main part of their diet. The weasel should be permitted to kill its own food, which it can do most efficiently and quickly.

In keeping animals belonging to this group, the matter of food is most important. They require considerably more food than their size would seem to indicate. A mink, for example, will eat three to four times its own weight of food daily. The reason for mortality in captivity for most of the weasels is starvation, because otherwise they are a fairly long-lived and hardy animal.

Weasels can climb, but they much prefer to remain on the ground, and their dens are burrows or rock piles. Their cages must have secure bottoms or they will dig out. They must be taken very young in order to become tame enough to be handled, and even then an individual may not permit you to hold it without a struggle.

Weasels, in common with the other members of the Mustelidae, have anal scent glands that give off an offensive odor when the animal is frightened or angry. Actually, the animal always has a slight musky odor, which is most unpleasant to some persons but does not bother others.

Young weasels can be fed Similac either plain or with iron. It is better if a small amount of blood from a freshly killed mouse, rat, or chipmunk is mixed with the formula. They can be weaned by cutting up a mouse into very small pieces and feeding these to the little animal. Feed the fur and intestines as well as their contents. As soon as the weasel can tear pieces of meat from the mouse by itself, let it have a whole mouse to eat. After a short time it will be able to kill its own prey, and then it should be given the mice alive. White mice are ideal food for weasels if you cannot trap enough wild field or meadow mice alive. Weasels will also eat birds, small snakes, and, when adult, can kill and eat rabbits, rats, and chipmunks. They are strictly carnivorous animals. Mink are another species of weasel.

ORDER: Carnivora.

FAMILY: Mustelidae.

SCIENTIFIC NAME: *Mephitis mephitis.*

POPULAR NAME: Common skunk.

RANGE: Over the entire United States.

GESTATION PERIOD: Fifty-one to sixty-three days.

BIRTH MONTH: May.

NUMBER OF YOUNG: From four to ten.

NURSING PERIOD: Six to seven weeks.

A young pet keeper playing with a pair of baby skunks.

LIFE SPAN: Ten years or more.

PHOTO PERIOD: Nocturnal, although sometimes seen in daylight.

Hardly any of you needs an introduction to this animal. Everyone is familiar with the pretty black-and-white creature that
possesses such effective armament. The story that a skunk cannot spray its scent if you are holding it up by the tail, by the
way, is not true. A skunk can sock-it-to-you in any position.
Whether or not it wants to is another story. Usually he isn't really interested in using his weapons and will give you every opportunity to stop scaring him so much that he has to let go. The
liquid he shoots at you does not make you blind, either, as so
many people believe. It will burn your eyes exceedingly, but
you will not lose your sight.

The skunk relies on its gaudy coloring to warn its enemies. If
the striking black-and-white flag does not stop the attacker, the
skunk will erect his tail and stamp his front feet. This is his last
warning. Now he's really getting scared. After the foot stamp-
ing, the next move is to turn his back, keeping his tail up in the
air, and let you have it! And his aim is as accurate as a sharp-
shooter's.

However, skunks would rather not spray and, if approached
quietly with no sudden moves or loud noises, they can actually
be picked up and petted with no attempts to become belligerent.
Skunks make ideal pets, becoming very tame, and it is not necessary to have them de-scented in order for this to be true. The
only reason for de-scenting the animal is because people other
than the immediate family who has it may frighten it, tease it,
or goad it into a frenzy.

It is therefore best to have the glands removed. Any veterinarian can do the job easily and quickly. Pet stores that carry
skunks for sale always have the de-scented variety.

Skunks can be kept in cages outdoors all winter. They do not hibernate and are active even when the snow is on the ground. Shelter can be provided in the form of a large hollow log, into which they will walk to curl up and keep warm. The sides of the log should be thick, to afford as much insulation against the elements as possible.

The cage for skunks should not be placed where it receives full sunshine. Remember that the animals are mostly nocturnal, and full sun would quickly kill them. Their fur is thick and black, absorbing the heat of the sun, and they would not be able to cool their bodies quickly enough to dissipate the killing temperature. Sudden and loud noises frighten skunks, as they do most all animals, and the animal should not be subjected to hysteria and screaming of children, as is often the case when children "play" with a pet animal. The racket and violent motions are just not to a skunk's liking, and will actually damage the sensitive creature if it cannot escape to quiet and hiding.

Feeding a skunk should present no problem. They are carnivorous, but they also relish fruits, berries and seeds, nuts, vegetables, eggs—they are extremely fond of eggs—mice and other small mammals, corn, peas, and other vegetables, and insects. They will eat with relish the large white beetle grubs that are so destructive to lawns and plant-root systems. At least once a week, better two or three times, they should be given a white mouse, or live field mouse if you can trap one, and be permitted to kill it itself and eat the entire animal. All carnivores need the full meat of prey—muscle meat in the form of the inner organs and intestines, the blood, fur, and small bones, for calcium, roughage, and a balanced diet. Feeding captive animals hamburger, for example, is an almost certain way to lead it into poor health, rickets, vitamin deficiencies, and other debilitating ailments.

Skunks also need a constant supply of fresh clean water, and they drink quite frequently. When they are young, and when you are weaning small ones, a very good food is Similac with iron, into which is beaten a raw egg. They will relish this and thrive on it. A few drops of liquid children's vitamins can be added once a day if desired. While the Similac has vitamins added, the little extra will do no harm.

Always provide dishes that are wide and flat enough to prevent them from tipping easily, to animals like skunks, raccoons, and others of the same size and bulk. They have the habit of putting their front paws on the edge of the dish, and if he doesn't have a broad steady base, they will dump out the contents. There are several species of skunks in the United States.

ORDER: Carnivora.

FAMILY: Canidae.

SCIENTIFIC NAME: *Vulpes fulva.*

POPULAR NAME: Red fox.

RANGE: Almost the entire United States except the western-central states.

GESTATION PERIOD: About fifty-one days.

BIRTH MONTH: March to April.

NUMBER OF YOUNG: Four to ten.

NURSING PERIOD: About five weeks.

LIFE SPAN: Up to twelve years.

PHOTO PERIOD: Mostly nocturnal, but often diurnal as well.

The fox is a much maligned animal, being treated as a pest in almost its entire range, with a bounty paid for killing it in many of the states. Actually, the fox is a valuable animal economically, since it is a superb mouser and ratter, killing thousands of these true pest animals each year. The fact that it also takes a chicken now and then is enough to condemn the animal in the eyes of most farmers, however, and it is a tribute to the sagacity of the creature that it is not extinct.

Foxes are wily enough to evade most hunters and have established themselves in places right next to human habitations, seemingly in derisive challenge to their hunters. When taken young enough, a fox can be tamed to the point where it can be handled and be called a pet. However, the animal must be constantly in contact with people, or it will quickly revert to a wild state. They must be handled and played with daily.

Fox cages must be large enough to give the animal considerable space to run and pace for exercise. There should also be something high to climb on. An old section of tree with several branches is good. There should also be provided a "den" of some kind for retreat. This can be large rocks piled in such a manner that there is a hollow cage within. Care should be taken to pile the rocks so they will not collapse if the animal jumps up on the outside of the pile. If they are set in mortar, it is even better.

Young foxes are weaned on small pieces of chicken, soft fruits, and some vegetables. When weaned, the diet should consist largely of mice, chipmunks, rabbits, rats, chickens, and pigeons. A fox will also eat fruit, vegetables, and carrion, and this varied diet must contribute largely to its ability to survive under adverse conditions such as the encroachment of mankind.

ORDER: Carnivora.

FAMILY: Felidae.

SCIENTIFIC NAME: *Lynx rufus.*

POPULAR NAME: Bobcat, wildcat.

RANGE: Western and southern United States, occasionally in the Northeast.

GESTATION PERIOD: Fifty to sixty days.

BIRTH MONTH: Throughout the year, but mostly in the spring.

NUMBER OF YOUNG: Two to four.

NURSING PERIOD: Eight weeks.

LIFE SPAN: Up to twenty-five years.

PHOTO PERIOD: Generally nocturnal.

The bobcat, and the lynx, *Lynx canadensis,* which it greatly resembles, are two of the smaller large cats in this country. These will be all the felines offered in this book. Both the lynx and the bobcat must be taken as small kittens in order to become tame. However, they do tame up and will live very much like a house cat if they have had enough care and attention while weaning and rearing. These animals are under protection in some parts of its range, and a bounty paid on their hides in others. When they get older, the bobcat and lynx prove unpredictable and may become dangerous, biting on little or no provocation and scratching deeply when touched.

They are clean animals and can be raised on cat foods, but their main staple diet is rodents. They are one of the excellent mouse and rat killers and also take enormous numbers of rabbits.

CHAPTER THIRTY-SEVEN

Rodents as Pets

The rodents comprise a very large group of animals, and specimens belonging to this order are more familiar to people than any others. Certainly the rodents are much more plentiful in any given location, are easier to trap or catch than the more wary predators, and more of them are kept in captivity as pets.

Some of the most endearing of all animals belong to the group of rodents. Also some of the most obnoxious. Rodents are found from tiny, tiny creatures to truly giant ones. They live in every possible climate and environment. They are very adaptable and take well to captive life if obtained when they are young.

All are more or less vegetarian, but almost all eat insects, and some are omnivorous, requiring meat in their diet as well as vegetable matter. Some of these animals will turn cannibal if they are not given enough meat to vary their diet.

We will list a number of rodents. They are easy to keep, easy to feed, and interesting animals in every way.

ORDER: Rodentia.
FAMILY: Sciuridae.
SCIENTIFIC NAME: *Marmota monax.*
POPULAR NAME: Woodchuck, ground hog, marmot.
RANGE: Most of eastern United States.
GESTATION PERIOD: Thirty-one to thirty-two days.

This little woodchuck decided that friendliness was better than fighting, especially when the reward was a delicious carrot.

BIRTH MONTH: April to May.
NUMBER OF YOUNG: Two to eight.
NURSING PERIOD: Five weeks.
LIFE SPAN: Four to five years.
PHOTO PERIOD: Mostly diurnal.

Surely everyone is familiar with the short-haired, shaggy little brown animal so numerous along the edges of highways and parkways. They sit up as the cars whiz by, chewing on the succulent grasses and leaves on which they feed. Stop your car, though, and they scoot for safety to the taller and thicker underbrush beyond the grassy strips.

Baby woodchucks are cuter than the adults. For that matter, baby anythings are cuter than their grown-up counterparts. Woodchucks live in deep and long burrows and must have concrete bottoms to their cages, or they will merely dig down far enough to clear the sides and merrily go their way. Heavy screened bottoms could be used, too, provided the animal cannot get the individual meshes in his jaws, or he will be able to gnaw through in time.

Woodchucks are one of the animals that give off an offensive odor from large and active glands near the anus. This makes them unattractive to predators and is an efficient means of defense. They eat mostly plant material, insects, and an occasional mouse or bird. Woodchucks normally hibernate from October through February. In captivity they could probably be kept active by feeding them winter-available vegetables.

Unweaned chucks can be fed with an eyedropper, but be sure to use the plastic kind, or there is a chance that the young animal will bite off the glass end and cut its mouth. Baby bottles can be tried, but the nipples will probably not last long. The animals have enormous front teeth.

ORDER: Rodentia.
FAMILY: Sciuridae.
SCIENTIFIC NAME: *Cynomys ludovicianus.*
POPULAR NAME: Prairie dog.
RANGE: West-central states.

GESTATION PERIOD: About one month.
BIRTH MONTH: March to April.
NUMBER OF YOUNG: Three or four.
NURSING PERIOD: Eight weeks.
LIFE SPAN: Eight to ten years.
PHOTO PERIOD: Diurnal.

This is an animal that is seldom seen east of the vast great plains country. In years past, great "towns" of prairie dogs lived in the plains, prairies, and deserts. Sometimes the animals numbered in the hundreds of thousands to a town. However, since the food of prairie dogs is the same as for cattle, poisoning programs were put into effect to kill off the population with such good success that the census has been reduced from hundreds of millions to a few thousand in protected areas, and the prairie dog is now one of the endangered species, near extinction.

This is a pity, since these interesting animals are a part of the heritage of the United States, and efforts should be made to see that they have a chance to survive. True, they eat forage plants. And true, their burrows are a hazard for horsemen, whose mounts step into the holes and break their legs. But there are plenty of places where cattle do not run, or men should not be riding horses, where the prairie dog can live in peace.

Prairie dogs make good pets because they will become tame when taken young. They eat grasses, succulent plants of many descriptions, some insects, berries, and other fruits.

Since they dig very deep burrows and have several of them in a colony, the cage for prairie dogs must have screen or concrete walls that go down many feet. This is impractical for most young people, and the next best thing is a concrete bed on which the cage is fastened. The cage can be made large enough to permit dividing it in two inside and, by laying concrete blocks on one another to build a wall two or three feet high, the resulting enclosure can be filled with dirt. Here the animals can build their tunnels and holes without digging out of the cage and thus have the security of their burrows.

They sit at the opening of the burrow, most of the time straight up like a sentinel. At the approach of any strange animal or man, they give a short sharp bark and dive into the hole, to pop out again as soon as they think it is safe. While prairie dogs will live in smaller cages indoors or outdoors, they are really not contented under those conditions. These animals should have the natural environmental conditions duplicated as nearly as possible in captivity. They estivate, but do not hibernate, although they may remain dormant for the colder winter months.

ORDERS. Rodentia.
FAMILY: Sciuridae.
SCIENTIFIC NAME: *Tamias striatus.*
POPULAR NAME: Chipmunk, Eastern chipmunk.
RANGE: Eastern half of the United States.
GESTATION PERIOD: Thirty-one or thirty-two days.
BIRTH MONTH: May and September. Two litters per year.
NUMBER OF YOUNG: Two to eight.
NURSING PERIOD: Eight weeks.
LIFE SPAN: Three to eight years.
PHOTO PERIOD: Diurnal.

Chipmunks are very pretty animals and make interesting pets. However, they do nothing to endear themselves to homeowners, because of their destructive habits. Plant bulbs around the house, and you are sure to have them dug up and eaten by the local chipmunk population. About the only way you can have any success with bulb flowers in some areas is to plant the bulbs under a heavy wire screen, then fill in the dirt on top of the screening. The bulbs will grow up through the screen to flower, but the metal mesh will foil the attempts to dig them up.

Wean tiny chipmunks on Similac with iron, adding vitamins for the first feeding of the day. They should be fed three to four times daily. Warm the formula until it is about body temperature. Chipmunks normally hibernate from the first frost through the winter until late March. In captivity they remain active through the year, but they do sleep a lot, and their feeding drops off too. Females caught in late April are almost sure to have their babies in captivity. The young can be suckled by the mother animal, but they should be played with and handled frequently every day in order to become tame. Then, as soon as they are weaned, they can be separated from the mother in order to remain tame. As long as the mother is with her babies, she will instill a fear of human beings into them. If they are removed from the parent, this fear seems to be considerably less. Second generation chipmunks are even more docile and permit handling almost from birth.

Chipmunks feed on roots, berries, nuts, vegetables, fruits, insects, mice, and small birds, and may turn cannibalistic if they do not have meat provided in their diet. The pair I kept for a year were very fond of dry, hard, elbow macaroni. They would sit and nibble at a piece of this tasteless material for as long as I would offer it. Sunflower seeds were probably their very favorite.

ORDER: Rodentia.

FAMILY: Sciuridae.

SCIENTIFIC NAME: *Sciurus carolinensis*.

POPULAR NAME: Gray squirrel, Eastern gray squirrel.

RANGE: Eastern half of the United States.

A delighted baby gray squirrel being fed with an eyedropper and formula.

GESTATION PERIOD: Forty-four days.

BIRTH MONTH: March–April and September–October. Two litters per year.

NUMBER OF YOUNG: One to six.

NURSING PERIOD: Eight weeks.

LIFE SPAN: Fifteen years.

PHOTO PERIOD: Diurnal.

Of all the rodents, this animal and the next one to be described are the most beautiful and endearing pets. If found just before they are weaned, gray squirrels are very tame and trusting and need no particular attention for them to continue so. They are playful and gentle, rarely attempting to bite, although they can bite to the bone if the occasion warrants. They do nibble, especially on your ears when sitting on your shoulder, which seems to be a favorite lodging spot when you have them out of the cage.

Gray squirrels are almost impossible to raise if you find them very young, although I have raised two, one from one day old and the other from about four weeks. I would certainly not recommend it, though.

After your squirrel has become completely tame and you know it will remain in the vicinity, you can make a cage for it out of hardware cloth that has a runway to the outside. One way to do this is make the runway window sill height and lead it to the window, which can be opened enough to admit the end of the runway. This will leave an opening beside the runway which would permit insects and pests to enter the room. This opening can be closed by cutting a board to fit, holding it in place by closing the window down tightly against the board and the runway. The squirrel will have the protection and shelter of the indoor cage, but will be free to go and come as it wishes. You will find that the animal will, in time, try to entice other squirrels into the cage. Whether or not it is successful depends on the temperament and fear of the visiting squirrels. We have had friends of our pet line up on the window sill, but none of them quite worked up the courage to enter the room. They all accepted food from our fingers though.

Every squirrel has its own personality. Some are inquisitive, others bold, still another may be shy and timid, tolerating attention only from its immediate family, but not from strangers.

In captivity, squirrels may eat more items than they do in the wild. This, perhaps because they are made available to the animal, whereas in the outdoors, the foods may not be found. Nuts, of course, are a staple part of the diet. Fruits, berries, grapes, and cherries are especially relished, an occasional grasshopper or cricket will do for their meat requirements. Raisins, cheese, lettuce, and celery all are eagerly accepted. Water is important, and squirrels will readily learn to drink from a tube bottle, obtainable from any pet store.

Their cage should have some kind of hollowed-out shelter, either a piece of hollow log, a box, basket, or anything the animal can get into. Newspapers laid on the bottom of the cage will provide material for shredding into nest-building fluff. The bottom of the cage could have a layer of Cat-Comfort to keep it clean and sweet smelling. Squirrels are not dirty animals and much prefer clean quarters.

Unless the cage does have an exit to the outside, the animal should be released for play for a time each day. This is important for the welfare of squirrels, both the play and the exercise, and they really are a lot better off for the attention.

ORDER: Rodentia.
FAMILY: Sciuridae.
SCIENTIFIC NAME: *Glaucomys volans.*
POPULAR NAME: Flying squirrel.

This baby flying squirrel was born in captivity, together with four more.

RANGE: Eastern half of the United States.
GESTATION PERIOD: Forty days.
BIRTH MONTH: March to May and August through September. Two litters annually.
NUMBER OF YOUNG: Two to six.
NURSING PERIOD: About ten weeks.
LIFE SPAN: About twelve years.
PHOTO PERIOD: Nocturnal.

Actually, flying squirrels do not fly—they glide. The skin on their sides forms a canopy from the inside of their forelegs to the outside of the rear legs. When gliding, their legs are extended, making a sail out of the skin flaps. The tail is long and flat, and is used as a rudder in flight. The glides can be very long, depending upon the height of the tree from which the animal launches itself.

Flying squirrels are much more common than most people think. Being entirely nocturnal, they are seldom seen. Since their flight is silent and they do not use their voices much, they are neither seen nor heard. They are the prey of owls and other night-hunting predators. They are, to me, the most lovable of all wild animals to have as pets.

I have at present a family of six—the mother and five young ones who are now fully grown, and the three females are about to have their own litters. They are now a little over one year old, and I overwintered them in a large walk-in cage outdoors, providing a heavy log which I dug out to make a nesting place, and which they have filled to the brim with the shells of nuts they have been fed. As a matter of fact, I have emptied out the log once already, because there were so many shells that there was no room for the squirrels.

Flying squirrels are so soft that it is almost impossible to hold them. Their little bodies seem to ooze right out of your grip unless you use so much pressure to hold them that you crush them. Mine were born in my cage. I had caught the female when she was about to have her young, so the ones in the cage now are second generation. I am waiting for the third generation to come along, which will be in about two weeks, at which time I will bring inside one of the females with her young and as soon as they are weaned separate them from their mother. I want to see how much effort it will take to tame the third generation. It should not take much, because the second ones are quite tame already.

These little animals eat all kinds of fruits and nuts, raisins, insects, celery, and other vegetables, and they will gnaw on a steak or pork chop bone. They require a constant supply of clean water. Their cage should be placed in a location that can be illuminated at night, because just after dusk and just before dawn they are very active, bouncing about inside the cage for their exercise. A well-branched part of a tree is an ideal exerciser for them, and they will clean off all the bark, then run up and down it leaping from side to side of the cage. One never tires of watching their sure-footed acrobatics.

ORDER: Rodentia.

FAMILY: Cricetidae.

SCIENTIFIC NAME: *Cricetus cricetus.*

POPULAR NAME: Hamster.

RANGE: Asia and Syria, but has become a domestic pet in the United States.

GESTATION PERIOD: Sixteen days.

BIRTH MONTH: Continuously brooded. Can have a litter every month or so.

NUMBER OF YOUNG: Up to fifteen.

NURSING PERIOD: From twelve to fourteen days.

LIFE SPAN: Two years or more.

PHOTO PERIOD: Can be active at all times of day and night.

The hamster is one of the wild mouselike animals of the Eastern countries, but, after introduction into this country as a laboratory animal, has become so well established that it is often thought of as a native species.

They are friendly and quite tame and have been made into house pets for many years. They breed readily in cages and care for their young. They are fairly clean animals and keep their sleeping quarters clean. They require some meat in their diet in the form of other, smaller animals, insects, or, in captivity, canned dog foods or cat foods. They have been known to eat their young if they lack animal protein.

Hamsters are sold by most pet stores, and so-called hamster cages are also sold in great quantities each year. Actually, these cages are not the best way of keeping the animals, since they do not afford room enough for proper exercise. To compensate for this lack of space, most of the cages have within them a wheel, inside of which the hamster is supposed to run, as on a tread-mill, and this is supposed to keep the poor creature in condition. My personal opinion is that it mostly drives the animal into a kind of near-hysteria and frustration, instead of conditioning it.

Hamsters are, for the most part, fed on "hamster pellets," which are good enough to eat, but this diet should be supple-mented with green foods such as lettuce, celery tops (and stalks), beet tops, corn, grains, and cereal. Prepared breakfast ce-reals are excellent, most hamsters love Cheerios, raisins are a good source of iron, almost any vegetable. The required meat can be in the form of grasshoppers, crickets, and other large in-sects in the summer, mealworms during the winter months, and a bit of meat on a steak bone or chop bone, preferably raw, will help. The butcher in your neighborhood will gladly give you a small bone with small scraps of meat left on it, usually for noth-ing, but at the most, he will charge a nickel or a dime.

You must be careful to keep a steady supply of fresh, clean water. This can be in the tube water bottles, or in a small flat dish.

ORDER: Rodentia.

FAMILY: Cricetidae.

SCIENTIFIC NAME: *Meriones unguiculatus.*

POPULAR NAME: Gerbil.

RANGE: Manchuria in nature. Captive pet animal in the United States.

GESTATION PERIOD: About twenty-five days.

BIRTH MONTH: Continuously brooded in captivity.

NUMBER OF YOUNG: One to twelve.

NURSING PERIOD: About three weeks.

LIFE SPAN: Two to five years.

PHOTO PERIOD: Diurnal.

Gerbils are the common field mice of Mongolia, and they occur in astronomical numbers at times. There is a plague of gerbils on record, which occurred in India, numbering countless hundreds of thousands of gerbils, and which totally destroyed the complete grain and vegetable crops over an area measuring eight thousand square miles. The resultant famine in turn destroyed countless numbers of human beings.

Perhaps the reason for the huge numbers of these animals is due to the fact that they breed rapidly, bearing large litters each time, and they live in places where it is comparatively easy to escape predation. Certainly great numbers of them are killed and eaten by other animals and predatory birds, but they seem to be able to breed fast enough to overcome the predation level.

The really interesting thing connected with gerbils is that they were permitted to be brought into this country, since, without any adaptation whatever, they are ideally suited for our climate and certainly their diet is such that they would have no trouble surviving. If an animal can breed to truly frightening proportions, as this one does, certainly there is a real danger of having imported a creature that could run rampant through our enormous grain belt, for example. Several of the little mice were imported in the early 1950s, and from this original stock we have gerbils in almost every pet store in the country, not to say thousands of them in laboratories from coast to coast.

Since gerbils can survive in hot, arid deserts, going for nearly a year without drinking water, you should be very careful about letting any of them escape to the wild. In captivity they will take water, but really do not need a lot. Many pet store owners will tell you that, because gerbils do not drink water, they do not urinate, or at best, urinate very little and, as a consequence, their cages do not smell and their bodies are odorless. This is not exactly the case. There is no animal that does not have a body odor, with the exception, perhaps, of a newly born fawn. No matter how clean an animal is, if it is kept in a cage, the cage will smell and has to be cleaned at regular and frequent intervals. This is merely part of the chore of keeping an animal, and, if you have the idea that you can get away from this duty, please forget it—you can't.

Their cage can be a large aquarium, the bottom of which has a thick layer of Cat-Comfort, for cleanliness and to keep them dry. A few rocks can be piled in one end in such a fashion as to leave large pockets within them. The gerbils will use these for their "dens," and, when you see that they have mated or that the female is swelling with young, place several squares of clean burlap in the cage. The female will carefully shred the burlap into fluff and use this to build her nest.

Food for gerbils is no great problem. They are practically omnivorous. Grains of all kinds, sunflower, squash, pumpkin, and watermelon seeds, birdseed, fruits and vegetables, hay is relished and is excellent roughage for gerbils. They like alfalfa too. Insects are also taken.

ORDER: Rodentia.

FAMILY: Cricetidae.

SCIENTIFIC NAME: *Peromyscus leucopus*.

POPULAR NAME: Deer mouse, white-footed mouse.

RANGE: United States, except for the Southeast.

GESTATION PERIOD: Three weeks.

BIRTH MONTH: Continuously brooded.

NUMBER OF YOUNG: Two to six.

NURSING PERIOD: Two to three weeks.

LIFE SPAN: Up to five years.

PHOTO PERIOD: Both nocturnal and diurnal.

Within the description of this little animal, we shall group a couple of other species, because all requirements are the same for them. White mice, white rats, and colored species of both, of which there are great numbers, all need the same treatment, food, and housing facilities.

Of the white and colored mouse and rat group, very little need be told since these animals have been common in pet stores for many years. The white-footed mouse is very like the "tame" ones, except it is found in the wild.

Almost every home in rural areas has been visited at one time or another by white-footed mice. Usually in the fall, when the weather becomes too cold for comfort, these little animals will come inside houses in search of food and warmth. Their usual fate is to step into a mouse trap and end up flushed down the drain. A small live-animal trap baited with a dab of peanut butter is sure to pick up a specimen, and, if it is young enough, you have an interesting pet. If it is a full adult, continue to set your trap each night and catch three or more, which number will almost definitely ensure you a male and a female. These will most certainly mate in your cage, and as soon as the resultant babies are weaned, you can separate them from their mother and they will grow up tame if you play with them for a time each day, feeding them tidbits from your fingers.

Food consists of fruits, vegetables, nuts, seeds of all kinds, green leaf vegetables such as lettuce, celery tops, beet tops, etc. Insects are a very important part of their diet. Large grasshoppers, crickets, and beetles are relished. Mealworms are good, especially in the winter, when these beetle larvae are readily available or you can rear them yourself in plastic boxes. White mice and rats will also take insects, and you should make sure that some animal food is available at all times.

All mice cages will smell if they are not kept scrupulously clean. One method is to use a cage with a sliding tray at the bottom. This tray can be filled with Cat-Comfort. The upper bottom in the cage is made of wire mesh, upon which the animals live, and their droppings and liquid waste falls through the mesh to be caught and absorbed by the litter material in the tray. This, then, can be slid out, emptied, and cleaned to be refilled and replaced, keeping the cage much cleaner and making maintenance easier.

ORDER: Rodentia.

FAMILY: Erethizontidae.

SCIENTIFIC NAME: *Erethizon dorsatum.*

POPULAR NAME: Porcupine, hedgehog.

RANGE: The western half and the northeastern corner of the United States.

GESTATION PERIOD: About seven months.

BIRTH MONTH: April to May.

NUMBER OF YOUNG: One.

NURSING PERIOD: Up to four months, but takes solid food in a few hours.

LIFE SPAN: Up to ten years.

PHOTO PERIOD: Mostly nocturnal, but sometimes seen in daytime.

Porcupines are certainly familiar enough to most people who live in the country, especially where there are wooded areas nearby. Many hundreds of these animals are killed each year at night along the highways.

They are slow, lumbering animals, inoffensive enough, but

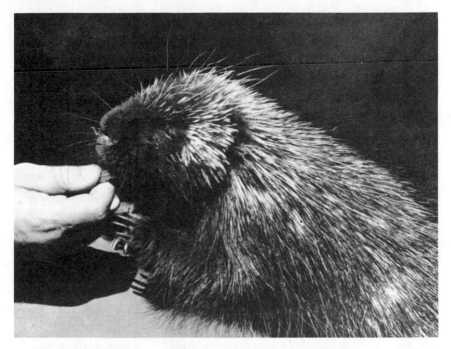

The way to a pin-cushiony porcupine's heart is with a piece of Hershey bar, or a Life Saver. They also like lots of salt.

instantly ready to defend themselves with their truly effective armament. The stories about porcupines being able to shoot their quills at their enemies are not true. The quills are loosely attached to the body, and sometimes it only requires a brushing against them to dislodge them and fasten them into your skin. Porcupine quills have small barbs on their tips, shaped in such fashion that they cause the quill to work its way deeper and deeper into the flesh with each muscle contraction of the victim.

Porcupines do not attack, but merely bunch themselves up into a ball with the rear presented to the enemy and raise the quills. If it is touched, the animal gives a violent hump of its back, driving the quills into whatever touched it. There is also the tail to consider. This is short, flat, and very muscular, and is covered with equally effective quills. Approached, the frightened animal will flip its tail in an attempt to strike the attacker. Needless to say, it is a sorry predator that tries anything with a porky. It has a few enemies in the wild, the fisher being perhaps the main one, since they have learned to turn a porcupine over on its back, attacking the victim on the belly which is free of quills.

Porcupines eat vegetation of many kinds. Tender twigs of trees, evergreen foliage, buds, roots, and berries. In captivity they will eat such foods as carrots, celery, lettuce, and similar greens. These animals require a lot of salt in their diet, and a salt block as is used for cattle is welcomed. These can be purchased from most feed stores.

Until and unless your porcupine is completely tamed, it is dangerous to handle it. Anything that frightens the creature will cause it to hump or flip its tail, with possibly disastrous results to the person holding it. However, when tame, they make interesting pets, if you can tolerate their smell, which is certainly not fragrant. They love sweets, and will readily take candy out of your fingers. As a matter of fact, this is one of the ways to get the animal to become tame. Feed it bits of Hershey bar, and you will quickly make a friend of the animal. They also take Life Savers with relish, sitting on their haunches and nibbling the candy with loud crunching noises.

ORDER: Rodentia.
FAMILY: Caviidae.
SCIENTIFIC NAME: *Cavia cobaya.*

POPULAR NAME: Guinea pig, cavy.

RANGE: Originally from Guiana, South America. Introduced to the United States.

GESTATION PERIOD: From sixty-one to sixty-five days.

BIRTH MONTH: Throughout the year.

NUMBER OF YOUNG: From one to twelve.

NURSING PERIOD: About three weeks.

LIFE SPAN: Up to eight years.

PHOTO PERIOD: Diurnal. In captivity, both nocturnal and diurnal.

To begin with, guinea pigs are not in any way related to pigs, nor do they come from Guinea. Guiana pig would be more accurate, and even this is not really descriptive. The pig part of this animal's name probably comes from the fact that they grunt like a pig when hungry or frightened.

These animals have been kept in captivity for so long that they could almost be called a domestic species. Many varieties have been bred into them until three major ones have become accepted. These are called English, which is the standard short-haired animal; Peruvian or Angora, which has very luxuriant long hair and which is the aristocrat of the group; and Abyssinian, which is the cross between the long and the short-haired varieties.

Many pet store owners and several "information" pamphlets will tell you that guinea pigs do not smell, that you can let their cage go uncleaned for six or seven weeks with no odor coming from it. These statements are not true. In fact, guinea pigs have an unpleasant odor, and, like every other animal in the world, if their cage is not cleaned daily, it will smell. A good thick layer of Cat-Comfort on the bottom of their cage, covered with a layer of hay, in which they will bed, and on which they will also nibble, will help to reduce the odors of the animals and their wastes. Water should be provided in a tube bottle, since they would foul a water dish or tip it over.

Guinea pigs are of great value in laboratories, where thousands are used in biological experiments. They breed as readily as mice or rabbits, and one male will service up to eight females. As a matter of fact, two males cannot be kept together in the same cage or they will fight.

These animals cannot stand drafts or cold air. They catch colds in drafts, which can quickly develop into pneumonia and kill the animal. They also cannot tolerate high temperatures.

The food of guinea pigs is varied: fruits, almost any green vegetable, carrots, or dandelions. They' love clover when it is picked fresh for them. Pet stores also sell pellets for guinea pigs, and these are good for the winter months.

Female guinea pigs that are going to have babies should be given bread soaked in milk, or better still, soaked in Similac with iron.

ORDER: Rodentia.
FAMILY: Leporidae.
SCIENTIFIC NAME: *Lepus cuniculus.*
POPULAR NAME: Rabbit.
RANGE: World-wide.
GESTATION PERIOD: About thirty days.
BIRTH MONTH: Continuously brooded.
NUMBER OF YOUNG: Four to twelve.
NURSING PERIOD: About three weeks.
LIFE SPAN: Three years or more.
PHOTO PERIOD: Diurnal, and sometimes nocturnal.

In the classification above, we have listed the domestic rabbit rather than the wild one. There is a difference of scientific name, but there is also a reason for not identifying the wild species. Domesticated rabbits are available everywhere, and they are safe to handle and keep as pets. The wild rabbits have many diseases, some of which are transmissible to man, and some of them are fatal to man, tularemia being one of the latter. It is unsafe to handle wild rabbits with bare hands. Perhaps they will not have tularemia, but they could have. Perhaps you would not contract it, but you could do so. It is better to leave the wild ones alone and concentrate on a tame one.

I don't think very much has to be told about keeping a rabbit. The young can be weaned with a baby bottle and Similac. When weaned, the food of rabbits is entirely vegetable—lettuce, carrots, almost any root vegetable, leafy greens, grasses, dandelions, clover, plantain, especially the wide-leaved variety, hay, and alfalfa. Rabbit pellets are available in every pet store. Rabbits require a constant supply of water and will take it from a tube bottle.

Cages for keeping rabbits should have a screen floor raised above the ground. A cleanout tray may or may not be used under the cage. If the animals are kept outdoors, the wastes can be permitted to drop on the ground under the cage, moving the location from time to time to permit the elements to dissolve the droppings and return them to the earth.

Cages for rabbits should be kept in a place where they receive shade during the hotter part of the day. Full sunlight causes acute distress to most animals, and especially to rabbits, with their heavy coat of fur. Full sunlight will rapidly kill animals like skunks!

Rabbits do not as a rule try to bite. However, if roughly handled or frightened while you are holding them, they will struggle violently and finally kick with their hind legs. The kick of a fully grown rabbit is not to be discounted! They can knock the breath right out of you with a double-whammy to your belly.

CHAPTER THIRTY-EIGHT

A Wacky Mammal

ORDER: Edentata.

FAMILY: Dasypodidae.

SCIENTIFIC NAME: *Dasypus novemcinctus.*

POPULAR NAME: Armadillo, Nine-banded armadillo.

RANGE: Southeastern United States.

GESTATION PERIOD: About five months.

BIRTH MONTH: March to April.

NUMBER OF YOUNG: Four.

NURSING PERIOD: Unknown to me.

LIFE SPAN: Up to ten years.

PHOTO PERIOD: Crepuscular, or moonlit nights, sometimes active by day.

Here is a creature, about which the famous statement must have been said, "There ain't no such animal!" And truly, closer examination of an armadillo merely serves to bring home the truth, that such a creature should belong to another planet, not our own familiar earth. Essentially a tropical animal, this one has made its way into the extreme southern states, until it can be classed as indigenous.

The body of this strange creature is covered with hard plates, as is the head and tail. When alarmed it can roll up into a tight ball, protecting its soft vulnerable belly, with the plate on the top of the head closing the opening in the ball. A predator can roll the animal around on the ground, but will find it difficult or impossible to get enough of a bite on it to force it to unwind.

The belly is covered with large warts and long, scraggly hairs. The snout is long and tapering with a small opening, and, although it has thirty-two teeth, it never tries to bite with its tiny mouth. The claws, however, are a different thing. They are, especially on the front paws, extremely long, heavy, hard, and are capable of stripping you to the bone, although when tamed, it does not use these very efficient weapons.

Armadillos make marvelous pets just because they are so weird. Their food consists of grubs, earthworms, insects of all kinds, eggs, berries, roots, and fruits. One I had was simply batty over hot scrambled eggs, snuffling them up off the plate like a vacuum cleaner!

These animals always have four young at a time. Never three or five—but only four, and always the same sex. The offspring may be males or females, but there are never mixed sexes in the same litter. They have four teats to suckle their babies with, which seems to be much more practical than, say, an opossum, which has thirteen teats and can have up to twenty young, seven of them doomed before they even get started.

Armadillos are slow, deliberate animals, trusting, rightly, in the protection of their armor. They can, however, move rapidly if the need arises, and then take off with a lumbering gait over the fields.

Water should be provided in a heavy flat dish that is not easy to overturn, and armadillos must have deep water to get into to bathe. They like to go under water to soak for long periods of time, keeping their nose above the surface to breathe. A tank, so constructed that they can easily climb into and out of it, should be a part of their cage.

The cage must have a concrete bottom or you will not long

have your pet. It can dig out no matter how hard the ground. Even a screened bottom will not contain them for long, since screening is made short work of with their front claws. The bottom of the cage could be made of hard wood, covered with a piece of sheet metal, which should prove invulnerable to the animal's claws.

As with almost any animal, but more so with this one, keep the cage in the shade. Since the normal activity period is early dawn, or early evening, this is an indication that they shun bright sunlight.

Regardless of the fact that the animal may root up a bit of your lawn, or a flowerbed or two, the armadillo is beneficial to mankind. The rooting is only in search of harmful grubs and burrowing insects that would otherwise take their toll of your garden and grounds. The damage done by the digging is slight compared to that done by the insects if they were left to mature.

INDEX

Note: Page references in italic type indicate illustrations.

Acriflavine, 46
Adders, 227–28
Adipose fin, 22, 65
Aerators, aquarium, 5–6, 18–19
Affinis (plant), 32–33
African lovebirds, 304
Agassizi's Catfish, 87
Alco Carrying Cases, 345
Algae, 11–12, 31, 42, 152, 207
Alligator lizard, 244
Alligators, 192–93
Alpine salamanders, 122, 124
Amazon Sword (plant), 33
Ambystoma gracile,
    (Northwestern
    salamander), *162*
Ambystoma maculatum
    (spotted salamander),
    147
American toad (*Bufo
    americanus*), 130–34,
    131
Amoebic disease, 201–2
Amphibians, 97–125
    anatomy, 97–114
    aquariums for, 150–54

buying, 166–67
diseases, 160–167
egg collecting, 149–50
feeding, 156–60
finding, 145–50
Jacobson's gland, 106
Jacobson's organ, 106–7
life span, 125
limb girdles, 112–13
reproduction, 114–24
terraria, *153*, 154–56
    caecilians, see Caecilians
    frogs, see Frogs
    newts, see Newts
    salamanders, see
        Salamanders
    toads, see Toads
Amphiuma (Congo eel), 109,
    112
Amplexus, 117
Anabantids (Labyrinth fish),
    22–23, 70, 76–78
    breeding, 76–77
Anacharis (plant), 24, 36, 61,
    238
Anacondas (snakes), 200–1

Anal fins, 21
Anal plate, 177
Anchor worms, 50
Angelfish, 14, 29
Anoles (chameleon lizards),
    192, 205–6, 214,
    241–243
  Anolis carolinensis, 242
Ant eggs, 193, 197
Antibiotics
  amphibians, for, 162–63
  aquarium use, 45–46
  birds, for, 319–20, 323
  reptiles, for, 200
Aquariums, 3–20
  amphibian, for, 150–63
  fresh-water fish, for, 5–12,
    17–20
    algae, 11–12, 207
    breeding, 61
    covering, 19–20
    pebble layer, 62
    planting, 16–19
  light for, 11, 13, 20, 26, 27,
    151
  salt-water fish, for, 88–93
  scavengers in, 64
  sizes, 14–16, 54, 61, 63
  turtle ponds, 206–7
  water
    chemicals in, 6, 7, 11
    filling with, 18–19
    filtering, 10–11, 89
    fresh, 5–12, 150–53
    salt, 88–89
    standing before use,
      7, 8

temperature, 8, 20, 151
Arched Corydoras (*Corydoras
    arcuatus,* Elwin),
    (catfish), 87
Armadillos (*Dasypus novem-
    cinctus*), 328, 348,
    394–96
Arrow poison frog, 124
Asthma in birds, 321
Atelopus zeteki (Zetek's frog),
    167
A-200-Pyrinate, 202–3
Aureomycin (chlortetracy-
    cline), 319–20
Aviaries, breeding in, 279–80

Bacitracin, 323
Bacopa (plant), 34, 72
Baking soda (calcium
    carbonate), 321
Balancing aquariums, 6
Banding, birds, 290, 301, 303
Bandit catfish (*Corydoras
    metae,* Eigenmann), 87
Banjo Catfish, 84–85
Barbs (fish), 61, 70
  Sumatra (*Capoeta tetrazona,*
    Bleeker), 74–75
  Tiger (*Capoeta tetrazona,*
    Bleeker), 74–75
Barking tree frog (*Hyla
    gratiosa*), 99
Basilisk (lizard), 181
Beef hearts, 41–42, 64
Beetles, 129, 157, 159
Betta splendens, Regan

(Siamese Fighting
Fish), 78, 79–82, 80
Bird baths, 266, 267
Birds, 264–77
  altricial, 256
  antibiotics, 319–20, 323
  bathing, 266, 267, 271–72
  bills, 261–62
  bones, 260–61, 323–24
  breeding
    finches and canaries,
      278–96
    methods, 279–80
    nestling food, 278–79,
      288–90
    nests, 282, 298–303
    psittacines, 278, 297–307
  cages, 265–67
    breeding, 280–82, 303
    cleaning, 268, 318–19
    door, 269
    drafts, 269
    flight, 288–90, 299–300
    hospital, 318
    perches, 266
    seed guards, 274
    size, 268–69, 273–74
    temperature, 269, 271,
      317–18
  claw clipping, 274–75
  cuttlebone, 292, 297
  diseases, 254–55, 269,
    317–24
    asthma, 321
    colds, 320
    constipation, 321–22
    diarrhea, 321–22

    egg binding, 322
    plugged oil gland, 321
    pneumonia, 320
    rickets, 320–21
    scaly face, 322–23
    scaly leg, 322–23
    sour crop, 321
  feathers, 259–60
  feeding, 264–65, 276–77
    charcoal, 265, 292, 297
    gravel, 265, 268, 292, 297
    nestling food, 278–79,
      288–90
    oystershell, 265, 292, 297
    weaning, 289–90
  imported, 254, 255
  isolation, 318, 319
  light, 269
  medicines, 319–20, 322, 323
  precocial, 256
  reptiles and, 215–16, 256–57
  training
    finger perch, 308, 310–14
    rewards, 313, 314
    talking, 314–16
  varieties
    cardinal, 323
    passeriformes, see
      Passeriformes (perching
      birds)
    psittaciformes, see
      Psittaciformes
      (hook-billed birds)
  vision, 261
  water for, 265, 266
  wing clipping, 309, 310–11

Birdseed, 276–77

Black-masked lovebirds, 305–7, 306

Black-spotted catfish (*Corydoras melanistius,* Regan), 87

Blacktop catfish (*Corydoras acutus,* Cope), 86

Blanding's turtle, 240

Blowfly larvae, 165

Blowing adder (hog-nose), 227–28

Blue-bellied swifts, 243–44

Blue-masked lovebirds, 307

Boa constrictors, 223–26, 224
  diseases, 200–1
  feeding, 215
  rubber boa, 230

Bobcat, *see* Wildcat

Bog terrarium, 155

Bone meal, 164

Bones, bird, 260–61, 323–24

Box turtle, 239–40

Brachydanio rerio, Hamilton-Buchanan, (fish), 68–69

Breathing
  amphibians, 110–12
  newts, 137
  skin, 101

Breeding cages, 280–82, 303

Breeding tanks, 13

Breeding traps, 27

Brine shrimp, 26, 37–38, 42, 63, 78, 82

Broken bones, bird, 323–24

Bronze Catfish (*Corydoras aeneus*), 85

Bubble nest builders, 76–82

Budgerigars
  bathing, 271
  breeding, 254, 263, 297–303
  cages for, 268–69, 272
  chick, 301
  feeding, 265–66, 297
  price, 298
  taming, 274
  toys, 268
  training, 304, 308
    finger perch, 310–13
    talking, 314–15

Bufo americanus (American toad), 130–34, 131

Bufonidae (toad genus), 130–34

Bullfrog (*Rana catesbeiana*), 103, 127

Bunch plants, 34, 35, 36

Butterfly fish, 40

Cabomba (plant), 24, 36, 61, 71, 238

Caecilians, 97
  anatomy, 101–2, 104, 106–7, 109, 112, 114
  reproduction, 117, 118–19, 120–21, 122, 124

Cages
  bird, 265–67
    breeding, 280–82, 303
    cleaning, 268, 318–19
    door, 269
    flight, 288–90, 299–300

hospital, 318
seed guards, 274
size, 268–69, 273–74
mammals, 339–46
concrete floor, 341–43
holding cages, 345
live traps as, 346–47
reptile, 205–7
humidity, 209
outdoor, 207–8
planting, 210
requirements, 209–12
temperature, 209–10, 211
Caimans, 193, 215
Calcium in bird diet, 320–21
Canaries, 253–54
bathing, 271
breeding, 278–96
eggs, 284–86
feeding, 287–89
nests, 282–84
cage size, 272
equipment, 265, 268
life expectancy, 254
mother and chick, 287
taming, 274
temperature, 271
wild, 262–63
Candling eggs, 285
Canidae (fox family), 369–70
Canned seafood as fish food,
42
Capoeta tetrazona, Bleeker
(Barb), 74–75
Carapace, 235
Carbon dioxide cycle, 6, 31,
101, 110

Cardinal (bird), 323
Cardinal Tetra (*Cheirdon
axelrodi*, Schultz), 17,
66–67
Carnivora, 359–71
Carp, 70
Carpenter frogs, 126
Carriers, animal, 345–46
Carrots as bird food, 278, 299
Cat-Comfort (litter), 346, 380,
386, 388, 391
Catfish, *see Corydoras*
Caudal fins, *see* Tail fins
Cavia cobaya (Guinea pig)
390–92
Cavy, *see* Guinea pigs
Caymans, 193, 215
Chameleon lizard (*anole*),
192, 194, 205–6, 214,
241, 243
Anolis carolinensis, 242
Chameleons (true), 248–50
Characins, 22, 64–66
Charcoal, 265, 292, 297, 321
Cheridon axelrodi, Schultz
(Cardinal fish), 66–67
Chemicals in aquarium, 7–9
Chicken snakes (*Elaphe*), 185,
222, 223
Chipmunks (*Tamias
striatus*), 376
cages, 339, 344
Chlorine, 7
Chloromycetin, 45–46, 47, 49,
50
Chlortetracycline, 319–20

Chordata (plant), 32, 72
Chrysemys picta dorsalis
    (Southern painted
    turtle), 235–36, 236
Cichlids, 48, 70
Coatimundi (Procyon narica),
    362–63, 363
Cobra, 228
Cockatiels, 263
    breeding, 278
    cage size, 269, 273
    diet, 297
    training, 304, 308, 310–13
Cockatoos
    cage size, 269
    sulphur-crested, 258
Cockroaches, 159
Cod liver oil, 319
Cold-blooded animals, 21
Colds, bird, 320
Collared lizard, 245
Community tanks, 13
Concrete cage floors, 341–43
Condors (snakes), 262
Congo eel (Amphiuma), 109,
    112
Constipation, 163, 321–22
Constrictors (snakes), 180–81
    boa (Constrictor constrictor),
        see Boa constrictors
    king, see King snake
        (Lampropeltis)
    rat, see Rat snakes (Elaphe)
    reticulated python,
        223–26
Consumption, 50
Copper

aquarium water, in, 7
    salts, 46–47
Copper-Blue Cure, 47
Copperhead snakes, 186, 219,
    223
Coral, 90
Coral snakes, 177–79, 186, 187
Corkscrew Val (plant), 24
Corn meal, 151–52
Corn snake (Elaphe), 171,
    172, 185, 222
Corydoras (Catfish), 22, 64,
    83–87
    scavengers, as, 54
    varieties
        acutus, Cope (Blacktop
            catfish), 86
        aeneus (Bronze catfish),
            86
        agassizi, Steindachner, 87
        arcuatus, Elwin (Arched
            Corydoras, Skunk
            catfish), 87
        elegans, 86
        julii, Steindachner
            (Leopard catfish), 87
        melanistius, Regan
            (Black-spotted catfish),
            87
        metae, Eigenmann
            (Bandit or Masked
            catfish), 87
        multimaculatus,
            Steindachner (Soldier
            catfish), 87
        myersi, H. Ribeiro
            (Myers' catfish), 87

paleatus, Jenyns
    (Peppered Corydoras),
    87
punctatus, Bloch (Spotted
    catfish), 87
rabauti, LaMonte (Dwarf
    catfish), 87
reticulatus, Fraser-Brunner
    (Norfolk catfish), 87
Crabs, 90, 91
Cramps, 165
Cricetidae (rodents)
  deer mice (*Peromyscus
    leucopus*), 386–88
  gerbils (*Meriones
    unguiculatus*), 384–86
  hamsters (*Cricetus
    cricetus*), 383–84
  mice (pet), 386–88
  rats (pet), 386–88
Cricket frogs, 160
Crickets, 129, 157–58, 164,
    213, 245, 354
Crocodilians, 172–73, 202
Crop (bird's) sour, 321
Crows, 257, 308
Crustaceans as fish food, 41
Cryptocorynes (plants),
    32–33, 72–73
Crystal Manufacturing
    Company, 89
Cuttlebone, 292, 297
Cutthroat finch (ribbon
    finch), 294, 295, 296
Cynomys ludovicianus (prairie
    dog), 374–76

Danios (fish), 27, 61, 67
  Brachydanio rerio,
    Hamilton-Buchanan,
    68–69
  Danio malabaricus, Jerdon
    (giant danio), 71–72
Danner Manufacturing
    Company, Eugene, G.,
    89
Daphnia, 26, 41, 63
Darwin's frog, 123–24
Dasypus novemcinctus
    (armadillo), 328, 348,
    394–96
DDT, 9
Decro-Corners, 19
Deer mouse (*Peromyscus
    leucopus*), 386–88
DeKay's snake, 229
Desmognathus fuscus (dusky
    salamander), 139–41
Diarrhea in birds, 321–22
Didelphiidae (marsupials),
    351–55
Digestion, amphibians, 109–10
Dip tubes, 151–52
Discus fish, 14, 29
Diseases
  bird, 317–24
    Newcastle disease, 255
  fish, 41–51
  rabbit, 254
  transmissible to humans
    psittacosis, 254
    tularemia, 393
Ditmars, Raymond, 201

Dorsal fins, 21
    double dorsal, 22
Downfeathers, 259
Dragonflies, 159
Dri-Die, 67, 199–200
Dried foods for fish, 42
Dropsy, 50
Dusky salamander
        (*Desmognathus
        fuscus*), 139–41
Dwarf Amazon Sword plant,
    33
Dwarf Catfish (*Corydoras
    rabauti*, LaMonte), 87

Eagles, 262
Eardrums of amphibians, 105
Earthworms, 38–39, 64,
        156–57, 213, 356
Echinodorus (plants), 33
Eel grasses, 36
Eels, Congo (*Amphiuma*),
        109, 112
Efts, 137
Egg binding, 322
Eggs
    amphibian, 114, 119–20,
        149–50
    birds, of, 284, 285–86, 322
    candling, 285
    pet food, as, 64, 278, 279,
        355
    protection, 29, 62, 70
Elaphe (rat snake), *see* Rat
        snake
Elegant Corydoras (catfish),
    86

Enchytraeus (White worms),
    157
English Nestling Food, 278
Epsom salts, 322
Erethizontidae (porcupines),
    388–90
Estivation, 376
Eureka Products Company, 89
Exotic fish
    aquarium conditions, *see*
        Aquariums
    captivity described, 3–4
    color; temperature of
        water and, 3
    feeding, 3
    mating, 4, 7
Exotic Newcastle disease, 255
Eyes
    glands, 104
    infections, 164
    lids, 102–3
    nictitating membrane, 103

Fear of humans, encouraging,
        340–41
Feathers, 259–60
Felidae (cat family), 370–71
Fence lizards, 243
Fence swifts, 243
Ferrets, 344
Fertilizer for aquarium plants,
    31
Field trips, 145–48
Fighting fish (Siamese), 16
Filoplumes, 259
Filters, aquarium

fresh-water, 10–11
salt-water, 89
Fin and tail rot, 49
Finches, 257–58, 262
  bathing, 271
  breeding, 278–96
    chicks, 287–89
    eggs, 284–86
    Lady Gould, 291–92
    nests, 282–84, 290, 293
    Society, 291, 292
  cage and equipment, 265,
    268, 271, 272
  feeding, 292
  varieties
    cutthroat, 294, 296
    Darwin's, 258
    Lady Gould, 291–92
    ribbon, 294, 295, 296
    Society, 291, 292–93
    Zebra, 272, 292, 293–94
Finger training birds, 308,
  310–14
Fins
  adipose, 22, 65
  disease of, 49
  structure, 22
  types, 21
Fire salamanders, 124
Fish
  air-breathing, 76–78
  aquariums for, see
    Aquariums
  breathing, 22–23, 76
  breeding, 13, 24–30, 62,
    76–78
    adhesive egg layers, 70–75

egg-scatterers, 65–69
live-bearing, 24, 25–27,
  52–60
tanks for, 13
diseases, 44–51
  anchor worms, 50
  consumption, 50
  dropsy, 50
  fin and tail rot, 49
  fungus, 48–49
  Ich, 44–46
  remedies, 45–46
  rust, 46–47
  shimmies, 50
  swim bladder trouble, 50
  velvet, 46–47
eating young, 26, 53
egg-scatterers, 61–70
feeding, 28, 37–43, 53,
  62–66, 90
fins, 21, 22, 49, 65
fry, 62–63, 70, 71, 77–78
salt-water, 88–93
scavengers, 54, 90–91
sexes, distinguishing, 27–28
temperature
  body, 21
  water, 45–46
turtles and, 235
varieties, see individual fish
  or genus
Five-Way Breeding Trap, 27
Flat-headed adder (hog-nose),
  227–28
Fleas, 350
Flies, 159
Flight cages, 273, 289–90, 303

Floating plants, 31
Flying squirrels, *see* Squirrels
Foam nests, 122
Fox, red (*Vulpes fulva*),
    369–70
Fox snake (*Elaphe*), 223
Frogs, 97, 98, 126–29
  anatomy, 102–15
  breathing, 110–11
  breeding, 100, 107, 111,
    115–18, 120–22, 128–29
  croaking, 116, 136
  diseases, 164
  eggs, care of, 122–23
  feeding, 107–10, 158,
    159–60
  foam nests, 122
  Jacobson's organ, 106
  varieties
    aglossid, 108
    arrow poison, 124
    bullfrog (*Rana
      catesbeiana*), 103, 160
    cricket, 160
    Darwin's, 123–24
    hairy, 115
    horned, South African,
      108
    Leopard (*Rana pipiens*),
      126–29, 127
    poisonous, 100, 117, 124
    tailed, 118
    tree (*Hyla gratiosa*), 99
    tree (*Hyla versicolor*), 120
      122, 123, 134–36
  Zetek's (*Atelopus zeteki*),
    167

Frozen foods for fish, 42
Fruit, 354
Fruit flies, 158, 160, 214
Fry (fish)
  bubble-nest varieties, 77–78
  protection, 62–63, 70, 71
Fumes, toxic, aquarium water
    and, 6
Fungus infections
  fish, 48–49
  salamanders, 161

Game farms, 333, 337
Garter snakes (*Thamnophis
    sirtalis*), 218, 226–27
Gases, aquarium and, 5, 6
Geckos (lizard), 183
  buying, 195
  cages, 208
  eyes, 183–84
  feeding, 214
  varieties
    Madagascan day, 193
    tokay gecko, 184, 193, 214
  voice, 184
Georgia-Tennessee Mining
    and Chemical
    Company, 346
Gerbils (*Meriones
    unguiculatus*), 384–86
Gila monster, 186
Gills
  amphibians, 110–11
  newts, 137
Glands
  amphibians, 100
  bird; plugged oil gland, 321

Glass snakes (lizards), 182,
    245–46
Glaucomys volans (flying
    squirrel), 339, 343,
    380–83, *381*
Golden Cichlids, 29
Gonopodium, 53
Gopher snake, 226
Gouramis (fish), 23, 78
Granular glands, 100
Grasshoppers, 129, 159, 245,
    354
Gravel
    aquarium, 16–17
    bird, 265, 268, 292, 297, 321
Gray squirrel, *see* Squirrels
Green rat snake (*Elaphe*),
    222
Green tree frogs, 135
Green water, 43, 73, 78
Griffithii (plant), 32
Gro-Lux, 20
Groundhog, *see* Woodchuck
Grubs, 356
Guinea pigs (*Caria cobaya*),
    390–92
    reptile food, as, 214, 215
Guppies, 25, 37, 55–56, 235
    amphibians, food for, 158
    diseases, 45
    Rainbow fish (*Lebistes
        reticulatus*), 55

Hairy frogs, 115
Hairy toads, 115
Hamsters (*Cricetus cricetus*),
    339, 383–84

Harlequin fish (*Rasbora
        heteromorpha,*
    Duncker), 72–73
Hatchetfish, 65–66
Hawks, 262
Head and Tail Light
    (*Hemigrammus
        ocellifer,* Steindachner),
    67–68
Heaters
    aquarium, 20
    cage, 209, 338–39
Hedgehog, *see* Porcupines
Hellbender salamanders, 104,
    118
Hemigrammus ocellifer,
    Steindachner (Head
    and Tail Light), 67–68
Herpetologists, 172
Hershey Seed Company, 278,
    288
Hibernation, 108, 128, 129,
    377
Hippocampus hudsonius,
    DeKay (Sea horses),
    91, 92
Hissing viper (hog-nose),
    227–28
Hog-nosed snake, 227–28
Honey, 347, 348
Horned toads (lizards),
    244–45
Hospital tanks, 46
House snake, 222
Hunting for amphibians,
    145–48

Hybrid pine snake (*Pituophis melanoleucus*), 178
Hygrophila polysperma (plant), 34
Hyla versicolor (tree frog), 134–36
Hylidae (frog genus), 134

Ichthyophthiriasis, 44–46
Iguanas, 182, 192, 246–48
cages, 206
common, 247
feeding, 200, 213
Indigo snake, 226
Infections, fungus, *see* Fungus infections
Infusoria, 43, 63, 68–69, 77, 82, 158–59
Insects in amphibian diet, 107–8, 129, 134, 136, 139, 152

Jacobson's organ, 106, 179
Jays, 257
Jungle amphibians, 98

Katydids, 245
King snake (*Lampropeltis*), 171, 177, 185, 219–22
checkered adder, 222
common, 221
Eastern, 221
getulus, 220
house, 222
milk, 171, 185, 222
salt and pepper snake (Southern king), 221

Southern, 221
spotted adder, 222
Kissing Gouramis, 78

Labyrinth fish (Anabantids), 22–23, 70, 76–78
breeding, 76–77
Lacerta (lizard), 246
Lady Gould finches, 291–92
Lampropeltis (King snake), *see* King snake
Larks, 257
Lateral-line (fish), 22
Lateral-line organs, 107, 137
Laxatives, 322
Leaches, 85
Leaf-nosed snake, 188
Lebistes reticulatus (guppy), 55
Leopard catfish (*Corydoras julii*, Steindachner), 87
Leopard frog (*Rana pipiens*), 126–29, 127
Leporidae, 392–93
Leprosy, salamander, 163
Lepus caniculus (rabbits), 392–93
Licenses (wild animal), 333
Light for aquarium, 11, 13, 20, 26, 27, 151
Limb girdles, 112–13
Listerine, 201
Lizards
anatomy, 106, 181–82
bites, 172
cages, 205, 206, 208
catching, 189–91

desert, 190–91, 206, 209–10, 211
diseases, deficiency, 202
feeding, 194, 202, 213, 214–15, 245, 248
mites, 198–99
parental instinct, lack of, 173
poisonous, 172
reptiles, as, 172
temperature requirements, 209–10, 211
varieties
  alligator, 244
  anoles, see Anoles (Chameleon lizards)
  basilisks, 181
  chameleons, 248–50
  collared, 245
  fence, 243
  geckos, *see* Geckos
  glass snake, 182, 245–46
  horned toad, 244–45
  iguanas, *see* Iguanas
  lacerta, 246
  rail, 243
  skinks, 182–83, 187–88
  swifts, 243–44
Locusts, 245
Lovebirds
  African, 304
  Black-masked, 305–6
  Blue-masked, 307
  breeding, 304–5
  diet, 297
  Peach-face, 305
Ludwigia (plant), 34–35

Lung fish, 76
Lungless salamanders, 122
Lungs, amphibians, 110–12
Lustar Products Company, 26–27
Lynx
  canadensis (lynx), 371
  rufus (wildcat), 370–71

Macaws
  cage size, 269
  red and yellow, 270
  scarlet, 270
Macropodus opercularis, Linnaeus (Paradise Fish), 78–79
Maggots, 350
Malachite green, 49
Mammals, wild
  buying, 333
  cages, 339–45, 346–47
  defined, 329
  disposal, 336–37
  extinction of species, 330
  feeding, 329, 330, 331–32, 347–50
  injured, 327, 331–32
  laws concerning, 327–28
  "lost" or orphaned, 330, 331, 332, 347
  taming, limits of, 335–36
  temperature requirements, 338–39
  transporting, 345–46
  trapping, 346–47
  types, 329–30
    carnivores, 359–71

insectivores, 356–58
marsupials, 351–55
rodents, see Rodents
Mannikins, 293
Map turtles, 235
Marine (salt-water) fish,
    88–93
Marine toad, 100
Marmot (*Marmota monax*),
    372–74, 373
Marsupials, 351–55
Masked Corydoras (*Corydoras
    metae*, Eigenmann), 87
Mealworms, 39–40, 157, 213
Medicine, giving, 166, 319–20,
    322, 323
Mephitis mephitis (skunk),
    365, 366, 367–69
Meriones unguiculatus
    (gerbil), 384–86
Metals in aquarium water, 7
Metamorphosis, frog, 135
Methylene blue dye, 45, 46
Mice (food), 171, 214–15
Mice (pets), 386–88
Midwife toads, 123
Milk snakes, 171, 185, 222
Minerals in aquarium water, 7,
    11
Mink, 364, 365
    ranches, 337
Minnows, 70, 158, 235
Miracle Fry Treet, 26
Miracle Pet Products, Inc., 26,
    47
Mites, 195, *198*, 199–200,
    322–23

Molasses as laxative, 322
Moles, 356–58
    Parascalops breweri
        (hairy-tailed), 358
    Scalopus aguatiaus
        (common), 356–58
Mollienisia (Mollies)
    latipinna, 54
    midnight, 60
    sphenops, 60
    velifera, Regan, 59–60
Mollies, see *Mollienisia*
Mollusks, 91
Molting, 260, 290–91
Moonfish (*Xiphophorus
    maculatus*, Gunther),
        58–49
Mosquitoes, 146
    larvae, 26, 41
Moss, terrarium, 154
Moths, 159
Mountain lions, 336
Mucous glands, amphibian, 98,
    100
Mucous membrane, 130
Mud puppies (*Necturus
    maculosus*), 141–44,
        160
Mud turtle, 237–38
Musk turtle, 237–38
Mustang Manufacturing
    Company (trapmaker),
        346
Mustelidae
    Mephitis mephitis
        (skunk), 365
    Mustela erminea

(Bonaparte weasel),
    363–65
Myers' Corydoras, 87
Mynah bird, 263, 273, 309
Myriophyllum (plant), 36, 61,
    71
    proserpinacoides (Parrot's-
        Feather), 24, 35, 36,
        61, 71

National Aquarium Supplies
    and Accessories
    Company, 19
Nauplii, see Brine shrimp
Necturus maculosus (mud
    puppy), 141–44, 160
Neon tetras, 17, 66
    diseases, 51
Neosporin, 200, 323
Neoteny, 124–25
Neptune salts, 88
Nests
    bird, 282, 298–303
    bubble, 23
    foam, 122
    liners, 282
Network catfish (Corydoras
    reticulatus,
    Fraser-Brunner), 87
Newcastle disease, 255
Newts, 104, 105, 107, 137
    breeding, 115, 116, 119,
        138–39
    feeding, 159, 160
    red-spotted (Notophthalmus
        viridescens), 136–39
Nictitating membrane, 103

Northwestern salamanders
    (Ambystoma gracile),
    162
Nostrils, amphibian, 106
Notebooks, 147–48
Notophthalmus viridescens
    (red-spotted newt),
    136–39

Opossums, 340, 344, 351–55,
    353
Ornamental tanks, 14
"Oscars" (fish), 14
Oviparous reptiles, 176
Oviviparous reptiles, 176
Owls, 261, 262
Oxygen–carbon dioxide cycle,
    see Carbon dioxide cycle
Oxygen in aquarium water, 5
Oystershell, ground, 265, 292,
    297, 321

Painted turtles, 235
    Eastern, 235
    Southern (Chrysemys picta
        dorsalis), 235–36, 236
    Western, 235
Paint fumes in aquarium water,
    6
Panchax (fish), 70
Paradise Fish (Macropodus
    opercularis, Linnaeus),
    78–79
Parakeets, 263
Paralysis, 165
Parascalops breweri
    (hairy-tailed mole), 358

Parasites
    mites, 198
    reptiles, on, 195
    roundworms, 164
Parotid glands, 130
Parrot fever (*psittacosis*), 254
Parrots, 253, 263, 268, 269,
        273
    training, 308–13
Parrot's-Feather, 24, 35, 36, 61,
        71
Passeriformes (perching)
        birds, 257, 259
    bills, 262
    canaries, *see* Canaries
    claw clipping, 274–75
    eyesight, 261
    feathers, 259–60
    feet, 262
    finches, *see* Finches
    lovebirds, *see* Lovebirds
Peach-face lovebirds, 305
Peanut butter, 319
Pectoral fins, 21–22
Penicillin in aquarium, 49
Peppered Corydoras
        (*Corydoras paleatus*,
        Jenyns), 87
Perches, bird, 266–67, 273–74
Perching birds, *see*
        Passeriformes
        (perching) birds
pH balance of aquarium, 9–10
Pickerel frogs, 127, 165
Picture Window Fish Breeder,
        27

Pilot black snake (*Elaphe*),
        223
Pituophis melanoleucus
        (hybrid pine snake),
        178
Plant lice as amphibian food,
        159
Plants
    aquarium, 13, 16–19, 24,
        28–29, 31–36
    terrarium, 154
Plastron, 235
Platies, 42
    wagtail, 59
    Xiphophorus maculatus,
        Gunther, 58–59
Plethodontidae
        (Salamanders), 139
Pneumonia, bird, 269, 320
Poisonous animals
    frogs, 100, 117, 124
    snakes, 172, 177–79, 186,
        187, 189
    toads, 100
Ponds, turtle, 206–7
Pond snails, 152
Porcupines (*Erethizon
        dorsatum*), 388–90, 389
Potassium permanganate, 161,
        163
Poultry, 355
Prairie dog (*Cynomys
        ludovicianus*), 374–76
Procyonidae
    lotor (raccoon), 340, 344,
        349, 359–61

Nasua narica (coatimundi), 362–63, 363
Proteidae (salamander genus), 141
Protozoans, 175
Psittaciformes (birds), *see* Psittacines (hook-billed birds)
Psittacines (hook-billed birds)
  breeding, 297–307
  Budgerigars, *see* Budgerigars
  Cockatiels, *see* Cockatiels
  Cockatoos, *see* Cockatoos
  Parakeets, 263
  Parrots, *see* Parrots
  training, 308–16
Psittacosis (parrot fever), 254
Puff adder (hog-nose), 227–28
Pythons (Constrictor), 180–81, 223–26
  diseases, 200–1
  feeding, 215
  reticulated, 223–24

Quarantine, 201–2
Quills, porcupine, 389–90
Quinine hydrochloride, 45

Rabaut's catfish (*Corydoras rabauti*, LaMonte), 87
Rabbits (*Lepus caniculus*), 392–93
  reptile food, as, 214, 215
Raccoons (*Procyon lotor*), 332, 334, 335, 340, 344, 349, 359–61
Rail lizards, 243

Rain frogs, *see* Tree frogs
Rana catesbeiana (bullfrog), 103
Rana pipiens (Leopard frog), 126–29, 127
Ranidae, *see* Frogs
Raptors, 262
Rasbora (fish)
  heteromorpha, Duncker, 72–73
  trilineata, Steindachner (scissor-tail), 73–74, 74
Rats, white
  pets, as, 386–88
  snake food, as, 171
Rat snake (*Elaphe*), 171–72, 180–81, 185
  chicken snake, 185, 222, 223
  corn snake, 171, 172, 185, 222
  fox snake, 223
  green rat snake, 222
  pilot black snake, 223
  red rat snake, 222
Rattlesnakes, 186, 219, 223
Rectal plugs, 203–4
Red-backed salamander, 139
Red-eared terrapin (*Pseudemys scripta*), 234
Red fox (*Vulpes fulva*), 369–70
Red leg disease, 165
Red rat snake (*Elaphe*), 222
Red salamander, 139
Red-spotted newt (*Notophthalmus viridescens*), 136–39

Reflectors, 20
Reliance Sales, 346
Reniket (Exotic Newcastle disease), 255
Reptiles
  birds, descended from, 256–57
  breeding, 175–76
  buying, 173, 191–95
  cages, 204–8
  crocodiles, *see* Crocodilians
  diseases, 195–96, 197–204
  eggs, 176
  fear of, 171
  feeding, 213–16
  humidity requirements, 209
  lizards, *see* Lizards
  locomotion, 76–77
  markings, 177
  parental instinct, lack of, 172–73
  searching for, 185–88
  skin shedding, 179–80
  snakes, *see* Snakes
  temperature requirements, 209–10, 211
  tree dwelling, 185
  turtles, *see* Turtles
  waking hours, 173, 188
  water supply, 210–11
Reptiles of the World, 201
Reticulated python (constrictor), 223–25
Ribbon finch, 294, 295, 296
Rickets, 164, 320–21
Rila Marine Mix, 88
Rila Products, 11, 88

Ring-necked snakes, 230
Roaches, 159
Rocks, aquarium, 17
Rodents, 359, 364
  Caviidae, 390–92
  Cricetidae, 383–88
  Erethizontidae, 388–90
  Leporidae, 392–93
  Sciuridae, 372–83
  snakes and, 171
Ross Laboratories, 347
Roundworms, 164, 165
Royal Lunch crackers, 278, 279
Rubber boa, 230
Rust (fish disease), 46–47

Sagittaria (plant), 29, 36, 72
Sailfin Mollies (Mollienisia)
  latipinna, 54, 60
  Midnight, 60
  sphenops, 60
  velifera, Regan, 59–60
Salamanders, 97–98
  anatomy, 100–14
  aquatic, 159
  birth, 120–21, 122–23, 124
  diseases, 161
  feeding, 152, 159, 160
  mating, 116–18, *119,* 140–41, 143
  sex characteristics, 100, 115
  varieties
    alpine, 122, 124
    dusky (*Desmognathus fuscus*), 139–141
    fire, 124

green tree, 160
Hellbenders, 118
lungless, 122
mud puppies (*Necturus maculosus*), 141–44, 160
northwestern (*Ambystoma gracile*), 162
spotted (*Ambystoma maculatum*), 147
tiger, 115
Salamandridae (newts), 136
Salmonella, 197, 231–32
Salt, use in aquarium, 48–49
Salt-water fish, 88–93
Sawback turtles, 235
Scales, reptile, 177
Scalex, 323
Scalopus aquaticus (mole), 356–58
Scaly face, bird, 322–23
Scaly leg, bird, 322–23
Scavengers
bird, 62
fish, 83–87
Scissor-tail (*Rasbora trilineata*), Steindachner, 73–74, 74
Sciuridae
chipmunk (*Tamias striatus*), 376–77, 378
flying squirrel (*Glaucomys volans*), 339, 343, 380–83, 381
gray squirrel (*Sciurus carolinensis*), 377–80
prairie dog (*Cynomys ludovicianus*), 374–76

woodchuck (*marmota monax*), 372–74, 373
Sciurus carolinensis (gray squirrel), 378–80
Scorpions, 362
Scutes, 176–77
Sea anemones, 90, 91
Seafood as fish food, 42
Sea horses (*Hippocampus hudsonius*, DeKay), 37, 91, 92
Seals, 331
Seeds as bird food, 276–77
Shedding of skin
amphibians, 101, 133
reptiles, 179–80, 181
Shells
aquarium, effect on water in, 11
oyster, ground, 265, 297
Shimmies, 50
Shoulder training birds, 313
Shrew, 329, 332, 356–58
Shrimp, 61, 90
coral shrimp, 90–91
Siamese Fighting Fish (*Betta splendens*, Regan), 78, 79–82, 80
Similac, 347–48, 360–61, 365, 369
Siren lacertina, 111
Skin
amphibians, 98, 100, 101
shedding, 101, 133
reptiles, shedding, 179–80, 181

Skink (lizard), 182–83,
    187–88
Skunk Catfish (*Corydoras
    arcuatus*, Elwin), 87
Skunks (*Mephitis mephitis*),
    365, 366, 367–69
  cages, 340, 344
Sleeping hours, reptiles, 173
Snails, 64, 152, 235
Snakes
  anatomy, 106, 176–80
  bites by, 172
  cages, 205, 208
  catching, 188–89
  desert, 217–18
  diseases, 195–96, 198–200
  eggs, 176
  escaping, 219
  exotic, 218
  fear of, 171
  feeding, 219
  locomotion, 176–77
  markings, 177
  parental instinct, lack of,
      173
  poisonous, 172, 177–79, 186,
      187, 189
  skin shedding, 179–80
  temperament, 216
  temperate zone, 217, 218–19
  tropical, 218
  varieties
    anaconda, 200–1
    bull, 171, 172
    chicken, 171–72, 180–81,
        185
    constrictors, 180–81

copperhead, 186
coral, 177–79, 186, 187
corn, 171, 172, 185, 222
DeKay's, 229
garter (*Thamnophis
    sirtalis*), 218
hog-nosed, 227–28
hybrid pine (*Pituophis
    melanoleucus*), 178
*King, see King snake
    (Lampropeltis)*
leaf-nosed, 188
milk, 171, 185, 222
pythons, 180–81
rat, 171, 172, 180–81,
    185
rattlesnakes, 186
ring-necked, 230
rubber boa, 230
Sonora, 229
water, 177
water moccasin, 186–87
Snapping turtles, 236–37
Society finches, 291, 292–93
Sodium dihydrogen phosphate,
    9
Sodium fluoride solution, 200
Sodium monohydrogen
    phosphate, 9
Soldier Catfish
    (*Multimaculatus*,
    Steindachner), 87
Sonora snakes, 229
Sore throat in salamanders,
    163–64
South African horned frog,
    108

Space Farm, 337
Spadefoot toad, 105
Spawning, 28–30
  artificial refuges, 24, 61
  breeding traps, 27
  egg-laying, 27–28
  egg-scatterers, 62
  egg supports, 29
  food for mother, 26, 27,
    62–63
  light requirements, 26, 27
  live-bearing, 24, 25–27
  mops, 71–72
  prevention, 25–26
  water chemistry, 27, 28
  water temperature and, 26,
    27, 28
Speech training of birds,
  314–16
Spermatophore, 118
Spiders, 129, 213–14
Spinach as fish food, 42
Spotted Catfish (Corydoras
  punctatus, Bloch), 87
Spotted salamander
  (Ambystoma
  maculatum), 147, 160
Spotted turtles, 237
Spreading adder (hog-nose),
  227–28
Spring peepers, 135
Spring salamander, 139
Squirrels
  cages, 339
  flying (Glaucomys volans),
    339, 343, 380–83, 381
  gray (Sciurus carolinensis),

378–80
Squirrel tree frogs, 135
Starlings, 257
Start Right (water
  conditioner), 7–8
Striped Danio (Brachydanio
  rerio, Hamilton-
  Buchanan), 68–69
Swifts (lizard), 243–44
Swim bladder trouble, 50
Sword tail (Xiphophorus
  hellerii, Heckel), 50,
  56–58
Sulfa drugs, 163
Sumatra Barb (Capoeta
  tetrazona, Bleeker),
  74–75
Sylvania Electric Products,
  Inc., 20

Tadpoles
  development, see Frogs
  turtle food, as, 235
Tail fins, 21
Tailed frog, 118
Talpidae (insectivores),
  356–58
Tamias striatus (chipmunk),
  376–77, 378
Taming birds, 308–13
Tarantulas, 362
Taricha (newt genus), 136
Teeth
  amphibians, 108, 109
  fish, 64
Temperature of aquarium
  water, 8, 20, 151

Terrariums, 153
  cleanliness, 163, 165
  crowding, 163
  land-water, 155
  making, 154–55
  stocking, 156
Tetras, 61
  Characins called, 65
  diseases, 51
  neon, 17, 51, 66
Thamnophis sirtalis (garter
    snake), 218, 226–27
Thigmotaxis, 140
Three-toed box turtle, 240
Thrushes, 257
Ticks, 202–3
Tiger Barb (*Capoeta tetrazona,*
    Bleeker), 74–75
Tiger salamander, 115
Toads, 97–98
  anatomy, 100–9, 112–15
  diseases, 164
  eggs, 132
  feeding, 107–8, 158, 159–60
  hibernation, 133
  mating, 115–16, 117, 120
  poisonous, 100
  sex characteristics, 115
  shedding skin, 133
  tadpoles, 121, 122
  varieties
    American (*Bufo
      americanus*), 130–34,
      131
    hairy, 115
    marine, 100
    midwife, 123

  voices, 134
  warts, 130, 132
Tongues, amphibians, 108–9
Tooth-carp, 70
Top Minnows, 70
Transferring fish, 8
Traps, live, 346–47
Tree frogs, 120, 122, 123
  diseases, 165
  feeding, 158, 160
  toe glands, 100
  varieties
    Hyla gratiosa (barking),
      99
    Hyla versicolor, 134–36
Tree toad, *see* Tree frog
Tubifex worms, 37, 40, 42,
    159, 160
Tularemia, 393
Turtles, 231–40
  bites, 172
  cages, 206
  care of, 184, 231–32
  diseases, 195, 197
  feeding, 193, 213, 233–35,
    238, 239
  hibernation, 240
  ponds for, 206–7
  reptiles, as, 172
  temperature requirements,
    211
  varieties
    box, 239–40
    map, 235
    mud, 237–38
    musk, 237–38
    painted, 235–36, 236

pond, 232–37
red-ears (*Pseudemys scripta*), 193
sawback, 235
slider, 193, 232–33
snapping, 232, 235, 236–37
Southern painted (*Chrysemys picta doralis*), 236
spotted, 237
water, 237
wood, 238–39, 239

Underwater plants, 31
Undulating reptiles, 176

Velvet (fish disease), 46–47
Vent, reptilian, 177
Ventral fins, 21
Vipers, 228
Vitamin E, 202
Vitamins
amphibians, for, 164, 165
mammals, for, 348
reptiles, 202
Vole, 330–31
Vulpes fulva (red fox), 369–70
Vultures, 262

Warts, 130
Water, aquarium
fresh, 5–12, 26, 27
fumes in, 6
salt, 88–89
Water dogs, 141

Water fleas, *see* Daphnia
Water moccasins, 186–87
Watersnakes, 229
diseases, 201
water moccasins, 186–87
Water Sprite (plant), 36
Water turtles, 237
Waxbills, 293, 296
Weasels, 328, 339, 344
Bonaparte (*Mustela erminea*), 363–65
Weaverbird, 259
Westchester Aquarium Supply Company, 88
Whale, blue, 329
Wheat germ oil, 288, 319
White footed mouse, *see* Deer mouse
White spot disease, 44–45
White worms (*Enchytraeus*), 157
Wildcat (*Lynx rufus*), 370–71
Wildlife refuges, 337
Willissi (plant), 33
Woodchuck (*Marmota monax*), 372–74, 373
Woodcock, 261
Wood turtle (*Clemmys insculpta*), 238–39, 239
Worms, 107–8
anchor, 50
meal, 157
tubifex, 159, 160
white (*Enchytraeus*), 157

Xiphophorus hellerii, Heckel, (swordtail), 56–57

maculatus, Gunther
  (moonfish, Platy), 58
variatus, (Platy), 59

Zebra Danio (*Brachydanio
  rerio*, Hamilton-

Buchanan), 68–69
Zebra finches, 272, 292,
  293–94
Zetek's frog (*Atelopus zeteki*),
  167